On the Outskirts of Hope

Educating Youth from Poverty Areas

On the Outskirts of Hope

Educating Youth from Poverty Areas

HELAINE DAWSON

McGraw-Hill Book Company

*New York • St. Louis • San Francisco • Dallas
London • Toronto • Sydney*

Illustrated by Robert Carter

First McGraw-Hill Paperback Edition, 1970

Dedication

I dedicate this book with deep affection to my students, the young men and women whom it has been my privilege to meet and with whom it has been my pleasure to work. May the mutual respect and warm relationship we have developed be extended to others from similar backgrounds.

Preface

ON THE OUTSKIRTS OF HOPE is written for anyone who is interested in the education of ghetto youth—and will be particularly useful for teachers, social workers, and anti-poverty program administrators. It tells how to communicate with young people who have never been given a real chance to advance in life—young men and women who have turned their backs on a society they hate and mistrust. It explains why they equate authority with abuse, and why traditional teaching will not work with them. They are "on the outskirts of hope," yet, with teachers who understand their problems and who respect them as human beings, there is indeed promise for their future.

The book is not a theoretical exposition. It takes the reader into the classroom to observe real situations and real people. Slowly they grow toward maturity as they begin to realize that their new skills will free them from the bondage of ghetto life. They meet obstacles and, with the teacher's help, overcome them. For the first time in their lives, they experience success in the classroom.

The author's reflections and discussions are based on first-hand experience with two hundred young people over a three-year period. Her presentation of the characteristics of such students—their short attention spans, their restlessness, their inability to listen—will help any teacher or administrator understand and deal effectively with them.

Mrs. Dawson's approach to teaching is unorthodox and highly successful. She describes it simply, with no educational, psychological, or sociological jargon. It is based on practical solutions. At the same time, it is scientific in its treatment of behavioral problems.

Helaine Dawson has had a varied professional background. Her vast experience in the United States and in Europe—as social worker, magazine columnist, teacher, and medical-education consultant—has been with people from different cultures and different educational levels. In each capacity she has met challenge with innovation and effected desirable changes in attitudes. At present she is an adult educator with the San Francisco Unified School District.

The Publisher

Acknowledgments

THE ORIGINAL DRAFT of this book was vastly improved by the judicious editing of my patient, loving husband. To him, too, do I publicly declare my gratitude for his insistence on dialogue rather than exposition. I did not always agree with his suggestions, but at least I listened. I owe thanks to him, too, for his willingness to be interrupted at inopportune moments to listen to ideas as they bounced off the top of my head.

I am also indebted to my many friends who have given me encouragement along the way, among them "Buzz" Anderson, the producer and host of *Where Is Jim Crow?*, a program of the Bay Area's educational channel KQED. He also gave my students their first opportunity to express their points of view to the public via television.

Helaine S. Dawson

Contents

bennies pep pills

blood a black

blow pot smoke marijuana

bread money

brother someone of the same race

bullet one year in prison

bus a slob steal a kiss

bush marijuana

canine unattractive, undesirable woman

cat man

chuck eat

come on right be honest

con pretend

cop get drugs illegally

cop a matchbox buy a small quantity of drugs

crystal methedrine

devils 1. benzedrine pills;

2. whites, a derogatory term

dog woman, good or bad depending on circumstances

dude man

fronting putting on, pretending; as an adjective, superficial

get a slave get a job

get loaded get high on drugs

gigging partying

grass marijuana

grease feed

head frequent drug user

the heat the police

heavy knowledgeable

high state after injection of drugs or smoking marijuana

hustle earn money in an illegal way

in a bag set in a condition of

life, a pattern of behavior (e.g., youths in ghettos may be in a bag consisting of pimping, prostitution, shoplifting, wine drinking, etc.)

lace money

lame square, outside the group and not accepted

mac, macarone 1. fool around; 2. encroach on another pimp's territory

mellow high on drugs, but still aware of one's surroundings

nitty gritty down-to-earth level; matter relating to actual problems of poverty

ofay short for "old faded," a derogatory southern experssion for whites; "fay" also means foe

on a trip 1. high on narcotics; 2. introducing materials not in a textbook but arising from free association of ideas

on time satisfactory

out of sight especially good or bad, depending on the situation (e.g., someone who shows sincere interest is "out of sight," but someone who is not liked or does something not liked can also be "out of sight")

pin get down to specifics

play it cool be nonchalant

polish up flatter someone

poor cracker poor whites, a derogatory southern expression

popcorn sucker (obsolete)

pull my coat expose me to a good thing

put me on pretend to me that conditions are satisfactory

reds benzedrine pills

rip me off do something for or to me, good or bad depending on circumstances (e.g., "He ripped me off" could mean either "told me about a good job" or "took my girl away from me")

score a cop find drugs

seditty affected, pretending to be sophisticated

the set the setting; where the action is

shine him on snub him, ignore him

shortneck small bottle of wine

slave job

smack heroin

soul deep feeling

soul food southern cooking; especially fried foods such as ham and turkey, corn bread, etc.

stable prostitutes that a pimp maintains

stuff marijuana

swift satisfactory

tough good-looking

turned on high on narcotics

Uncle Tom a black who yields to whites' influence

weed marijuana

yellows dexedrine pills

On the Outskirts of Hope

Educating Youth from Poverty Areas

Introduction

THIS BOOK is about educating people, young people who have known nothing but poverty and deprivation, whose problems have been compounded by racial prejudice in various strata of our society. Most of the experiences on which this book is based have been with black youths, but what I saw and learned is not peculiar to blacks. A negative outlook on life, so discernible in our initial contacts, chameleon manifestations of hostility toward authority symbols, classification of anyone outside gangs or peer groups as "square," distrust of outsiders, feelings of hopelessness, and fear of continued failure—these are just as common among youths anywhere in the world who have been forced to grow up in slums and invisibly walled ghettoes, no matter what their racial or ethnic heritage. There are a few who can surmount these walls, but they are the exceptions.

If you are a social worker, teacher, policeman, probation officer, mental health educator, physician, community action aide, administrator, or housing authority, how do you communicate with such a youth? Where do you begin? Do you impose your preconceived plans on him? Do you feel that you know what is good for him and that therefore he had better abide by acceptable middle-class standards or suffer continued ostracism from the mainstream of society? If your task is to prepare such youths for the world of work by developing their marketable skills, and they look upon you with disgust and suspicion before you even open your mouth, how do you reach them?

What you do depends on how you view this complex problem. Trying to solve it piecemeal, without perceiving the relationships of a social structure interwoven with conflicting cultural and economic values, will produce continued failure. For example, providing jobs is considered a panacea by many. Surely jobs are important to maintain human dignity, but providing jobs without understanding attitudes won't turn the tide. Jobs go hand in hand with job training. The training has to be so conceived, however, that it will be adequate preparation for electronics-type jobs in a computerized era. Contrived jobs are a myopic solution; they have no future. Viewing jobs in proper perspective means relating job getting, job training, and job holding to attitudes of employers toward the hiring of blacks, Mexican-Americans, other minority groups, and those with police records.

Whenever these youths' resentment flares up into overt anarchical behavior, the finger of accusation and blame is pointed at "hoodlums" and "criminal elements." Certainly disregard for law and order cannot be condoned, but it can be understood as a manifestation of frustration and ineffective communication. When there is trouble, the people directly involved are not called in to settle it. This is unfortunate; they may not be able to express themselves in language understood by those in higher economic or educational brackets, but they understand their own problems. The usual procedure is to call in consultants from government circles and bookish professionals who have neither experienced poverty nor had face-to-face contacts with youths who have. After much talk and repeated investigations, they produce hackneyed solutions which have never worked and never will work.

Rather than promises or halfhearted action, youths want and need acceptance and understanding of their world, which is so different from the middle-class world. Without changes in attitudes on the part of people at different levels of financial and intellectual achievement, jobs won't alleviate the explosive situations existing in slum areas. Those who have grown up in ghettoes display unsocial attitudes and behavior that germinate in their environment. Young blacks want no part of the genuflection to whites that may have been their parents' means of survival. They want to be accepted, respected, and treated with the dignity befitting human beings. When they are not treated this way, their feelings of worthlessness and hopelessness are intensified, and they develop a smouldering hatred of whites and middle-class blacks. Human understanding and compassion cannot be legislated.

Many attempts have been made to discipline and control these youths by law enforcement and community, social, and educational agencies, but these attempts have failed for the same reason: inability to communicate. Communication is an active process. It is also a two-way process. Simply telling another person what is good for him is not communicating. You have to do more than that. You have to listen to him, and he has to listen to you. Without mutuality, and an open mind on both sides, there can be no effective communication. If more people listened to these youths' feelings and thoughts and followed this up with understanding and appropriate action toward job training, job getting, nondiscriminatory housing, increased health services, and person-to-person respect regardless of color and background, no such tragedy as the Watts, Los Angeles, riots might occur. Increasing police surveillance or sending in the National Guard may suppress a riot, but it amounts to shutting the lid quickly on Pandora's box. The lid can pop open any time.

For example, shortsightedness by the government led to the outbreak that occurred in the Hunters Point ghetto area of San Francisco in September, 1966. San Francisco, considered "quiet" by the Manpower Development Training Office in Washington, was not made a recipient of Manpower Development Training appropriations. Instead, the 27 million dollars allotted to California for MDTA programs was distributed among the "trouble" spots: Watts, Stockton, and Oakland. This meant that whatever job training programs were in existence in the fall of 1966 would be completed, but no new ones would be instituted. When the outbreaks occurred, the mayor frantically beseeched Washington for immediate reversal of the MDTA decision on funds for San Francisco. San Francisco was now added to the inevitably growing list of "explosive" cities.

This after-the-fact and piecemeal approach to a national problem solves nothing. It only delays the black revolution, which is a reality. "Explosions" in the various cities cannot be treated singly as peculiar to a particular locality. They are part of the pattern of revolt being fashioned by a dissatisfied minority. Such outbreaks will continue to occur until deeper understanding, creative planning, and action at the grass-roots level become a way of coping with economic, social, and political problems.

Fortunately there are some people in government, business, education, and social agencies who have had the courage and vision to institute boldly conceived projects to help youths in ghettoes. These projects are called by different names, but their main reason for existence is the same: to curb violence and reduce the rate of juvenile delinquency by providing job training and counseling services. The Youth Opportunities Center, established in San Francisco in September,

1963 by the San Francisco Committee on Youth, was such an innovative approach to the problem. Financed by the Ford Foundation, the President's Committee on Delinquency and Youth Crime, and the United States Department of Labor, it worked to develop a job training program with the cooperation of at least eight other agencies. Among these were the California State Department of Employment and the Adult Education Division of the San Francisco Board of Education. The largest appropriation, however, came from the Federal government's Office of Manpower and Development Training, established by the Manpower Development Training Act of 1962 and later amendments. This act provides states with funds for a designated period to set up job training programs in cooperation with established public and private educational agencies. The state departments of employment recruit the trainees; the accredited educational institutions provide the teaching staffs and determine the curricula and the duration of the particular job training program. The kinds of job training programs reflect the needs of the job market. After job surveys have been made, the state departments of employment are supposed to continue their programs of job development so that graduates from the job training programs can immediately be placed in jobs for which they have been trained. Throughout this book, such programs will be referred to as MDTA programs.

The Youth Opportunities Center in Hunters Point, San Francisco, was one of the first of its kind in the nation. Many mistakes were made, as is natural with any experimental undertaking: there were ineffective lines of inter- and intra-agency communication, lack of understanding of the problems of poverty, and inadequate contacts with the youths and parents of the community. This is a national problem, however, and is not peculiar to San Francisco. The first programs — the programs for general office clerks and office boys — were the most difficult to administer. The trainee, the primary focus of the Youth Opportunities program, sometimes seemed to be relegated to a secondary position while inner politics were untangled.

In San Francisco the Adult Education Division of the San Francisco Unified School District has the responsibility of supervising the job training, setting up the curricula, determining the duration of each job training program, and providing the necessary teaching staffs. The initial programs suffered because so little was known about the world of poverty. As a result of what was learned from the early programs, radical changes in curricula concepts were effected. The main problem still exists, however: the educational approach of the teacher. In this complex venture, where highly skilled and experienced teachers with new outlooks on education are needed, few are available. Most teachers are not trained to cope with the attitudes, problems, and daily crises of these youths. Not having been exposed to young people from this kind of environment, the teacher is not able to communicate with them at their own level. The teacher is therefore unable to withstand the verbal attacks and other forms of aggressive behavior exhibited in initial contacts. The traditionally oriented teacher, who is in the majority, feels personally threatened and becomes defensive; gamesmanship between him and the trainees ensues, with little learning possible under the circumstances.

Teaching young people from poverty areas and ghettoes requires someone who is flexible and able to cope with unexpected daily crises. Teaching in this milieu is strenuous. The daily struggle is sometimes so intense that you begin to think you won't be able to go on. Teachers need physical stamina and the skin of a crocodile to survive. If you can endure it, however, you will be rewarded by changes in the attitudes and behavior of your students and by a permanently close relationship between them and you. Those teachers unable or unwilling to commit their whole beings to such a program should move on to positions less strenuous and calling for less emotional involvement.

The services of the Center were separated from the job training facilities financially as well as physically and psychologically: Ford Foundation paid the salaries of the Center staff on an annual basis, while the Office of Manpower Development, through the accredited educational facilities, paid the salaries of the teaching staff on a per-diem basis.

The state departments of employment have improved their methods of recruiting because they have learned that ghetto youths have to be reached where they are—on the streets, in pool halls, in recreation centers. Young people from poverty areas and ghettoes are suspicious of "do-gooders" and therefore do not respond to signs or other forms of publicity available in established agencies.

As an incentive for high school dropouts and other young people to prepare themselves for skilled jobs, trainees accepted for each program are paid a weekly stipend. This begins at a minimum of twenty dollars a week and increases depending on family status and work experience. Transportation expenses, omitted from the early programs, are now included.

It was in connection with the job training phase of the Youth Opportunities Center project that I entered the initial program in December, 1963. I asked for a teaching assignment, and I have been teaching with the program ever since. My responsibility has been to set up and teach Personal Development to young men and women, 18 to 22 years of age, who are being prepared to enter the world of work. In the first program I also worked as counselor, which gave me an added opportunity to learn about the world of these young people. More than half were high school dropouts, the majority with police records. A minority of the young women had children out of wedlock. I saw firsthand their crippled spirits, self-hatred, fears, and inner confusion. I learned what it means to grow up in poverty and to be so filled with self-disgust and hopelessness that the only way out seems to be through gangs, narcotics, pimping, gambling, or hustling.

Fortunately, my superiors in the Adult Education Division of the San Francisco Board of Education gave me a free rein, encouraging me to implement ideas that I felt would help change antisocial habits and attitudes. From the very beginning I shared ideas and experiences with the students, accepting them as they were. I listened much more than I talked. I learned their language and began to realize that they had to be bilingual, as did I. They were well versed in their own "in" language, the language of gangs and peer groups; but they had to become more conversant with the "out" language of the world of work. I had fun and success in learning their language, so that many of them consider me a "soul sister," the highest compliment an outsider can receive.

How we—the trainees and I—evolved Personal Development, so that it aroused their interest and touched their daily lives, is recorded in this book. Our successes resulted from mutual involvement in the teaching-learning process. From the beginning, I had to work at a down-to-earth level—what the students call the "gut" or "nitty-gritty" level.

My method of operation is decidedly unorthodox compared with traditional standards. However, the trainees became involved—they learned vocabulary, increased their interest in reading, became aware of their potentialities, began to be able to accept criticism, and therefore became less hostile and more self-confident. Thirty out of the thirty-four members of the original group of general office clerks and office boys are still employed as clerks in banks and in industrial establishments. Some are telephone operators or warehouse clerks. Those from the duplicating machine operators program are working as typists and file clerks rather than duplicating machine operators; this implies that there was poor analysis of job opportunities in this particular category. Unfortunately, this coeducational group suffered the longest period of inactivity before finding employment. The continuation of telephone contacts between me and my former students provided a little comfort and buoyed up their spirits. Many of these students sought jobs on their own rather than depending on the Center's services. At the time of this writing, 75 percent are employed.

The group of young men who were in training as telephone frame-men fared much better when the category was enlarged to include preparation for employment by utilities companies and elevator installations and in airline maintenance and computer manufacturing and servicing, rather than aiming only at employment by telephone companies. Ninety-five percent of these students are now employed in capacities for which they were trained, having passed the necessary pre-employment tests. Only 5 percent failed to adapt to the work-habit patterns, returning to the streets and their familiar life. Ten male students were so interested in continuing their education they requested letters of recommendation from me to the University of California.

This book is, therefore, an operational research study based on close daily relationships with 200 young men and women, the majority of whom were from Hunters Point. How the respect and affection we have for each other developed, and how we think of each other as human beings, I would like to share with you. If you are planning to work or are now working with young people from similar backgrounds, or if you are interested in general, you may find the material pertinent.

None of the anecdotes is contrived. Each is recorded as it occurred to demonstrate the interaction between the trainees and me and the application of the principles I espouse. The names used are those the students chose.

I experimented with role playing, used the tape recorder almost daily, interspersed films and instructional materials such as books and newspapers, and utilized community resources; but I found group discussions most conducive to learning.

The glossary contains only those words and expressions I learned while working with my students. Acquiring this new vocabulary has been helpful to me in effecting communication between us. The bibliography includes new publications on black history, a topic in which the students were greatly interested. The appendixes include various teaching techniques, such as criteria, tours procedure, and sample educating materials; material for preparing students for employment, including self-evaluation questionnaires and simulated pre-employment tests; a list of audio-visual materials; sources of instructional materials; and suggested supplementary reading for teachers.

This is not a "how to" book. There can be no magic formulas for instant education, instant job training, or instant dissolving of hostility. To achieve warm interpersonal relations, to destroy man-made barriers of "we" and "they," takes patience, compassion, deep understanding, skill, and time.

I hope that the actual class demonstrations, illustrating the principles and practices which I found effective, give you ideas that can be adapted to your particular situation. Good luck!

1 • Getting Started

GETTING STARTED on any type of program is a process filled with anxiety and risks. Especially is this true in working with young people from poverty areas or ghettoes. Their world is strange to us. Their values are not the values of the middle-class world; their attitude toward learning seems alien; their language is different, and their behavior may be shocking. But if you enter the picture with courage, imagination, warmth, understanding, a sense of humor, and physical stamina, you stand a chance of reaching them and establishing rapport — without which no effective communication or learning can take place.

They are extremely sensitive to labels such as "culturally disadvantaged," "culturally deprived," "hoodlums," "delinquents," "dropouts." Too frequently these are hurled at them by people traditionally accepted as experts, who may have visited poverty areas, spoken to agency leaders to obtain research data, and then written "inside" revelations. Such labels are no aid to understanding. Take the simple term "dropout." The fact that the majority of youths in these areas are high school dropouts only increases their feelings of failure. Youths who find excitement in the streets think of school as boring. Too often they are justified. Classes *are* often boring — textbooks are followed daily with little attempt made to encourage spontaneity, and subject matter is not related to their daily lives.

If your primary goal is to teach personal development or any other subject in which attitudes and acceptable work habits are to be developed, whether it be sponsored by the Manpower Development Training Act (MDTA), Economic Opportunity Act (EOA), or private industry, where do you begin? How do you begin? What materials do you use?

What do you know about your students' communication skills? What do you know about them as individuals? How do you handle discipline problems? How do you reach them?

How you answer these questions depends on your concept of your role. You can't consider yourself an authority to be listened to and obeyed. If you do, you will only perpetuate your students' dislike of authority symbols and intensify their hostility toward you. But neither should you go to the opposite extreme of complete permissiveness. Some guidelines are necessary. These can't just be stated, however. They must be practiced daily by both you and your students. Otherwise the students will consider you insincere. Apply what you profess.

The teaching of any subject depends not so much on techniques as on understanding of human behavior. Techniques are easy to master. A good teacher has to play many roles. He has to be a counselor, psychologist, sociologist, cultural anthropologist, and friend. If he gets to know his students as individuals and they feel his interest, they begin to feel like people. Their initial feelings of worthlessness and shame, mingled with feelings of stupidity and failure, slowly diminish. By all means, *be yourself.* Encourage them to be *themselves.* Working with these youths presents countless challenges for you and them. If you conceive the teaching-learning process as a mutual one, you will learn something daily.

Learn how to play things by ear and, whatever you do, try not to get excited. In their language, "play it cool, man." How you react to the many tests they impose on you daily will reveal your vulnerability. In the beginning, they may do many things to test you: display complete indifference, sleep in class, and subject you to verbal abuse.

Listen to them if you want them to listen to you. There is too little listening, especially in the classroom. Many teachers talk too much. These students who have dropped out of school know how to tune you out. Listening to them will provide you with feedback from which you can evaluate your effectiveness and extract ideas for future content.

Accept your students as they are, both educationally and behaviorally. Don't judge them by middle-class standards. If you show them that you accept them, the time it takes to earn their acceptance will be shortened.

Create situations that will stimulate their interest, relate to their daily lives, and involve them in the learning process. Teaching by telling is, in my opinion, not teaching. What you are telling has to filter through the students' nervous system. This implies that you should be sensitive to the students in order to generate reactions. Learning is active. It is also personal. Each student learns what he wants to at his individual rate of learning. You have to get feedback and encourage thinking, not memorizing. Encourage creativity. In addition, give your students opportunities to be exposed to new experiences. Try the untried. Don't be afraid of failure; progress results from learning from our mistakes. Experiment and then evaluate. These activities must be continuous. Try to consider yourself and your students as in a perpetual state of becoming.

The basic precepts which I followed can be summed up and easily remembered by a mnemonic device, L A C E.

L   Listen and Learn
A   Accept
C   Create and Communicate
E   Experiment and Evaluate

These imply mutuality. You will be successful in communicating only to the degree that you enter into the process. The more you learn from your students, the more effective you will be.

Before You Start

Before you meet your students for the first time, certain preliminaries should be followed.

Spell out your objectives.

Familiarize yourself with the neighborhood.

Get to know inter- and intra-agency structure, and lines of communication.

Check to see if necessary equipment is on hand.

Such planning will be a great help. It is understood that you will be changing your objectives after you have become better acquainted with the students' needs and interests.

SPELL OUT YOUR OBJECTIVES

The primary objective of the Youth Opportunities School program is to develop marketable skills and prepare youths for the world of work. This is too vague; more specific objectives have to be spelled out. You will probably change your objectives after you get to know the students' needs and interests, but at least you will have a tentative plan from which to work. To give any program stability and direction, objectives should become an integral part of the planning stage. They will provide you with criteria for evaluating the effectiveness of each phase of the course.

The following objectives — and some of the methods used to attain them — were formulated specifically for Personal Development, but you may find them applicable to your particular situation:

1. To get each student to feel good about himself as a person by creating an atmosphere of friendliness and personal interest

2. To develop awareness in the student of the world around him and of his responsibility to it by interrelating subject matter with personal experiences

3. To arouse each student's motivation so that he becomes personally involved and interested in pursuing what he needs

4. To help him communicate by developing his ability to express his thoughts both orally and in writing

5. To help him develop new patterns of thinking which will be reflected in changes in attitudes and behavior

6. To increase his self-confidence by praising every indication of progress and to help him develop an understanding of himself

7. To give him opportunities to develop aptitudes, such as writing, painting, acting, etc.

8. To broaden his horizons by exposing him to new experiences, people, and places

9. To help him think critically and keep an open mind rather than react violently to people and situations; to stop thinking in stereotypes

10. To help him develop more flexibility in adjusting to the unexpected

FAMILIARIZE YOURSELF WITH THE NEIGHBORHOOD

A tour of the neighborhood in which you will be teaching will help you understand your students better. You can't be expected to visit individual homes. You are an outsider in the eyes of the parents and young people in these areas. They will be suspicious because they have had too many experiences with study groups, investigating committees, and the like, who have visited, questioned, recorded, and published reports in sociological or psychological jargon. The people in these areas never saw any changes resulting from these visits. You won't be able to visit them until you have been working for a long time and have earned their acceptance and the people in the area request your visit. Even then, you may not be able to go unescorted. I don't mean that you must be escorted for safety's sake; but your relationship, even after you have been accepted, may be improved if you are accompanied by someone indigenous to the neighborhood for whom they have respect.

Your initial familiarization with the neighborhood, therefore, doesn't imply thorough knowledge. This can't possibly be gained before you meet your students. You will be in a continual process of gathering data. However, you can get the overall picture by looking around the neighborhood. City transportation rather than an automobile is suggested for your initial survey. What industries do you notice? Do bars and cocktail lounges predominate? Are there restaurants? Churches? Schools? Who owns the small businesses? Does the neighborhood contain several ethnic groups or only one? Are there recreational facilities? How many? The picture you get from this superficial once-over can help you understand the interests and value system of the students. Don't underestimate the local environment as a factor in human development.

GET TO KNOW INTER- AND INTRA-AGENCY STRUCTURE

Before you meet your students, it is important to find out what you can about all possible sources of referral to help students with vocational, family, and health problems. Your knowledge of the various agencies' functions and the degree of centralization of services will be useful in changing students' attitudes about the callousness of agency representatives. As a teacher you are one of the few professionals who meet the student regularly. You can give him the opportunity to develop a meaningful relationship by showing him that someone really cares what happens to him.

Unfortunately the hierarchy in many agencies does not consider teachers or other professional practitioners as possible consultants. Administrators are consulted whenever programs are set up or evaluated; this is the traditional practice. It would be interesting, however, if occasionally practitioners at the grass-roots level were invited to participate. Perhaps in your agency you can advocate this after you have proved your effectiveness. Only you will be able to judge the efficacy of such innovation. Don't jeopardize your position in the process.

See that some kind of machinery is set up within the training program so that you and the other faculty members can meet with the administrator at least once a month to discuss individual behavior problems of students and possible referrals.

TRY TO HAVE NECESSARY EQUIPMENT ON HAND

Too frequently programs are begun before the necessary equipment has been delivered. Even when requisitions are filed in advance, there are bottlenecks along the way which hold up delivery. This is frustrating for all concerned. When the first program of general office clerks began, there were no typewriters, in spite of the fact that they had been duly authorized and requisitioned. They didn't arrive until six weeks later. Can you imagine teaching typing without typewriters?

You Begin

With this preparation, you are now ready to face your students for the first time. What you encounter may startle you, but try to maintain perspective and a sense of humor. For example, on my first day I followed what I have suggested. I investigated the neighborhood. I saw a highly industrialized, densely populated, predominantly black area of San Francisco. This section, referred to as Hunters Point, borders the rim of Candlestick Park, the baseball home of the San Francisco Giants. It is sometimes referred to as "Candlestink" Park because of its proximity to garbage dumps. I saw meat-packing plants, fish-processing plants, scrap-iron plants, canning factories, a naval shipyard, and housing projects of tacky fiberboard. There were a few restaurants, a couple of corner hot-dog stands, gasoline stations, laundromats (but no coin-operated dry-cleaning stores), a few churches, a junior high school and an elementary school, and two recreation centers.

Most of the students lived in the public housing project on the top of the hill. These rat-infested, paper-thin buildings, originally only temporary shelters during World War II, are scheduled for razing.

What were the job training facilities like? Picture an old church. Its auditorium provided a large classroom. It had a stage and four gas heaters, two in front on either side and two in the rear. Downstairs were rest rooms for men and women, with one toilet each. A room adjacent to the auditorium, and accessible from it, served as another classroom. This room had a gas heater, usually unable to be adjusted. The gas heaters were so obsolete in structure that fumes continually escaped, polluting the air already dense with stench from the meat-packing plants. On days of little wind, or sometimes with a sudden shift in wind direction, the smell of decaying fish was added to the atmosphere.

I shall never forget the first day. The bell for class rang at one o'clock, but this didn't seem to matter to the students. Some were gathered on the steps in front of the church. Others, with their transistor radios, were laughing, yelling, and dancing. Still others were sitting in cars, nestling up to friends loaded with wine and marijuana.

When I entered the classroom, I saw two young, attractive women sitting in the front row with their highly coiffed heads on the desk. I said nothing, but simply observed, listened, and waited to see what would happen. Slowly, but very slowly, two young men wandered in, looked at me with seeming hostility and disgust and then, even more slowly, wandered to the men's room. Now it was 1:20 P.M. The rest of the men began to saunter in, so slowly that they seemed hardly to be moving. They wore narrow-brimmed black fedoras, bound in velvet, sport shirts, no ties, and sunglasses. Those not wearing hats displayed hair long on top, with ends bleached red and standing out stiffly like overstarched shirts. Their long sideburns, heavily greased, reached almost to the chin. When they finally sat down, they sat at right angles to the front of the room and to me, so that the blackboard was out of sight. They never removed their hats or sunglasses, and they chewed bubble gum noisily. They talked to each other loudly: "Hey, man, I sees this cat and he's on a trip. . . . What a broad. . . ." They giggled and yawned with looks of utter boredom. I wondered how I was to prepare them for office jobs in thirty-nine weeks!

While they ignored me, I observed and waited. I said nothing. I didn't introduce myself yet. Soon the two men returned from the rest room, and four others went out. I was curious, because I knew there was only one toilet. Much later I learned that in the rest room they smoked marijuana, drank wine, and shot craps.

In the midst of this traffic, more girls wandered in. It was now 1:30 P.M. They seemed totally oblivious of the time. They were heavily made up with eyeliner, mascara, and streaked hair. Several wore capri pants so tight that their expansive rears begged for release. Others wore skirts so short that when they sat down the skirts almost became bikinis. A few had scarves tied around their heads and wore coats with fur collars. These students didn't sit down, but stood with their backs to the gas heaters. Others pushed their chairs closer to each other, chewed bubble gum, chattered, filed their nails, or took out their mirrors and applied mascara, shooting side glances at me. Then groups of four girls left for the women's rest room, where there was also only one toilet. This procedure was repeated until there were only three women and three men left in the classroom.

At about 1:40 P.M. everyone had returned, and we had our full complement. Now it was time to introduce myself. "I'm happy to see you finally settling down." Piercing looks of disgust and boredom mingled with hostility confronted me. "I'd like to introduce myself." A few crossed their legs and turned their backs, while two girls in the front row passed notes to each other, completely disregarding me. "I'm Mrs. Dawson." They couldn't care less. Yawns and guttural sounds greeted this. "Nobody sent me here! I asked to come; I have a great deal of experience outside of teaching which may help you. I want to share this with you." Even this didn't have any demonstrable effect. A few were listening, however, and this was encouraging.

"Let's understand from the very beginning how we're going to operate. I don't teach the way you're used to. You may find it strange in the beginning, but you'll get used to it. I won't talk as much as this on any other day. Today it's necessary so that we can understand what to expect. In this class we're going to discuss topics you're interested in. We want to get to know each other well and to know ourselves well."

One fellow blurted out, "Hey, you some sort of nut or something? I knows me."

"Maybe I am some sort of a nut. You can think that if you want to. I hope that by the time we finish the course you change your mind."

This response had an immediate effect. Several turned around and faced me.

"I don't want you to consider me an authority. Question everything I say. You don't have to agree with me. You do have to have reasons for not agreeing. As long as you show you're thinking, that's what counts."

A few more seemed to be listening and turned around. The looks of disgust and lack of interest of the majority still persisted.

"The course I'll be working with you on is Personal Development. What does that mean to you?"

John, in the middle of a yawn, said, "Gee, you must be stupid or something. Anyone'd know that—developing your person, of course."

"Developing yourself in what way?"

Silence. Finally a young woman with a sullen look on her face— Jessie—answered. "You aksed me? How you dress, how you talk, you know, you know."

"That's good, Jessie."

I put A K S E D on the blackboard and next to it A S K E D. I pronounced both and asked the students if they heard a difference. I went around the room and had each one pronounce the two words. Both were pronounced the same way, *aksed*. I knew then and there that pronunciation and speech would be an essential part of our daily sessions. When the students finally heard the difference, I said, "You are being prepared for jobs. On a job interview this could be a factor in your not getting the job."

"Right," said Jessie[1]. Several others chimed in, too. I was beginning to get some interaction. I laughed.

"What must we do, you and I, to understand each other? This is important on a job, at home, in school, anywhere. An author has to be able to do this in books, or you'll stop reading them. You have to do this with your boy friend, wife, husband, or children if you want to prevent arguments."

Jessie said, "Get through to the person."

"That's good. Can anyone think of a better way of expressing the same thing—one word, maybe?"

There were many tries, and John, whose vocabulary was good, said, "Communicate."

"Good, John," and I wrote it on the blackboard. I pronounced it, and the class did.

---

[1] Jessie later proved to be one of the brightest but most undisciplined in the group. She was nineteen, had been living out of wedlock for three years with the same man, who had fathered two children, now two years old and nine months old. She was a high school dropout. Her face was mobile, with large brown eyes and pert nose. She was extremely perceptive and had a dry sense of humor.

"John, if you talk to Jessie, are you communicating?"

"I don't know."

"Why?"

"Because she may not be listening."

"Communication means what, then?"

Belle said, "It means someone talks and the other listens."

This is how we began to develop the concept that communication is a two-way process.

"In this class we won't be using a textbook regularly. We'll use it occasionally. In fact, we'll evolve our own text." When I realized I had used the word *evolve*, I immediately put it on the blackboard and asked what it meant.

"Turn around," said Dick.[2]

"What's the word he's confusing this with?"

"'Revolve,'" said Jessie.

"We'll make a note of this and take it up later. Let's talk about 'evolve' first. If you, Belle, were home alone with your baby and heard screams, what would you do?"

"I'd look out to see what was happening. Maybe I'd call the police, maybe open the window and yell, I don't know, you know."

"You'd be evolving a plan of action. This course will evolve, too. It will grow, develop, and change as we go along. The vocabulary and what we do will depend on you. We will evolve this course together. This has never been done before in this way in this kind of program. You will be among the first students."

"We're going to be pioneers?"

"In a way, yes. Everything we do will be to help you develop yourself for living as well as for working. Let's have a few more illustrations of 'evolve' to see if you understand the idea."

Pointing to John, I said, "John, suppose your car broke down on the freeway, what plan of action would you evolve?"

"I'd get to a phone and call if I had a dime." Laughter.

"Anything else?"

"I'd flag another car and ask the driver to get help."

---

[2] Dick later proved to be interested. He wanted a job badly. He had a sick wife, eighteen years old, who had just returned from the hospital after a mastectomy; there was a diagnosis of malignancy. His two children were two years old and eight months old. He was twenty and a high school dropout.

I saw that they were beginning to understand. I was encouraged. I then put REVOLVE on the blackboard and began to develop that, again using illustrations involving students.

Each time I called on someone, I asked his or her name. "Please be patient with me for about a week while I learn your names. Would you like me to call you by your surname — your last name — or by your first name?" They preferred first names, and so I used first names.

"Tomorrow, we'll move the seats into a semicircle so that we can see each other, and then we'll put them back the way they are now for the next teacher. One other thing, and then we'll stop. Everything we do we want to relate to a job. Think about appearance on a job. Ask yourself some questions: 'Would I wear a hat inside an office?' 'Would I chew gum?' 'Would I wear sunglasses indoors?' We'll discuss your answers at the next session. Remember, the bell rings at one o'clock. I'm happy to be working with you. Hope you'll feel the same soon. See you tomorrow."

It was obvious that first day that there are many problems to tackle if impoverished youths are to be readied for job training in a technological era. Their antisocial attitudes, conveyed by their defiance, insolence, and hostility, constitute a major problem. At first, until you have penetrated their "bag" — their set way of thinking and acting — their seemingly apathetic attitude toward learning overwhelms and shocks. Their attitude about their appearance and their extremes in hair styles and dress, their indifference to time schedules and to the observance of amenities of daily living to which middle-class people are accustomed, challenge your patience and understanding. The students' low level of communication skills and brief spans of attention test your ingenuity. This is a laboratory of human behavior in which you are privileged to operate. To make headway in solving any of these problems in a designated number of weeks requires vast inner resources of the teacher.

One thing is very clear, however. You will not succeed by using the traditional methods and techniques. For example, there was the problem of indifference to time. Although the bell had rung at one o'clock, the full complement of students didn't gather until 1:40 P.M. I followed my precepts. I didn't yell. I waited, observed, and listened. The students were unaccustomed to this approach and were watching while testing me. I concluded the first meeting by casually indicating that I expected to see them at one o'clock. The next day and several weeks thereafter, many more were there before the bell rang. Not all were on time. It's impossible to reach each student, so don't be discouraged. I didn't talk about dress. I didn't criticize.

When a student responded to my question, "What is personal development?" by calling me a "nut," again he was testing. The others were also watching very closely to note my reaction. They expected to be sent to the principal's office for insubordination; this is what they had been accustomed to. This was the traditional approach. When I admitted that I could see his point of view, I was on the road to establishing a friendly relationship. I caught the other students' attention. Soon thereafter I was able to get some interaction.

I tried to relate explanations to the lives of the students. This is how I began to get them involved and introduce them to vocabulary. In explaining words, I did not define or quote dictionary meanings. These students, as a result of their insulated environment and limited acquaintance with books, find it difficult to conceptualize. Therefore, in the beginning they are not equipped to think at abstract levels. Examples have to be in terms that allow visualization.

When I realized I had used the word *evolve*, I stopped to find out what the students understood by it. This is something to be alert to — your own vocabulary. Unconsciously you may express thoughts in language totally unfamiliar to them. If you listen to yourself, you can catch that. Your students will be too fearful of being considered stupid to ask what you mean.

Notice how incorrect pronunciation was used as a starting point to focus on vocabulary. *Asked* is still a pronunciation difficulty. Language patterns and how to change them will be discussed later. As you read further, you will also observe how every unexpected incident can be turned into a meaningful learning experience.

In getting started, tell the students how you plan to operate. Be direct. I told them my *modus operandi* and also added that I planned to share experiences with them. When I told them they could disagree with me, they repeatedly checked me out on this.

In the very first session I showed them that I was interested in what they thought by asking them how they wished to be addressed, by first names or surnames. The mutuality of the teaching-learning process began right then.

In subsequent sessions we did move the chairs into a semicircle. I sat in the center. I have found that so simple a thing as the physical layout can influence the atmosphere. Partly because I removed any barrier between the students and me, their dislike of "authority symbols" slowly evaporated.

They could talk to me. I was easily accessible. There was no feeling of condescension. We were exchanging thoughts in a friendly atmosphere.

Getting started in subsequent programs has never been as difficult. Communication in the ghetto or in an impoverished area, once established, is fast and effective. Your reputation travels quickly, and this makes some problems easier to handle. But don't fall into a rut. This is deadly. Treat each new group individually by respecting its differences.

Summary

What you do the very first·day you meet your students will influence your future relationship with these young people from poverty areas, whose spirit and outlook on life have been tainted by the exigencies of their daily struggle for survival. Prepare yourself in advance by familiarizing yourself with the physical and social environment so that you can understand the character of the area in which you will have to operate. You must also find out what you can about each student in your group. In the beginning this can only be superficial. Deeper understanding will come later through various sources. To understand the student so that you can relate to him, you have to listen and perceive and to be patient, receptive, interested, and enthusiastic about your subject — and quick to give him hope. Reinforce any change toward more acceptable behavior, no matter how slight.

In your planning before your first meeting, it is essential to think about your tentative goals. These you may revise as the needs of your students indicate. Goals or objectives will provide the criteria for evaluating the effectiveness of your daily sessions and suggest content for future sessions.

If you follow the principles implicit in L A C E — Listen and Learn, Accept, Communicate and Create, Experiment and Evaluate — and understand the mutuality of each principle, getting started will be a less formidable undertaking.

After you have met your students, you have to be ready to try new approaches. You have to relate examples to their lives, and you have to learn their language. If you are direct and share ideas and experiences with them from the beginning, they will realize your sincerity, realize that you do what you say. Under such circumstances rapport will come naturally.

2 • *Establishing Rapport*

ESTABLISHING RAPPORT is a continuing process which begins with your first contact with your students. You must show them that you are sincerely interested in their welfare. To be effective in working with these youths you have to learn more about them: how they think; how they communicate with each other in their private lives; how they live; what their attitudes and feelings are toward their families, the opposite sex, peer groups, the police, jobs, and the community; how they spend their leisure; and what their food and health patterns are.

The information you obtain will be most helpful as a foundation for developing a meaningful course in personal development that will touch the students' lives. The data provided will be analogous to data obtained in a research study. In subsequent chapters discussion will focus on how such data can be used in helping to change attitudes and behavior.

There are several sources for this type of information:

1. Listening to your students
2. Observing them
3. Taking clues from class discussions
4. Having individual conferences with your students
5. Having conferences with representatives from other agencies working with the students or their parents

Many of these activities occur simultaneously. For example, in the beginning program, I listened, observed, counseled, and also worked at learning their language.

Learning Their "In" Language

For the first two weeks of the initial Manpower Development Training program for general office clerks, I noticed that Wilbert arrived daily in the Personal Development class eating potato chips and a candy bar, which he washed down with a Coke. I soon discovered why this was.

"This class meets immediately after lunch. If you're on a job, why do you have a lunch hour?"

"To eat lunch, of course," said Belle.

"What if you're not hungry?" asked Susie.

"This is a habit you'll develop if you begin to eat regularly."

"Wilbert couldn't eat lunch, Mrs. Dawson, because he ain't got no lace."

"No what?" I asked.

"Boy, you're square, huh?"

"I guess I am. What does 'lace' mean in this sense?" I wrote it down in my notebook. "In order to understand you, I'll have to learn your language. I'm going to make my own notebook, and we'll both be learning."

"'Lace' means money," volunteered Jim, the gang leader.

"Wilbert ain't got no money," said Dick.

"Why not say, 'He hasn't any lace'?"[1]

"Gee, Mrs. Dawson, that ain't right. That's not hip. How square can you get? It don't make no sense. It's got to be, 'He ain't got no lace,' see?"

I wrote this expression down while all eyes were on me. "Wouldn't it be funny," I said, "if after the course is completed I speak your language and you mine?"

"Ooh, please don't, for your sake," they said.

As I had promised in the first session, I shared my plans and thoughts about programs with my students. When we decided we were ready for tours to businesses and industrial plants, I contacted the

---

[1] It is interesting to know that "in" language is regional. Therefore some words and expressions are peculiar to a region and not understood by other groups in other regions. For example, *lace* does not have the same connotation in San Francisco as in New York's Harlem, but *bread* means money among groups in poverty areas in Philadelphia, Chicago, New York, San Francisco, and Los Angeles. According to my students, obsolescence in word use occurs quickly. *Lace* in two years was no longer used by those under twenty-four.

Metropolitan Life Insurance Company and arranged for a tour to their offices. The company graciously invited us to be their guests at lunch. I was thrilled and excitedly told my students about the tour, but not about the lunch.

"We going to be greased?" asked Bailey.

I didn't understand and looked puzzled.

"We going to be fed?" James blurted out.

"Hurry, Mrs. Dawson, that's another one for your glossary," said the class, laughing.

In one of the programs in which I had been working with young men only, we were discussing words and what different reactions people have to the same words. Unknowingly, I mentioned as an example the word *mother*. There was giggling and tittering, but I didn't get the message. I continued, "If, for example, your mother abandoned you when you were an infant, that would give you an unpleasant reaction. If, on the other hand, your mother was kind and helped you, your reaction would be tender and loving." More laughter. I now know their connotation of *mother*; usually combined with a four-letter word, it has an entirely different meaning.

At another time, when we were discussing the meaning of *glossary*, Edward Emile Edlow used the expression "cop a matchbox." When I showed ignorance, he explained that it means to buy a small quantity of narcotics.

In addition to the commonly used four-letter words, they love "out of sight." This expression has two meanings, depending on the context. I heard it for the first time from Duke. Duke was belligerent from the beginning of the telephone framemen course. He blurted out four-letter words, mentioned irrelevant incidents, constantly interrupted, and sometimes came in reeling, insisting he never drank.[2] He would come to class a half-hour late, and he was too impatient to listen to explanations.

"Give me the definition, and quit the talk. I ain't interested in all that shit!"

"Now, Duke," I said, "hold that language. These are language habits, and when you go for an interview these words may spill out, especially when you're taken off guard by the interviewer."

"Gee," said Duke. "You know what? You're out of sight."

"Is that good or bad?" I asked.

[2] Duke was twenty-one and on probation for attempted assault.

"Now, it's good. I don't know another teacher who wouldn't yell, but because you don't you're good, different, and we like it. I'll tell you when 'out of sight' means bad."

He did. Before grades were due, I explained that in arriving at a grade I considered attitude in class, participation in discussions and activities, interest, and courtesy to other students as well as to me. When Duke got his grade, he snarled, "You're out of sight, Mrs. Dawson, and now it ain't good."

In the Basic Education program, Demo, who wore sideburns down to his chin, was absent frequently, never brought a notebook, and showed little interest in learning. He interrupted a discussion to say, "What's the sense of all this vocabulary? I don't need it. All I want to be is the biggest pimp in the world."

"He's not fooling, either, Mrs. Dawson."

Several fellows disagreed with him. Edward Emile Edlow's voice could be heard above the din. "Man, you sure in a bag. I was in that bag, once, too. Now I'm getting out. I don't want to reach ninety and still be drinking wine and hanging around the street doing nothing. I's going to make it, see. You ain't going to stop me. If you don't like it, don't come."

"In a bag" is highly descriptive of a condition, in this case theirs, of being boxed in, like captives. This is characterized by hustling, pimping, smoking marijuana, drinking wine, gambling, staying up all night, driving with revoked licenses, dropping out of school, and provoking authorities.

As new vocabulary arose in our daily sessions, there was discussion and practice in using it. The approach fascinated the students. Early in the first program, the students could be heard on their breaks competing with each other in using such words as *stereotype*, *procrastinate*, *obsolete*, *irrelevant*, etc. One afternoon Bailey asked, "Mrs. Dawson, you know I've been using the big words we had because you said we haven't learned until we use them, and you know what? My friends look at me as if I am crazy or something and say, 'Man, don't you go seditty on us, see, because we don't like it.' So, I want to know, what's the use of learning this vocabulary if I can't use it? I don't want to be laughed at."

"Bailey, you do have a problem, and let's talk about it. But, before we do that — This is the first time I heard 'seditty.' What does it mean? I can guess if you want me to."

"OK. Guess."

"Sophisticated, uppity, putting on. Do I have the idea?"

"You certainly have. Hurry up, add this to your special list."

Bailey's problem was a persistent one that each student had to face soon after each program got under way. The student's relationship to his gang or peer group was threatened by his newly gained knowledge. In the discussion which ensued it was agreed that using the new vocabulary might act as an incentive to get friends into the program who were still wary of returning to school. If these friends still wouldn't go to school, at least the students could transmit to them some of what they were learning and help each other in the process. I urged Bailey and other students in subsequent programs to be patient with their friends, taking their ribbing, but continue to practice using the new vocabulary, so necessary for getting more highly skilled jobs.

Throughout our sessions I stressed the fact that I realized that the language they used with their friends was an "in" language, not for the ears of squares. They had become more aware of their language habits and alert to use more acceptable language.

"What if on an interview you become angry or frustrated and you blurt out, 'You're out of sight'?"

"What do you take me for, Mrs. Dawson? I ain't a dope."

"Certainly, Bailey. I don't think you're a dope. But habits are difficult to change, and when you're provoked, you just might accidentally drop such words, including four-letter words."

"That's right," said Wilbert. "It might just happen."

"You mean I'd be so stupid I'd go up to an interviewer at the state employment office and say, 'Hey, dude, get me a slave'?"

"I can figure that out — 'Get me a job.'"

"You're practically in by now, Mrs. Dawson, because you know almost fifty words or expressions. You're really no square."

By taking an interest in their language, you are taking an interest in them; and it is only natural that rapport should be enhanced.

Understanding Their World

HOUSING

Parents of these students did not find the Promised Land in San Francisco any more than their relatives or neighbors found it in New York City, Philadelphia, Chicago, or any other urban area. They were restricted to living in the public housing project at Hunters Point because they couldn't afford rents elsewhere and were not welcomed in most white areas. Discrimination in housing exists in subtle forms. During World War II these housing projects were actual barracks for the defense workers in the naval shipyards. The rooms are small and rat-infested, and the walls are paper-thin. The one advantage of the area is the view. It is ruined, however, by the accumulated garbage and the stench emanating therefrom. Before World War II there were few blacks living on the hill. Whites lived there; the blacks lived at the foot of the hill. This section was an old working-class neighborhood in San Francisco. The changes here are similar to those in other urban areas, for example, the area behind the stockyards in Chicago.

During World War II, minority groups were welcomed in San Francisco for working in defense plants, meat-packing plants, and naval shipyards. After World War II, the whites on the hill moved out of Hunters Point and the blacks moved up into the projects.

Overcrowding here has become worse in recent years as ghettoes or slums in other parts of San Francisco were torn down and displaced families descended on Hunters Point. Landlords reneged on making repairs but charged higher rents.

An unwed mother with two children, for example, may occupy a three-room apartment. The bathroom will have either a shower and no tub or a tub and no shower. There is central heating, however. Several of my students—Belle, Jessie, Roberta, and Cindy, unwed mothers with one and two children—lived in this type of accommodation.

Take another sort of family, in which a young man of nineteen or twenty-one might live. This family may include a working mother, or a mother in the hospital, and a twenty-year-old brother. There could be a sixteen-year-old sister who is thinking of dropping out of school, an eleven-year-old brother, and a nine-year-old brother. If the mother is unable to work, the Welfare Department pays the rent. The apartment may have three bedrooms, but these would be very small. There would be no dining room, nor any room for study or entertaining.

In another family, a mother, a single daughter, three boys, and an unwed daughter with two children might live. The mother and one daughter sleep on a sofa in the living room, the boys in one bedroom, and the other daughter and her children in another.

Several students often spoke about their fear of living on lower floors facing streets. At night youngsters, eight years old and up, deliberately throw rocks through windows.

One morning, Selma, a student in the training program for duplicating machine operators, seemed especially depressed. Usually vivacious and eager to participate in our discussions, she now sat listless and forlorn. Even her appearance was in contrast to her usual well-groomed look; she was wearing no makeup, and her hair was disheveled.

After class I asked if she were ill.

"I can't talk, Mrs. Dawson," she said weepingly. "Last night while we were out, someone came in and stole my husband's suits and sliced the furniture covers and curtains."

"Do you live in the project?"

"Yes, and I face the street. I don't know what to do. We have no money to replace these things now, and my weekly Manpower Development Training allowance is three weeks overdue."

FAMILY LIFE

Instability in the black family can be traced to the history of blacks in the United States. Hundreds of years of economic, social, and psychological brutalization have emasculated the black man to such a degree that he has lost his stabilizing influence on the family. Black family structure, therefore, has been robbed of what immigrant family structure has been able to retain—a strong male image serving as a cohesive and stabilizing force for the family. A strong family unit is crucially important in our society. An amorphous and unstable family structure contributes to lawlessness; when crime rates increase, the rest of society is also adversely affected. The sordid history of the American Negro has systematically denied him the solidarity of culture that has been granted to the immigrant poor. It is fallacious reasoning, therefore, for the Irish, the Jews, the Poles, and the Italians to say, "We pulled ourselves up by the bootstraps. Why don't they? They're primitive and uncivilized." With no strong male image to emulate, it is no wonder that young black men fail to develop a positive self-image.

Because there is so often no constructive male influence in the black family, the burden of household responsibility, economically and socially, has fallen upon the black woman. The woman has found it easier to get domestic work than the man. The man's resentment of the woman's domination, consequently, is exhibited in various behavior patterns, such as drinking, gambling, sleeping all day, staying out all night, and beating wife and children.

Where there is no father or husband living in the home, there may be callers or hangers-on whenever welfare checks arrive. My students refer to the days when checks arrive as "Mother's Day." They tell me, "The men stay until the money is used up. They drink and carry on, and then they leave when the money is gone."

"Mrs. Dawson, we don't ever be like that," said Alma and Elizabeth.[3]

Meals are catch as catch can. There is no regular hour for eating. At an early age, children gravitate to the street. This is where the action is — the bright lights, gambling, pimping, and narcotics pushing. Shoplifting comes easily, especially when basic necessities not covered in welfare budgets are needed.

Not every black family in the ghetto or slum area suffers from such instability. There are some families in which parents provide a comfortable, cheerful atmosphere where there is time to talk about problems at the dinner table. In these families, the father may be a carpenter or other skilled worker who is the head of the household. Parents in families like these show concern for the children's welfare. They are likely to be fearful that their daughters will become pregnant while in high school. They often arrange to be home when their children come home from school.

Leadership and community cooperation usually have come from these families. The disorganized family is difficult to reach. By the end of our first program, however, some of the parents in disorganized families were beginning to realize the benefits to their sons and daughters as well as to themselves and as a result began to cooperate.

According to Peter Ribicoff, formerly a welfare representative on the staff of the Center, those who are third-generation welfare recipients often hate their status. They may offer to repay the government as soon as they receive steady employment.

Many of our students were born in San Francisco during World War II. Other students have migrated from the South, with or without their families, sometimes to live with grandparents or aunts and uncles.

At first they are continually taunted in class and called such names

---

[3] Both were still single, without children. Alma, twenty, was rather obese but always well groomed. She was quiet, cooperative, and intelligent. Elizabeth, eighteen, was the youngest of ten children. She was tall, slender, and seldom carefully groomed. She found it difficult to part with her head scarf. Both were in the duplicating machine operators program.

as "cotton seed," "country boy," and even "Uncle Tom" because they are more motivated to learn than those born in San Francisco and present no behavior problems in class.

Parents from the Southern rural areas try to discipline their children. But their rural upbringing conflicts with urban ways of life. As a result, these youths do not pay attention to their parents' attempts to discipline them.

The transition from rural to urban life creates many conflicts within these young people. The diverse value systems with which they have to contend intensify these conflicts. Their parents may have one set of values; their own neighborhood groups have another set of values; at school they meet their peers from other neighborhoods with still another set of values; and their teachers have yet another set of values. Growing up in a ghetto, therefore, amid such confusion, has negative results as far as the values of these young people themselves are concerned. My students have had to learn how to act and what to say in varying situations, in order simply to get along.

The young women who have children out of wedlock either leave their children with relatives while they are in school or pay for a baby-sitter out of their allowances. Often they are late or absent because their baby-sitters are unavailable. The pre-nursery centers provided by child care agencies have no facilities for caring for infants. Whenever children are ill, the young mothers stay home. There is awareness of this problem, but it is still left for the young mother to solve it in some way that will not interfere with gainful employment later. Yet these young women are devoted mothers.

The problem of out-of-wedlock children is a serious one because in many cases the fathers are unemployed teen-agers ordered by the courts to provide child support. Frequently young men who become fathers are so busy hustling at night to get money for the mother's medical expenses that they are unable to attend school regularly. This may be their only means of meeting their responsibility.

Behavior toward women may seem strange when judged by middle-class standards. Wiz, for example, says he had been having trouble with his wife because she was too attached to her mother. He allowed his wife to visit her mother on Saturdays. Because she refused to cook dinner or clean the house, he gave her an ultimatum—thirty days' separation. He thinks he is acting like a boss. As soon as she left to live with her mother, he began going out on the town. About two days later, his wife called and begged him to come back. She is back; but he says they still don't get along, so he goes out any time he wants.

"She has to grow up. But she knows I'm boss, and that's what counts. I hit her when she needs it."

Beating wives seems to be a common practice. We were discussing love and marriage one day. Allen Williams said, "For the first months after I got married everything was fine. My wife obeyed my orders. Then a few months later she got wise and didn't do nothing. She didn't keep the house clean, didn't cook, and so I thought she needed a lesson so I busted her on the side of the head. It didn't hurt much, and things began to go better. Women need to be beat at least once a month to let them know who's boss."

Edward Emile Edlow said, "You think you have experience? I had it once, but I got rid of her. It's not right when a girl marries and she's too immature. All she wanted to do was have a good time. She didn't even want to take care of the baby." (Edward, now twenty-one, has one child out of wedlock.)

Stewart commented, "I don't believe in beating a woman. That's the last thing to do when nothing else works. When my wife don't clean the house, I sit down and talk to her. If she don't listen, I try again another way. And if that don't work, I give her one. I still think girls shouldn't get married if they don't want to do these things!"

GANGS AND PEER GROUPS AND THEIR IMPACT

Every person needs a feeling of belonging. To know that someone cares adds security in a world of insecurity. A child is a human being with thoughts and feelings. He does not always understand the reasons for certain behavior he observes, and therefore he may make incorrect assumptions about it.

His mother, his sole parent, may be employed and on her return home too tired to listen to him. He may assume she does not love him. Because circumstances force her to be out of the home a great part of the day, he receives his feeling of belonging elsewhere. At six or seven, he gravitates to the street. He has no parental supervision, no males in his home to set examples of acceptable behavior, no books in the home or time for conversation; gangs become the growing child's parents, and the street his home. Here he belongs. The gang code becomes his moral code; the gang values become his values. He is unwilling and often afraid to upset his status in the gang hierarchy. If going to school, learning, and reading are considered a waste of time by the gang, he too adopts that attitude. If he doesn't follow this pattern, he loses the gang's approval and he feels ostracized.

He doesn't want to be considered "seditty" or "chicken" by going along with the teacher and showing an interest in learning. He cuts school because members of his gang do; he provokes teachers because that is part of the gang code. Many of those who have dropped out of high school have given reasons like "Learning was a bore"; "I was fed up with being bored"; "I did nothing but put a knife to the science teacher's throat because he showed me no respect." By the time the ghetto child has grown into a young adult, he has evolved a value system: "School is a bore"; "Get the other guy before he gets you"; "Jumping him shows him how strong you are"; "Using strategy hustling puts you one ahead of Mr. Charley"; "You can only get so far as the white man lets you"; and "Blowing weed makes you think clear and is not as bad as alcohol."

"The police is out to get us, no matter what."

"We know what we want, and no one's going to tell us what to do."

"The church ain't never got our parents nothing and they's always praying, but they don't listen to us."

"I don't care about tomorrow. I'm having fun today. I may be dead tomorrow."

Let's listen to Arnold, seventeen years old, who came from Chicago and now lives with his uncle and aunt in San Francisco:

"At nine I was in trouble in Chicago, for stealing. I belonged to a gang since I was seven. When I was fifteen I was kicked out of school for beating up guys."

"Why did you do it?" asked a fellow student.

"For the name. You get a name when you beat up a fellow bigger than you. If I beat up Sam," he laughed (Sam, slender and short, is the same size as Arnold), "that'd be silly, and the fellows'd laugh.[4]

"Gee," Arnold continued, "when I was in school or outside, it's kill or be killed. In gang fights we used guns and I'd get in the middle, close my eyes, and shoot. I didn't care who. I hate to see suffering, and so I'd be glad when I got him so he wouldn't yell.

"There was one fight I remember. It was good, only I destroyed those new shoes. They was hundred-dollar shoes, stolen, that I paid

[4] Sam, from Dallas, was one of the quietest and brightest in this class. He had no police record and was interested in school.

five for. This dude was from another gang. I didn't like him nohow. He crossed over and I got him. I hit him so hard, he hit the ground. What a mess — over my shoes. That's what bothered me. I had to get a new pair."

"What about him? Did he get a fractured skull?"

"I guess, but I didn't care."

"Now, you're out here to start a new life. What about it?"

"I go to church every Sunday. My uncle, the Reverend, asked me when I going to be saved. I ain't never going to be saved. I'm going to get me money and a gun. I got to write back for one . . . to protect my aunt and uncle. People think they wealthy, just because they got a '65 Cadillac, a '64 Impala, and own a cleaning shop. I'm in school just to please my aunt. I don't figure on staying. Money is my God. I'll make more when I start fighting in the ring when I turn eighteen in November."

The gang influences dress and hair styles. Daily, new hair trends are introduced. If it's stylish to process hair, several students appear with this style. On other days two may come in with hair streaked and wearing long sideburns down to the chin. Some girls, for a while, bleached their hair. Now the style is to dye hair black.

The gang code operated in the classroom. Students intent on learning and getting out of the bag they were in tried to buck the gang, but they were afraid to incur the wrath of the gang leaders. In the office boy training program, those who were considered the "good guys" went to the rest rooms or to the office or just walked out of the class if they sensed trouble. They stayed out until the outburst blew over. These disturbances often occurred in the English class because the students resented the teacher's authoritative manner and wished to vex him. If they absented themselves, the "good" fellows could not be accused by their peers of going along with the teacher. This was one way of staying in with the gang.

Once after an exciting discussion on what fraudulent advertising meant and how important critical thinking was, Stewart came up to me.

"Mrs. Dawson, Coolsann and me's having a hard time. This morning during the break we were in the men's room and I happened to say how much I was learning in this class and how I could see how much I got to do to get ahead. Three of the fellows heard me, and they were ready to jump me. They called me all kinds of names for wanting to learn."

EATING HABITS

These young people do not eat properly. Their daily diet consists of potato chips, sweet rolls, hamburgers, hot dogs, and carbonated drinks. They are not accustomed to eating breakfast and wait until they arrive at school to grab a Coke from the vending machine early in the morning. Seldom do they have dinner at a regular hour. Many lunch hours I watched my students as they dashed down to the corner and purchased hamburgers so thin they were practically invisible, drenched with catsup, mustard, and relish. Sometimes they eat an apple or an orange. Once a week, they go to the Chinese restaurant two blocks away for fried rice and shrimp, the soy sauce oozing from the paper container down their clean blouses. This item costs one dollar and a portion appears to be about four tablespoons.

The women never shop for several meals at a time in order to save money, but purchase frozen foods and TV dinners for each meal individually. The young men who still live at home with their parents go to the refrigerator any hour of the day or night and find something. Several married men said, "My wife don't cook when she don't want to, so I has to go out."

SLEEP HABITS

Sleep habits follow a pattern often established by the peers in the social group. Going dancing or "gigging" means staying out all night. At first I was shocked to learn that many young men and women often stayed up all night, many times away from home. Partying is not restricted to weekends. It goes on nightly. Under such circumstances, the trainee's readiness for learning follows a sort of curve.

Monday morning is sad. At eight o'clock only a handful appear ready for learning. Others straggle in throughout the morning. On Tuesday there is some improvement and an increase in their readiness for learning. By Wednesday the climax has been reached. On Thursday their interest begins to wane as they prepare for a "popping" weekend. Friday is, like Monday, an off day.

Not all students stay up late to enjoy themselves. There are a few who work at night. Dick, the twenty-year-old with two infants and a wife with incipient cancer, works as a television serviceman at night after attending school for seven hours during the day.

Others have hobbies which keep them out late. Henry, for example, has only four hours of sleep nightly because he works out in a gym to tune up for weekly boxing bouts. Instead of going to bed when he finishes his workout, he goes out with "the fellows and girls" and sometimes doesn't get in before 6 A.M. His pattern is slowly changing because he is now attending a city junior college at night.

RECREATION

Nearly all these youths listen to progressive jazz. Louis Armstrong, Duke Ellington, and Ella Fitzgerald are not for them. They love Cannonball Adderly, Lou Rawls, John Handy, Yusaf Lateef, Brenda Calloway, and the Impressions, a quartet of singers and instrumentalists. A few prefer rock 'n' roll. They know their styles so well from continuous listening that they gesticulate in imitation whenever records of their favorite singers are played.

A few young men practice in the gyms in the San Francisco Park and Recreation Department facilities. These recreational centers are too few for the increasing number of young adults. Moreover, they close at 9:30 P.M. Full of life, the young men crowd the streets looking for action.

Some of those who practice weight lifting have won prizes for their prowess, proudly displaying their photographs at the slightest sign of interest. These few eat and sleep in accordance with healthful regimens advocated by health educators.

HEALTH AND HEALTH FACILITIES

At the beginning of each program, I distributed a health questionnaire I had prepared. From the replies I was not surprised to learn that the majority didn't attend clinics regularly. However, women went more frequently than men. Only one city hospital, woefully understaffed and overcrowded, with obsolete facilities, was available. Few of these young people go for annual checkups. They frequent clinics for emergencies — accidents, pregnancy, venereal disease. Many have nervous indigestion. A few have asthma, ulcers, or diabetes. Surprisingly enough, eye examinations reveal that most have almost perfect vision. Only a few need eyeglasses.

As regards dental care, the responses indicate that students visit the dentist only when they are plagued by toothaches. When they go, it is often too late to save decayed teeth.

As is understandable, poverty and ghetto living have destructive effects on the mental health of youths who have been exposed to them. When discrimination and rejection are added to the picture, youths flounder in their search for an identity. Community mental health services on a twenty-four-hour basis are needed. These young people must have some place to vent their wrath and air their problems as they arise. They must learn more about themselves and understand who they are and what favorable influence they can exert on their younger brothers and sisters. They need reinforcement to develop a strong identity.

ATTITUDE TOWARD NARCOTICS AND ALCOHOL

It would seem, from discussions, counseling sessions, and topics chosen by the students, that narcotics and alcohol are of primary interest to them. What do they think about narcotics, and how deeply involved are they?

They think that marijuana is not a narcotic. "It's good for you. Ever blown weed, Mrs. Dawson? It makes you think clearer."

"It makes you feel good."

"You get a joint and start tripping out or get loaded, man!"

"You know, it puts you into a state of euphoria." (We had learned the word *euphoria*, and now it was used correctly.)

My students began the habit of smoking marijuana—"blowing weed"—early in high school, some even in elementary school. Nearly every student in this program has tried it. In fact, it is considered a regular feature of partying, or "popping." Few, to my knowledge, use heroin—"horse" or "smack." You can tell when they are still high on marijuana: their movements are uncoordinated; their eyelids are swollen; their speech is unintelligible and the tongue seemingly inflexible.

In addition to the usual narcotics, some ghetto youths are now getting narcotic effects from crystals used in the breeding of chickens. According to my students, who keep me posted on the latest trends, these crystals are more potent than heroin or cocaine.

A few have tried LSD. Allen Williams said his "trip" helped him creatively and communicatively: he now claims he communicates more effectively with his wife.

Those who smoke marijuana regularly or are addicted to heroin do not take alcoholic beverages. They are most vehement in discussions on the topic of alcohol, blaming delinquency on alcohol and minimizing the detrimental effects of narcotics. Drinking wine is a common habit, and this begins early in the morning. Whenever checks arrive or hustling money is obtained, a few young men can be observed heading for the liquor stores and carrying out wine or whiskey, which they drink straight. At parties they bring their own liquor, usually a fifth of gin or vodka. The young women drink too. Early in the first program, these drinking habits presented problems. Drinking in the men's room was common practice. "When I get home today, I'll get me a shortneck," said Deacon.

ATTITUDE TOWARD WORK: HUSTLING

Hustling—any illegal activity to make money—is a way of life to these youths. Welfare budgets provide only a substandard income which must be supplemented. Early in life, therefore, children in many welfare families are initiated into ways of hustling. Under gang influence they learn how to get along by shoplifting items such as food, clothing, candy, and toys. When they reach adolescence they are well schooled and pass their information down to their brothers and sisters. Hustling, to the younger child, assumes an aura of prestige. Later, pimping, gambling, and petty stealing make you more acceptable in the gang hierarchy.

"Each offense has to be evaluated in context," says a representative of the Bureau of Community Relations in the San Francisco Police Department. "A young woman, seventeen years old, who had had a child born out of wedlock, needed diapers and safety pins so badly that she took them from a five-and-ten, was arrested, and now has a police record." The judge was sympathetic to her plight and gave her a light sentence.

I was overjoyed one day when one of my seemingly apathetic men students, Dagger, gradually began to take an interest in our daily discussions, especially those on black history. He even stayed after class one morning on his coffee break—a rare occurrence—to talk to me about getting him another copy of the book *A Pictorial History of the Negro in America*,[5] priced at $6.95. We had few of these books, and I asked him why he wanted it.

[5] Langston Hughes and Milton Meltzer, *A Pictorial History of the Negro in America*, rev. ed., Crown Publishers, Inc., New York, 1963.

He said, "There's a bus driver I know who's mad about black history, and I think it'd do him good. So can you get it, huh?"

I noticed a twinkle in his eye, and something suddenly clicked in me. "Oh, no," I said to myself. "He's not going to hustle this! I'll ask him." I did.

"Well, uh, uh, yeah, Mrs. Dawson, I figures I can sell it to him for $8.00. I can use the money."

He never got the book. His seeming interest in learning vanished. It was interesting to see subsequent changes in his dress and behavior. His hair, which had been worn high already, was now worn even higher with more bleached red on top than before. He came in daily with new colored jackets, highly colored shirts, paisley-printed scarves in ascot fashion, polished nails, and shined shoes with pointed toes. His eyes were often swollen, however; he could rarely keep his head up in class, and it appeared that he was smoking marijuana or taking heroin. A few weeks later he was picked up for suspicion of possession of narcotics, and he is now in jail.

Before this happened, we had had several talks after class. What has happened is tragic, because he is extremely intelligent and realizes what he is doing to himself but is unwilling to sever relations with his associates or get professional help.

Not all students are engaged in illegal rackets or hustling, however. Many try to supplement their weekly MDTA allowances with income from part-time jobs as messengers, janitors, librarians' aides, or hospital orderlies, or take unskilled jobs. Soon, however, the hours at school plus the hours at work and the nightly partying conflict and something must be abandoned. It is sometimes the school and at other times both school and job, and once again they may be back in the street. In a few situations where the men involved have wives and several children to support, they have had to forgo school to keep the job. This is tragic, because such students have often shown superior ability to communicate and could have successfully completed this course.

ATTITUDE TOWARD WORK: JOBS AND SALARIES

During a tour we took to a newspaper plant our guide, a twenty-three-year-old copy boy, told us he had been on staff for seven years.

"How much do you make?" Bailey asked.

"Eighty-five dollars a week."

"Is that all? And you been here seven years?"

In our discussion the following day, Bailey said, "You know what? That fellow yesterday is a dope. I'd never stay no place for a lousy $85 a week." Several others echoed his sentiments.

"How much do you expect to get on your first job?"

"About $150 to $200 per week."

"Are you serious?" I asked.

"Yeah. Because I can make $150 a night hustling for a couple of hours. Why should I work for eight hours for such a little bit?"

"What about being caught and serving time for a while? Don't you figure you'd lose that way?"

"That's the chance you take. Life's a gamble, you know, Mrs. Dawson."

The youth born and brought up in the South thinks a job is important. He tries to keep it and is anxious to please the boss. This is not the case with the youth raised in the North. To him a job is needed to get nice clothes and a car. These are his goals. When they are met, he quits the job. Youths in the ghetto don't necessarily look down on something like a janitorial job. There are reasons for this attitude. In my students' eyes, a janitor's job, which they consider the lowest, can be managed successfully. They are afraid they will be rejected on a more highly skilled job. When the boss gives them orders which they don't like, they have an excuse for quitting a job.

ATTITUDE TOWARD THE POLICE

Youths who live in poverty areas and ghettoes, regardless of ethnic origin, seem united in their hostility toward law enforcement agencies. They continually complain about injustices practiced and feel that police attitudes show prejudice toward minority groups, especially toward blacks.

"If we're just standing near a car and talking to a friend, the police walks up. They tap you on the shoulder and say something bad. Sometime they frisk you. Sometime they ask you what you're doing out of your own neighborhood. What's it their business? If we ain't doing nothing, why can't we stand where we want?"

Early in the first program, our session was interrupted one afternoon by Bailey's dashing in breathlessly. "Hey, Wilbert, don't go home," he said. "The police looking for you with a warrant." Wilbert had been driving with a revoked license and had been arrested but had not answered the charges.

"Why did you wait until there was a warrant out for your arrest, Wilbert?" I asked him after class.

"I want to make him sweat, that's why. The police going to be after me, anyway, so what? They always harassing us." (*Harass* was a new word in our vocabulary.)

This charge that the police are "out to molester us" was repeated by a group of men students in the telephone framemen program. Their grievances, based on their personal experiences, were aired on an educational television channel. Allen Williams, twenty-one years old, a high school dropout and a former member of a gang, said, "If you're drunk on a Saturday night in Fillmore or Hunters Point," (these are black areas) "you can be picked up. That happened to me when I was younger. The police, they didn't talk pretty to me, either. It do matter where you live and what color your are. Because one night I visited some white friends in an all-white neighborhood. I was just as drunk, and all the officer said to me was, 'Young man, you've had too much. Why don't you go home?' He said it real polite, too."

These youths, therefore, have little respect for the police. Many times it seems as if they drive with revoked licenses, carry liquor in the car, speed, and take other risks because they want to provoke the police. This could be their way of communicating their frustrations and protesting against injustices.

Nearly all the men students in our program, and a few women, have police records. Whenever students are absent for two or more consecutive days, I fear they've been in trouble with the police. Early in the first program, Jim, a former gang leader with whom I was beginning to relate, was absent for several days. Bailey, his friend, said, "I guess Jim won't be around for a while. He was picked up last night. He was doing nothing. The police always do that — pick on us. They don't bother whites like that!" He continued, "Jim was riding with two fellas last night. They just left the Fillmore district when the police picked them up for speeding on Van Ness Avenue." (Van Ness is a prominent avenue in San Francisco.) "They examined the car and found narcotics. The three is now in jail. But Jim weren't to blame. He didn't know these fellows. He just out for a good time. The police — they always picking on us!"

During the program I was disturbed when Ali-Tees, a young man not yet twenty-one, who had been an example to his peers in the Basic Education course because he was attending a city college at night and participating enthusiastically in the program, suddenly got into difficulty. When he returned after several days' absence, I asked what had happened.

"Nothing really serious, Mrs. Dawson. I was waving a toy pistol at a friend who was teasing me with a knife, and the police picked me up for attempted assault. That's all. I'm going to be twenty-one in a few weeks, and I been clean since I was eighteen, and so nothing will happen." He didn't realize at the time that waving even a toy pistol would be considered serious by the police.

What is the solution to this complex problem? Many things have to be done simultaneously. The primary one, however, is to set up communication lines between law enforcement agencies, people in the ghettoes, and the middle-class members of society. The concepts necessary for establishing rapport in the education of these youths are equally necessary for changing attitudes of various groups — ghetto youths toward the police, the police toward ghetto youths, public toward police, and police toward public. Each group has to be able to accept feedback from the other, and sincerity has to be evident in attempts to understand each group's dissatisfactions.

In San Francisco, the police department has a Community Relations Bureau. A currently small staff of specially trained police officers, in civilian garb, listen to what these young people think, evaluate their grievances, and take action to change police approaches. There is evidence that this new approach works, but only if the assigned police officer is a warm personality who is capable of communicating with these youths. There has been such a community relations officer in the Hunters Point—Bayview district. This police officer earned his acceptance as an individual. His warm personal interest in each trainee with a police record, his attempts to get the youth's story, and his sincere desire to help earned him the youths' respect and acceptance.

In addition to the attempts of the police department's community relations division to change ghetto inhabitants' attitudes toward the police, a private agency was set up in San Francisco. Youth for Service, Inc., affiliated with the United Community Fund, has hired former gang leaders to roam the streets, visit teen-agers' hangouts, prevent gang fights, and try to interest youth in constructive activities while serving simultaneously as a safety valve for the release of tensions and frustrations.

The fact that the majority of our students have police records presents a very real problem. Students often mention their fear of not being able to get employment. This fear is well grounded. A few of their friends not in our program have tried to get jobs in industry by lying about previous arrests. If they were hired, they were later fired after company security investigations exposed their arrest records. This poses a serious problem. These youths are being trained for skilled jobs, but how can they get any if they have police records?

Education is needed to change attitudes of prospective employers. It is in this area that the specially assigned community relations officer is making a contribution. He makes it his business to sit down and talk with each youth who has a record. Then he visits individual employers to discuss the youth's record as it affects his chances for employment. Changing attitudes is slow, no matter at what level. Progress in changing employers' attitudes is being made, even if it seems imperceptible at times. Other groups are also working to persuade employers to hire such youths: the Urban League and the Committee on Youth, the latter responsible for initiating this first Youth Opportunities Center.

The attitude of young people in ghettoes toward the police is not peculiar to San Francisco. This complex problem is national, and crime is national; the solution, therefore, has to be national rather than local. The police throughout the country need special training; salaries of policemen have to be increased; and research is needed on the psychological effects of violence on the mental health of policemen. Little change in attitudes can take place, however, until effective communication lines are established between law enforcement agencies, ghetto inhabitants, and middle-class people. This is the foremost need.

ATTITUDE TOWARD RELIGION

In each program the topic of religion and the church was introduced by students as a selection for discussion. Early in the training program Allen Williams (one of the telephone frameman group), articulate and courageous, volunteered to be the first to be taped.

"I'm going to talk about a controversial subject, religion." (Everyone laughed, because *controversial* had been a new word the day before.)

"What I have to say may not please you. I don't know how many of you go to church, but I think religion is a bunch of hogwash." There were murmurs of shock from the class. "I can't believe that if I want something, praying will get it for me. I remember many times we had no food. The rent was due, and we were going to be evicted. My mother went to church and prayed, but nothing happened. Then I worked in a grocery store after school. I brought the money. I got the food, not God.

"We live on earth. The sun is a star—right, Mrs. Dawson?" I nodded. "No one yet has gone from star to star looking for God. Astronauts and cosmonauts have never found him in space, so I don't believe he exists. . . . Noah got two of each species for his Ark. That's nonsense. How could he find two of each species so quickly? I can't believe it. That's why I don't believe about Adam and Eve. Religious leaders just want to plant fear in you, that's all."

He had struck a sensitive spot. Immediately he was besieged.

"You mean you don't believe in heaven and hell?"

"You mean you don't believe in the Bible?"

"Man, you can't be serious about what you said."

"You an atheist, that's what."

Edward Emile Edlow raised his hand in Allen's face. "You are, too, an atheist. I was a few months ago, too. That was before I got with it. Then, being an atheist always got me in trouble. I even served time. How come now, since I believe in God, I'm straight?"

Deacon said, "Man, there must be something in it."

Allen said, "Do you want me to answer questions, or do you just want to hear yourself?"

"OK, talk."

"I don't believe in heaven and hell. I think that's told you to frighten you. I believe in science and evolution, not these stories."

"You think just because you can't see God, he doesn't exist. You're foolish. He's there all the time watching you."

Lionel said, "My mother believes in God, and I do, too. I was hit by a car and unconscious for weeks until my mother went to church and prayed for me. That day I became conscious. That was seven years ago, and I have believed in God even more since then."

The bell rang at this point. The topic was continued the following day. Several students who were born and raised in the South voiced their beliefs.

Bonnie, one of twelve children, now only eighteen years old, said, "That's all I remember as a kid . . . hearing my mother saying, 'Don't do this, don't do that, or the good Lord'll get you.' Every Sunday everybody'd be dressed up and off to church. They prayed and prayed, but they still be poor. The white man still their boss. I think they stupid, that's what. I had to go with them when I lived there, but not now. I never go to church."

The consensus seems to reflect dissatisfaction with what the church offers young adults. Many churches are aware of this problem and are trying to attract young people with innovative approaches such as jazz sessions and tutorial programs. In the last analysis, I believe the church has to prove its sincerity in wanting to help young people — in this world.

ATTITUDE TOWARD SCHOOL

Students enter our program expecting to find a perpetuation of practices they experienced in the secondary schools, practices which accounted for their dropping out or being dropped. Too often their expectations become a reality. Youths quickly respond to not being reached by appearing uninterested, even bored, by coming in late, and by being absent frequently. There are other factors in this behavior, too, but repetition of worn-out methods is a major cause.

"When I was in high school," said Anton, the only white student who entered the telephone framemen course, "I was bored. We all read at the same time. The teacher had to stick to the textbook. If I wanted to ask related questions not in the book, I was told to keep quiet. Whatever incentive I had was crushed. I got so fed up, I had to drop out in the eleventh grade. That's why I dig this class. I feel like somebody important. What I think I can talk about. I can read what I want and report on it."

Coolsann said, "When we were in high school, we didn't always catch on. Maybe we were slow, but it made no difference, the teacher never stopped to find out if we got it. Maybe there were too many children for her to teach. One thing, we never felt any teacher was interested in us. We thought, OK, we don't understand. So we don't understand, and we'd get feeling inferior and soon get a complex and try to get dropped."

These sentiments and experiences were common among these students. School was a sometime thing, an enigma to be tolerated rather than enjoyed.

ATTITUDE TOWARD WHITES

In the beginning the racial barrier may have afforded a basis for hostility in the classroom. But race was seldom mentioned. When the students' defenses were down, however, and rapport was established between them and me, their feelings toward whites were freely expressed.

In discussing employment, Deacon said, "Why fool ourselves, Mrs. Dawson? We can go only so far as the white man lets us."

Coolsann said, "The white man is prejudiced. When I fill out an application—before I'm seen, even—and the employer sees my address, he says to himself, 'Oh, that's the black belt.' I don't get the job. This has happened to me many times."

Duke, whenever he was annoyed with grades or outside problems, would blurt out in the middle of any discussion, "All whites are devils, and you can't tell me no different."

"Man, venerate Mrs. Dawson, and stop thinking in stereotypes." (We had discussed *venerate* and *stereotypes* as new vocabulary.)

"I didn't mean her, because she's mixed. We all know that."

It was at such times that I tried to develop the concept that no one knew all members of any group. "Duke," I said, "you don't know 'all' whites. Is it fair to put a label on a whole group for the actions of some?"

"That's prejudice, man," said Allen Williams, who continuously tried to counter the stereotyped thinking of his peers. "When you talk that way, like the Black Muslims, you don't make sense. What about the whites who gave their lives for civil rights in the South?"

"They just fronting, that's all."

"You're so crazy, I don't know if I should try. I'm wasting my breath. You're really ignorant, man. Conditions can improve only if we all work together—blacks, whites, Jews, Mexican-Americans, Chinese, and other ethnic groups." (*Ethnic* was a word introduced by Ali-Tees, who knew it from his study of sociology at a city college.) "You're really prejudiced," Allen added. "Twenty years from now things will be improved. You wait and see. You see more interracial marriages now than before. It just takes time."[6]

"We waited long enough," said Deacon. "If we depend on demonstrations only, it'll take another hundred years. We can't wait so long."

Allen said, "Well, if you're so anxious about rights, how come you aren't demonstrating out there? How come there are more whites than blacks on picket lines for civil rights?" He went on, "You think

[6] Allen is now married to a sweet-looking, understanding white girl who is working to send him to city college at night.

whites are prejudiced against us. Take my father and mother. They're still prejudiced against whites. Another thing. You think we're the only ones discriminated against. What about Jews, Mexican-Americans, and the most discriminated against, the American Indian? You never mention them."

Ray said, "The way I feel is, so long as there are people, there will always be prejudice." [7]

Wiz jumped on this. "I got something that bears on this. You go down to any one of the bathrooms in this school, and what do you see? Don't tell me prejudice is less."

"How many wrote that? You're stupid if you think that's the feeling of every white fellow in the building."

"It's on the walls. The janitor must be feeling that way. He never washed it off."

"We can stamp prejudice out."

"OK, you stamp it out, then. What are you doing to do that?"

"I think I'm doing a lot. By coming to school and educating myself," said Allen Williams.

"As long as there's an upper class, there's going to be discrimination. People who think they're better than others," said Deacon.

Allen Williams was right to mention other minority groups. These youths are prejudiced against other minority groups, especially Chinese and Jews. In the predominantly black area in San Francisco, the Chinese own small grocery stores. In some cases they do overcharge the black customers. In retaliation teen-agers often provoke the Chinese owners and pilfer whenever they can.

ATTITUDE TOWARD THEMSELVES; SELF-CONCEPTS

The majority of ghetto youth, as a result of their environment and cultural patterns, grow up in a sea of conflicts as to what to think about themselves. Most professionals and confused parents do not give them much help in improving their self-concepts. In many cases they only compound the confusion by not even listening to how youths feel about themselves and those around them.

[7] Ray, who usually remained quiet, had come from Louisiana only months ago. He was of French-Negro ancestry. Because he was quiet and eager to learn, he was pounced upon frequently. It took courage for him to disagree.

"I'm a dropout, and so I guess I'll never make it. Everyone else thinks I'll fail, too. So, what's the use? Even if I finish the course, I'll never be hired. Who'd hire me—with a police record?"

This lack of self-esteem may account for their negative outlook on life, their initial hostility in class, and their apparent lack of enthusiasm for learning.

Here and there, bright spots of hope appear, although only fleetingly at first. I remember how Emile Edlow answered Demo's expressed opposition to learning vocabulary. "You're in a bag, man. I'm getting out of it. I'm going to be somebody. I'm going to make it, see."

These youths have a very low opinion of themselves. They have tasted nothing but failure. And this attitude itself perpetuates failure. If their negative outlook is to be changed, they need warmth, sincere interest, and acceptance from teachers, prospective employers, and others. Only then can their self-hatred and distrust of others, especially whites, be changed to a more positive outlook.

Summary

Your understanding of how your students live, how they feel and think about themselves and others, what their attitudes are toward school, and how they occupy their leisure, and your familiarity with their language—these are fundamental to the establishment of rapport. Understanding of their world is necessary before teaching can be possible. It lays the groundwork for a partnership in a mutually meaningful teaching-learning experience.

Understanding their world gives you insights into handling behavior problems in a classroom setting, in addition to providing content for subsequent sessions. You perceive your students' needs. You now have the responsibility of opening windows in the mind for mental ventilation.

With knowledge like this you will be able to introduce new experiences that will have significance for them. You can introduce new approaches to help change attitudes and behavior, so that you will be preparing these young people not only for jobs, but for living even if jobs become obsolete. How you can utilize your information about their way of life is illustrated in later chapters.

3 • Communicating in the Classroom

Now that you have opened the door to another world, how do you proceed? How do you cut through these youths' hostility and reduce their resistance to change? How do you help them develop an awareness of themselves and the world around them? How do you increase their self-esteem, tap their inner resources, and prepare them for a world of ambiguities? What happens to you during this process? How do you know you are succeeding?

At the beginning of each new program, there was the same type of resistance to the seating arrangements. The fact that I never sat behind the desk but sat down with the students in the semicircle did not seem right to the students. There were individual differences in the intensity of their resistance. In one coeducational group, Saul, a heavy-set, small-eyed young man, entered the room with a sullen look and said, "Oh, not again! Why do we have to have family style? Why can't we sit like in other classes?"

When we were settled, I said, "We've been here only three days, and many of you aren't familiar with my method of operation. We'll be discussing many things. We want to be able to look at each other when we talk. We don't want to work with our backs to each other. We'll try to make this a friendly corner, not a classroom."

Several weeks later, I wanted to test reactions on seating arrangements. For the first time since we had changed to the semicircle arrangement, I left the chairs in the traditional classroom fashion. The bell rang, and the students entered aghast.

"Gee, Mrs. Dawson, what happened? Ain't we going to be friendly no more?"

Saul said, "I like it family style, now. Can we put the chairs in a circle again, please?"

Everyone got busy, and, more quickly than I had ever seen them move, rearranged the chairs in a semicircle.

Handling Discipline Problems

While a few students participated early in the first program, several still sat with their backs to me or completely ignored what was going on. Others carried on private talks, giggled, threw water at each other, poked their neighbors, stood up, and guffawed as if they were on the street. One young woman shrugged her shoulders, took out her lipstick, and proceeded to compare her shade with another girl's. A few had their heads on the desk. One or two were reading the sports pages of a newspaper they were now receiving daily in their English class.

When someone toward the front of the room turned around and said, "Shut up, I can't hear," she was slapped by her neighbor. Once an incipient fight between two women suddenly ended when Jim, the gang leader, just looked over at them. Quiet prevailed only momentarily, however.

Note passing between the young women persisted. I said on one of these occasions, "Enid, please stop passing notes. If you were on a job, how long do you think your supervisor would allow this?" [1]

"I ain't on a job. I ain't passing notes. Why always pick on me? Anyway, no one ain't going to tell me nothing! I does what I want, see!"

We talked about what it means to listen and show consideration to one another. I said, "Enid, when you have something important to tell Susie, how do you feel when she turns her head away or starts to talk to someone else?"

"I poke her real hard, and then she listens."

The same hostile attitude was revealed when we talked about extremes in hair styles and what effect this could have on an employment

---

[1] Enid wore her shiny, freshly pressed hair in different styles daily. Her attire was exotic, like a belly dancer's: balloon-like transparent pants with a décolleté blouse worn to the midriff. She was nineteen, married, and the mother of two children. Her husband was employed. She was a leader and from the first day expressed her defiance openly. She was a little spitfire, but I knew we could work together if her sporadic attendance improved.

interviewer's impressions. By the third week, we had a memo from the administration on the wearing of extreme hair styles, tight pants, ruffled shirts, goatees, etc. I read this to my students. It stimulated such discussion that it awoke a few sleepers. Even the uninterested soon got into the fray.

"No extremes?" said Jessie. "What if I want to wear my hair high? No one's going to tell me how to dress or to wear my hair. No one's going to tell me nothing."

"I'm my own boss, I knows things best," said Cindy, "I'll wear what I want." (Cindy, with her ever-present transistor radio and expansive rear, cavorted during coffee breaks with complete abandon. Her energy in class, however, was expended in watching the clock.)

We had been talking daily about the importance of showing respect to another person and stressing that this could happen only if we had respect for ourselves.

"I want to treat you like adults, as I told you the first day we met. I've shown respect for you from the beginning. I expect the same from you. I'm no prison matron. I have no intention of forcing you to do anything. You'll do certain things when you realize their importance to you. When you do, you'll open your mind—like opening a window—and you'll look outside. Then and only then will you be ready to learn. You don't believe me now, but you'll see as we go along. At this point we don't know when this will happen. Because each one of us is a different individual, our windows will open at different times. It's up to you whether you want to continue to keep your mental window closed and locked."

How could I show them how they looked to others without taking movies? I suddenly hit upon this idea. "I'm going to try to show you how you look to someone else—in this case, to me. I'm going to act this out without scenery or costumes. You will have to use your imagination. I'm not going to mention any names. I don't want to embarrass anyone. You can criticize me after I finish. Watch me closely. I may talk, but I will be using pantomime mostly."

Everyone was attentive as I arranged a chair on the platform, tightened my skirt while shortening it, and pushed my hair up into a bouffant effect.

"Maybe we'll understand each other better when I finish. First I'll make believe I'm the women, and then the men. Ready?"

"Ready!" came a unanimous response. Their attention was intense.

"OK. Curtain."

I came in swinging my rear, pretending that I was wearing a very short, tight skirt, so tight it outlined my derrière. I sat down on the chair with my legs stretched out in such a way that my imaginary skirt rode up around my thighs. I took out imaginary bubble gum and crackled it noisily. Spontaneous laughter arose from the students.

"Louise, did you hear about Amy last night at the dance? . . ." I said. (I chose names that belonged to no one in the class.) Then I giggled and, after passing notes, pointed to several imaginary class-mates, saying, "Who, me? Mrs. Dawson, why always pick on me? I ain't passing notes." There was more laughter. I proceeded to pretend to take out mascara and apply it. "What you say, Mrs. Dawson? I ain't putting on mascaree, I'm taking something out of my eye, see!" There was more laughter. Then I poked my imaginary neighbor, and I com-pared my lipstick shade with hers. More laughter. I concluded by dashing off with others to the rest room at the right of the stage. More laughter.

"OK, so much for the women. Now, the men." I put on sunglasses and pushed the brim of an imaginary hat far back on my head. I swag-gered in, swinging my hips from side to side while throwing my head back and forth as if pecking. The students laughed. I sat with my head on the desk. Then I swung around in the chair, so that I was facing the wall rather than the teacher or the blackboard, and yawned audibly. Suddenly I yelled in a most hostile manner, "Well, if you're going to dictate, dictate, see. I'm tired of all the talk." More laughter.

"That's you, Jim."

"No, that's Bailey."

"It ain't either."

I ended by taking out imaginary dice, rolling them, and then rushing out to the rest room to the left of the stage.

The next afternoon, before we officially began our class in Personal Development, Enid said, "Mrs. Dawson, I have something personal to say."

"I'll be happy to discuss it with you after class or in a counseling session tomorrow."

"No, it's not exactly my personal. It's everybody's personal. Uh, uh, uh, . . . we, that is, us, are very angry with you. You made fun of us yesterday. We don't like it. We here to improve."

"That's good, Enid. I'm glad to hear it."

"Mrs. Dawson," continued Enid, "you didn't have to mention names. Everybody knows it was me with the tight skirt and everything."

"If you could identify yourself, I'm sorry. I mentioned no names, but I did imitate what I saw and heard. Let's hear from others. Don't be afraid. Remember what I said the first day? One of the important things we hope to accomplish in this course is to be able to express our feelings and thoughts."

Jim, the gang leader, said, "It was funny yesterday, but when we talked about it after class, we decided we didn't like it."

"All right, do you think I was doing something that didn't happen?"

"No."

"Then this raises an important point. What you do shows how you feel and what you think. I'm trying to show you how you look to someone else. If I were your employer or a supervisor on a job and you acted this way, you know you wouldn't be there for long. As soon as you're willing to face up to yourself, you're on the bottom rung of the ladder to improvement. I'm not here to make you over. However, the way you look and the way you act now will never help you get a job. You have wonderful minds and a great deal of ability. I've seen that in these few weeks. How would you describe the behavior I dramatized yesterday?"

"Childish," said James.

"Infantile," said Jessie.

"Good. If this is true, you have to learn to take criticism. It is difficult for any of us. The less angry you get when you are criticized, the more you are growing up. You can't always block criticism by attacking the critic. I'm trying to teach you like adults; but remember, it's up to you to act like adults.

"I'm glad you reacted the way you did. It shows you're thinking and feeling. We're communicating. That's good. Keep it up. I'll do my share. You, too, have to help. You're developing personally when you feel it's important to learn. Only you know that. No one from the outside can tell you."

Duke was hostile, impatient, and defiant through most of the course. For the first week of basic education, which preceded the vocational training phase, he arrived a half hour late, sauntered in with his tardy pass, and sat down in front, disturbing his classmates to find his seat.

I looked at him, but I did not yell because he was late. During the session, we discussed the effect of tardiness on a job. I added, "I'd faint, Duke, if you ever came on time!"

"Mrs. Dawson, I can't promise you nothing, but maybe I'll come earlier. That is, if I feel like it." He was teasing and testing.

The next day he came fifteen minutes earlier than the day before. He sat down and said, "Did you notice? I'm fifteen minutes earlier. See, I'm improving, ain't I? You can say that!"

"That's right. Now see if you can make it on time."

The next day and each day thereafter he was in his seat before the bell rang. I said, "Duke, you're on time. That's wonderful. I hope you'll excuse me. I can't faint. I'm wearing a white blouse, and I don't want to get dirty." Laughter.

When I read the office memo outlawing goatees, beards, and extreme hairdos, Duke was furious. Stroking his goatee, he said, "Aw, shee-it, I'm going to wear what I likes. I'll dress how I likes. Look at these dudes, their hair's down to their shoulders, and no one says nothing about them."

I tried to explain the difference in our programs from the composition of the students in the regular school. Those in the regular vocational school were younger and were not receiving a weekly stipend as were our students. We also had to face reality, the world of work. Few, if any, of the students would be hired wearing goatees, beards, or any extreme styles that called attention to themselves. Several weeks later Duke came in with his hair closely cropped and without his goatee, looked at me quizzically, and sat down. He has been clean-shaven since then.

Duke never verbalized his pleasure with the way we operated as did many of his peers. He wouldn't give a teacher or any white authority symbol the satisfaction. This he had intimated often. I was surprised a few days later when Duke looked in through the glass half of the closed classroom door and motioned to me to come out. I excused myself from the class and went outside.

"Mrs. Dawson, Mr. X just kicked me out of Math. I told him I was bored doing the same shit every day in the week. Could I please sit in your room? I'll sit in the back and won't disturb no one."

"All right, Duke. Come in. Remember you have to show respect to others if you want them to show respect to you. You can't always do what you want to. On a job there may be many things that will annoy you. You have to learn to accept them."

I was pleased that Duke felt comfortable in my room. It seemed more advisable to me for him to have a refuge in the school than go back to the street and risk the danger of possible trouble.

He sat in the back quietly, as he had promised. As I learned, Duke's behavior was unpredictable. Some days he cooperated and seemed eager to learn, and then on other days he tried continuously to disrupt proceedings. He did this usually by using four-letter words or by introducing statements that were completely irrelevant or shocking.

On this day we were in the midst of a discussion of current events.

"What do you think about those paintings that were stolen from the museum?" asked Von. A lively discussion arose, including comments on the cost of such paintings.

Suddenly Duke said authoritatively, "Mona Lisa was a man."

This was a conversation stopper. We all looked at each other.

"What's that got to do with what we's saying?"

"It's art, ain't it? So . . . ?"

"Where did you get your information?" I asked.

"What's it to you? I knows, that's enough. I got it from a magazine, see?"

"Which one, Duke? This is important. Different publications have different points of view. Certain magazines are well known. In this course, we are trying to become more critical of what we see, hear, and read. That's why I asked you your source of information. To my knowledge the Mona Lisa was painted from a woman. I'd like to know what proof the author of the article you say you read had for his statements. Will you try to bring in the material?"

"If I can find it. I'll see."

The struggle between the students' concepts and experiences with former teachers on the handling of discipline and my own methods continued for many weeks. In the program in which Duke was a student, we were in the midst of an interesting discussion on the modern uses of the Laser beam when, suddenly, Randy and Monster began pushing each other. Monster, so designated by his gang, was short, slender, and neatly dressed.

"OK," said Randy, as he slapped his opponent, "step outside, and I'll show you who's chicken."

I stopped talking. The others watched me.

Several students yelled, "Mrs. Dawson, don't stop. Continue. We listening. We came to learn. They's immature. Kick them out."

"Yeah, don't be easy on them. You're too easy. You got to control us. They don't understand kindness. You got to be strict."

"All right, let's discuss discipline. If you sit attentively only when I force you to, you're not developing personally. If you need an authority to tell you what to do, that's coming from the outside. That means you haven't realized its importance yet. When you do, you won't have to have anyone tell you what to do or control you. You'll do this because it's part of you. You want me to act as a prison matron? I told you when we first met I would never do this. You have to do something about your own discipline. You are adults. Discipline is your responsibility. If any of you prevent others from learning, it's up to the rest of you to do something about it. I don't mean that you should react violently, either. I'm not going to send you to the principal's office. That solves nothing. I expect you to act like adults."

"That's right," said Ali-Tees, the only one attending junior college at night. "This is infantile group behavior." (He was studying sociology.)

When they left class at the end of the period, Ali-Tees said, "Mrs. Dawson, we all dig your method. We're learning. But you have to understand we have our bad days. Today is Friday. Please don't get discouraged."

Utilizing the Unexpected Incident for Teaching-Learning

A CONTROVERSIAL NEWSPAPER ARTICLE

Almost daily unexpected incidents arose which affected the students so intensely they naturally became topics for discussion. Such an incident arose early in the first general office clerk program.

Two weeks after we began training, the school was visited by a reporter and a photographer from the black weekly newspaper *Sun-Reporter*. They took pictures and made notes for an article. Several weeks later, the article appeared as follows:

THE SUN-REPORTER

WHAT IS THERE LEFT FOR HUNTER'S POINT?

On a hill in the Hunters Point–Bayview Area of San Francisco there is a street known as Oakdale, and between the 1400 and 1500 blocks of Oakdale a special type of school faces the back of one of our elementary public schools.

The school at 1509 Oakdale is operated by the Adult Division of the city's schools and is one of the most important parts of the Youth Opportunities Center at the Hunters Point project.

Both the Burnett Elementary and the YOC schools are under the administration of the San Francisco Board of Education. Both have the same objective of being "centers of learning," but they have different schedules. Their immediate goals are not the same either.

One of the schools has a good size recreation area; the other none. One has a large staff with different levels of classes, teachers and administrators. The other has one director, a supervisor who also teaches and three teachers. One is for children who are beginners in formal education; the other has students who either didn't finish school, better known as dropouts, or if they graduated from high school they didn't learn enough to be able to get the necessary training to become employable.

Some people who have been making a study of schools feel that lack of proper counselling and poor preparation has also contributed to making the young adults in this area unprepared for the current job market. There is a difference of opinion on this subject, which would be best to leave to a future article on schools.

The Burnett Elementary School has children just beginning to learn about life; whereas the YOC school has young adults not yet old enough to vote, but old enough to have fathered or mothered a child without benefit of matrimony. It also has students who are divorced. Both are in the minority.

In one of the schools the children, most of them, will go to junior and senior high school. Perhaps most of them will finish high school; hopefully most of them will be sufficiently educated and trained to meet the employment demands of this fast-paced automated world. It is also possible that a very few will go onto college and into a professional life, and be leaders of this country tomorrow.

But these 50 pupils at the YOC school located in old but adequate buildings of the Bayview Baptist Church are being trained to become employable in white collar jobs at the beginning level of office work. This is a tough task for both the students and the teachers.

The students were infuriated with the article. At the beginning of the session, Marietta opened with, "Mrs. Dawson, this was a terrible article. It . . . " She could go no further before she was interrupted by several speaking at once so that no one could be heard.

"Now let's give each other a chance to say why the article is so terrible. Marietta, finish what you started to say, will you please?"

"He compared us with children. We have nothing to do with the elementary school. We're adults. We're trying to better ourselves. That's why we be here."

"Look at the title," said Wilbert. "You'd think it was so hopeless. If this doesn't work, there's nothing left. How about that?"

"Anyway, we're not all dropouts. We're not all divorced, and we don't all have children out of wedlock," Rosetta broke in.

"So what if some of us do have children out of wedlock?" Cindy said. "So do many white kids. Why pick on Hunters Point?"

Jim, the gang leader, said, "Let's get that reporter here. We'll show him something. We can retaliate too." He smiled knowingly when using the new vocabulary.

"That's what I'm afraid of," I said. "Before we go any further, let's discuss the article paragraph by paragraph. Maybe your interpretation is not what the reporter intended."

The fourth paragraph especially aroused their ire. What if they were dropouts? Did they have to have that tag the rest of their lives? They said they would never get jobs with that kind of reputation.

"Get him down here," yelled Rosetta and Marietta, while the rest chimed in.

"Stop the chaos," said Belle, and they all laughed. *Chaos* was another new word.

"We're learning something, anyway," said Jessie, "but I still want to punch that reporter in the face."

"There we go," I said. "Jump him. Always violence for anyone who disagrees. Certainly I agree we should take action. First let's finish the whole article, and then let's talk about the kind of action to take."

The sixth paragraph created a furor: ". . . whereas the Youth Opportunity Schools have young adults not yet old enough to vote, but old enough to have fathered or mothered a child without benefit of matrimony. It also has students who are divorced. Both are in the minority."

Jim mispronounced *matrimony* by placing the accent over the second syllable. Several students laughed. This brought the boiling point down.

Roberta lambasted the reporter for putting the word *disadvantaged* on the caption below the picture of the students at their typewriters. "That implies we don't come from a good family. I never starved. My home was clean and is clean now. Yes, we have children out of wedlock. Whose business is that?"

I explained what was meant by the label "culturally disadvantaged," although I disagreed with the use of such labels.

"Just let him come here," said Cindy, raising her fist high. "I'll show him." Cindy always frankly expressed herself without regard to professional rank. When she was bored, she blithely turned her transistor radio on. She interrupted any time it pleased her fancy, as did Roberta, her pal. Both Roberta and Cindy had children out of wedlock and were receiving assistance from the Department of Public Welfare. They had much in common: they were articulate and fearless, born leaders.

Others resented the word *minority* at the end of the sixth paragraph. They had formed the erroneous impression that *minority* meant "black."

I brought up the point that the facts in the article were true: many were high school dropouts; many did have children out of wedlock. I asked them why they were disturbed by the truth. When they began to be able to accept criticism, they were beginning to show more mature reactions. These sessions were cathartic. They were beginning to practice articulating their anger rather than reacting with violence. I was not näive enough to think that this would be transferred to their solution of daily problems outside of school.

Roberta said angrily, "Just imagine what a future employer will think about hiring us when he sees our pictures right here. Even if our names are not mentioned, people can find out. They didn't have to put the picture in, you know."

Others began to complain about the role of the principal in their attempts to pin the responsibility for permission to print this article on someone. I said this was only an assumption on their part and that we would have to find out the truth.

Roberta said, "Well, someone at the top had to see it before it went to press. Isn't that right, Mrs. Dawson?"

"Roberta, that usually is the procedure. It doesn't always happen, however. You've had opportunity to express your feelings. Let's talk about action, not violence. Here's what I'll do. I'll discuss your displeasure with the principal. I'll try to find out what happened. Maybe we can have a meeting with the reporter, if you promise to treat him with courtesy. This is Friday. I'll report to you on Monday. How does that sound to you?"

They were satisfied. "Now you have things you can do. You're readers. You can telephone the editor and register your complaints. You can write letters to the editor."

"That's not enough. We want the reporter here. We want him to face us so that we can tell him directly how we feel."

Arrangements were made for the publisher to appear at an assembly the next afternoon. This gave us an opportunity to use this session for preparation.

"Let's work up our agenda," said Rosetta. (They used new words whenever they could.)

One of the students was made chairman by acclamation, another was made recorder, and discussion began. It was interesting to note that the chairman was stricter than the teacher and insisted upon complete attention and adult behavior. Several times at the beginning of the discussion on what to present the following day, there was so much commotion that Rosetta and Dick yelled, "Wow! What chaos! I thought we were adults." Quiet ensued for a few minutes, only to be broken by further outbursts. Finally Mahalia said, "Try to look at what we have to do without getting so excited. OK?"

Mahalia, the recorder, wrote on the blackboard the essence of what she heard. The points were:

1. Get the facts from the publisher. Did anyone see the galley proof before the article was published?
2. Why mention labels: "dropouts," "out of wedlock," "disadvantaged"?
3. Action to be demanded from publisher: apology, retraction, new article stressing the positive.

During this discussion I did not interrupt except when called on for advice. As an educational experience, I tried to have them learn what it means to think through an idea, not just accept it. I was fascinated. What evolved outdid any commercially produced drama. This was the chairman's first attempt in this capacity. She had never realized what abilities of leadership she had. Also, this unexpected incident added to their concept of "developing one's potentialities." It also emphasized the importance of planning, a habit I was trying to develop throughout the course.

At the assembly the following day, the publisher said he was setting a precedent. "I have never met with readers who disagreed with articles in my paper." He was a black physician who had practiced in this area for nineteen years. He spoke fearlessly and articulately, using some unfamiliar vocabulary.

"I came here because I'm interested in you. I respect you for trying to improve yourselves. At the same time, you have to learn to accept criticism. What are you afraid of? Whom are you fooling? Aren't most of you dropouts? Your having children 'without benefit of matrimony' is certainly no secret to me. I brought many of your babies into the world. Maybe you have to look more closely at yourselves. A façade of ignorance is no excuse. I'm adamant. I will not retract any statements in this article, just to appease readers." (*Façade, adamant,* and *appease* were discussed in subsequent sessions.)

The students wanted to show him how much they had learned in only two months.

Roberta said, "You're evasive. What you said was irrelevant. We ain't taking it lying down. We're here to improve ourselves. What if we have children out of wedlock? So do whites."

The publisher was patient and listened. Then he said he would not apologize, as they demanded, but would accept letters to the editor, which he promised to publish. Before the meeting broke up, the principal assigned me as adviser for the writing of these letters.

It was interesting to see the enthusiasm and activity in our sessions. The committee decided to get letters from each member, then combine the best paragraphs into two separate letters, each with the signatures of the entire class. The leaders rose to the occasion. Slackers were prodded.

"I don't have no ideas," said John. "I'm tired of thinking. I did too much today."

His peers would not listen, and he was shamed into working. He came up with excellent ideas, which I praised. I corrected errors, and then the students redid the letters until they were perfect. This process took a week. Students were so highly motivated that not a sound could be heard. Few went to the rest rooms. Everyone became involved in planning and in writing.

Before the letters were submitted, we discussed a plan to be given to the principal that would prevent a similar incident in the future. The students sighed with dismay. They wanted letters to be sent directly to the editor. We developed the concept of channels and related it to what they would encounter on a job.

"For a member of your Hunters Point social club to bypass its recognized leader to make arrangements with another social club could only result in trouble," I said.

"Right you are," said Jim.

"However, if you present your proposal to the club leader first, you would be using proper channels. In each agency there are channels. It's essential to find out the *who* and *what* of a situation before plunging into action. This is important when you hold a job."

The letters were later published in the *Sun-Reporter.* What an educational experience this unexpected incident provided!

SWITCH IN CLASSES DURING THE FIRST PROGRAM

Early in the general office clerk program, when my students and I were beginning to communicate and engage in controversial discussions, a new program was started to train "hard-core" youths to be office boys. With only an hour's advance notice, I was asked to switch my coeducational group of high school graduates in training for general office clerks and take over this "hard-core" group of men. I was to keep my coeducational class of dropouts. The majority of the office boys group had police records for assault and battery. They had provoked their teacher in this program by yelling profanity, refusing to apologize, squirting water at each other, sleeping in class, and walking out into the street whenever the spirit moved them. They absented themselves by going in groups to the rest room to shoot craps and smoke marijuana. They had no regard for property and had thrown their books out the window or onto the floor and then playfully stamped on them.

Their previous teacher was young, attractive, and black. This was her first experience teaching adults. She had had only elementary school experience with first-graders in another state. Conscientious, but traditionally oriented, she was constantly sending disturbers to the principal's office. This was no solution, since they returned to renew their practices. I could hear her scolding in a high-pitched voice daily. She was vulnerable. The students were winning by provoking her.

My immediate reaction to this switch was unfavorable. It had taken me almost three months to establish the kind of relationship which made it possible for my students and me to communicate. They were beginning to exhibit enthusiasm and seemed to be slowly coming out of their cocoons. Was this change fair to them?

I was to switch classes that very afternoon. I also discovered that the students had not been told of the new schedule. This administrative change would be a bombshell. I told the Education Director that I believed it would intensify the students' insecurity. Couldn't I begin the following Monday, I asked, and not interfere with their weekend?

The following Monday the classes were switched without the students' being notified in advance, and they reacted immediately.

Roberta, now the president of the student council, came out of her new room excitedly and gasped, "Mrs. Dawson, how could they do this to us? Just when we were learning so much!" Roberta's hair was peeking through her bandana, which she had not yet been able to part with, and her eyes flashed. She was volatile, in fact so much so that she was completing a five-year probationary period for attempted murder of her stepfather.

I explained that I was not the policy maker and that I had to abide by my superior's decisions, as she would if she were an office worker and her supervisor gave her instructions. Her eyes flashed, and the scarf, still circling her hair, fell off.

"Well, they'll see. We're not going to take this! We have something to say about how this school is run. Why do we have a student council if we can't be heard?"

"Roberta, calm yourself. Show what you learned in Personal Development. Let's use channels. Who is the head?"

"I don't care about him. . . . The principal or the supervising teacher. We'll go on strike. That's what we'll do. Tomorrow we'll picket."

"Roberta, why not try to operate as an experienced leader would in a labor-management situation? Get a committee together, plan what you want to say, and ask the principal for an appointment to discuss this with him. Tell him how you feel and why you feel this way. Sit down, talk it out. Then, if this isn't satisfactory, you can decide on other action."

"Mrs. Dawson, I'm only doing this because you say so."

"Roberta, this is learning how to work through channels. If you can do this, you'll be developing the kind of habit patterns you need for a job. I'm here, and I'll be available to you or your council members whenever you need me. I can use my morning counseling sessions for such problems, too." This satisfied her for the moment.

There was a tense climate in the "hard-core" class when I met them for the first time. Their leader, William,[2] was the most resentful. His black eyes flashed angrily whenever I could see them.

---

[2] He wore his sunglasses in class. His hat, small-brimmed and bound in velvet, hugged his head. Sturdily built, with broad shoulders, a thick neck, and a darkly expressive face, he walked with dignity and a sense of importance. He did not shuffle like some of his peers. He was a leader. The police knew it, too. His record went back to his twelfth year, when he beat up some boys from a rival gang. It continued on into high school; he was dropped for attempted assault on one of his teachers. I later discovered that he was an excellent reader and good in math; his quick mind made him a leader. He was moody and unpredictable in behavior, with a violent temper. He was also choked with hostility against himself, his family, the school, law enforcement agencies, the world, and whites. He, too, believed that "all whites are devils."

He showed his anger by feigning sleep. Quick to follow their leader, three others imitated him, leaving a crack between elbow and eye for watching my reactions.

"I intend to disturb no one," I said. "Nor will I send anyone to the principal's office. We will be talking about many subjects that will interest you. If you're sleeping, that will be your problem."

I repeated what I had told my other groups about how I conduct the class. I asked them to give this unfamiliar method a chance. Discipline was *their* problem. I would assume my responsibility, and I expected them to assume theirs because I believed that teaching and learning involved a sharing experience. The purpose of Personal Development was to help them develop *their* potentialities, increase *their* vocabulary, think, and improve *their* ability to communicate. Each one would be treated with dignity and respect. While I said this, some still pretended to be sleeping.

"I will not talk as much as this any other time, but I want you to know what to expect. How you act in class and your attitudes, revealed by your daily behavior, will be considered more important on my monthly reports than communication skills or vocabulary."

One fellow saved the day. "We going to get the big words your other classes get?"

"Yeah, what's 'stastistics'?" asked another.

I put the word on the blackboard and called their attention to the correct spelling and pronunciation: S T A T I S T I C S.

"Does anyone know what it means?" No one knew, and so I proceeded to give illustrations.

"We meet in Personal Development one and a half hours a day, five days a week. By the end of the month we've met thirty hours. If someone is sleeping," I said particularly loudly, "twenty-seven out of thirty hours, he can't learn much." I arranged a chart on the board.

NAME	NUMBERS OF CLASS HOURS PER MONTH	NUMBER OF HOURS ASLEEP IN CLASS	NUMBER OF HOURS AWAKE
Henry	30	27	3
George	30	25	5
Stanley	30	4	26

"Down the left side, let's put the names of three imaginary students, Henry, George, and Stanley. On the top, let's put headings and columns. At the top of the first column, we'll write the number of hours we meet a month, the number of hours asleep in this class, and the number awake. Henry sleeps twenty-seven out of thirty; George, twenty-five out of thirty; and Stanley, four out of thirty. This tells a story in figures and therefore is a form of statistics. Insurance companies offer statistics on the number of people who die from various diseases each year. Health departments publish statistics indicating the number of infants who die before they reach the age of two, etc."

I noticed one of the sleepers raising his arm and saw his eye peeking through. I said nothing. The next session, no one slept.

The next day, William said, "Notice something? I didn't sleep today."

"Good. What awakened you?"

"Your class is interesting. You know, you're always off on a trip."

I didn't know how to take it, but I said, "Well, it's a round trip, and I'll be back. Tell me, is 'on a trip' good or bad?"

"It's good, because you bring everything in the world into the classroom. Other classes are boring. Teachers never go on trips. They just follow the book."

"Thank you, William. I'm flattered."

"You're very intelligent. How do you get that way?"

"Again, thank you, William. I'm interested in people and things, and I'm always learning. It takes time, William. Remember, I'm much older than you. I read a great deal, and I enjoy being alive. You, too, William, are very intelligent. You have problems. When you sleep, I try to understand that you are trying to communicate something. Maybe you're escaping from your problems; maybe you're testing me or trying to provoke me as you did your former teachers. I don't know. We'll work more closely from now on, and maybe I can help you cut through some of the things that block you." I was thinking I might get to know William through counseling and then refer him, if he were willing, to a psychological counselor.

This talk with William made me feel good. However, I knew that was the way he felt this particular day. He, like the majority of students in this program, was very moody. The form their moods would be expressed in was unpredictable at first. An outside frustration would have its effect in the classroom. I therefore did not know how long William would continue to be so cooperative.

Soon thereafter he approached me before our class and said, "Mrs. Dawson, I want to tell you in advance, I just got an excuse from the principal. I have a terrible headache. I'm taking off the rest of the day. I'm sorry. I hate to miss this class."

"Do you have headaches often?"

"This is real. I ain't conning. I was hit on the head with a lead pipe, and I been having headaches since."

"Have you gone to the clinic?"

"Yes, but every once in a while I get them back. When this happens, I'm afraid. Maybe I won't think right, and I'll hurt someone." I told William I would discuss this with the principal to find out if we could refer him for further medical consultations and asked him if he were interested. He agreed.

In talking to him later, I understood that these headaches could also have been intensified by his personal problems: he was in the midst of a tug of war between two girls, both under eighteen, who claimed he was the father of their unborn children. William did not know if he loved either one, but he did know that he was in no position to marry. This problem was discussed with the principal and later with the Youth Opportunity staff.

As I had anticipated, William's mood changed several days later. I was working with another class. We were in the midst of discussing the importance of getting along with others on a job, when William burst in with a note in his hand. Pushing it under my nose, he said gruffly, "Sign it."

"William, I'm sorry, you're interrupting the class. You wouldn't like it if someone did this to you." He kept waving the note in front of me impatiently, with a hostile look. "William, please be polite. Even if you're angry, there's no reason to take it out on others." I refused to sign the note.

"To hell with you. You better watch out, that's what. I'll do something serious." He dashed off into the street.

I learned later that same afternoon that he threatened to shoot the principal the next time he was asked to take his hat off indoors. William was suspended for a week. The next day the principal received a call from William requesting permission to discuss his suspension and also to apologize to me. He was granted the interview. He said he was unable to control himself when his headaches returned. He begged to return to school. For the first time he felt he was learning and had decided to take advantage of this opportunity.

The day of his return, he visited me. I greeted him with a smile, not mentioning our previous confrontation.

"Mrs. Dawson, you're smiling at me. I can't understand it. I couldn't do that."

"I hope, William, you'll be able to before our course ends. That's much of what Personal Development is all about."

"Anyway, thank you. I never said this before to any teacher."

"That's a compliment, William, and I'm flattered. I'm glad you've returned and that your outside problems are being worked on. Now if you can control your temper when things don't go your way, you'll be making headway. Your reading ability is excellent. You're quick in understanding. In fact I would like to see you complete your high school requirements and then go on to college. I'll work with you. How about coming to counseling? Shall we discuss your high school transcripts and evaluate them tomorrow at 10 A.M.?"

"I'll be there." Since then we've been friends, as future episodes will show.

Getting the Students Involved in Teaching-Learning

ROLE PLAYING

At the end of each session, I reflected on and evaluated what had happened. Was I reaching the students? How well were we communicating? Were they listening more? Were they more involved? Did I notice any changes in behavior or habits? Were they developing more hopefulness? Was their span of attention increasing? Was hostility lessening? How could I draw out nonparticipants?

At the beginning of each program I met resistance to my methods. I did not lay down the law, but made them think. I was concerned about giving them opportunities to communicate and express whatever was bothering them. When the students saw how I reacted to their provocativeness and defiance, they accepted me. This might take several weeks.

In order to arouse their attention and sustain it for increasingly longer periods, I experimented with various techniques. Among these was role playing. This served many purposes related to our objectives and to each student's needs. It helped the student to communicate and listen; it made him aware of his relationship to others and of the need to cooperate; and it enabled him to understand himself better. Being able to step outside of himself and see how others look at him was another step on his road to self-development. Role playing could make learning pleasant rather than formidable and boring. It could also be a vehicle for creativity.

Role playing is simply assuming a role. Children often get so involved in role playing that they forget about eating. Psychiatrists call it "psychodrama." Sociologists refer to it as "sociodrama."

The time for introducing role playing will depend on how well you are getting along with your students and how well you are relating. It takes at least five weeks or more to reach the point where role playing can take place. Introducing this activity prematurely may bring about bedlam and consequently destroy its potential value as a teaching-learning technique.

"All right. Today we're going to try something different. We've talked about hair styles, attitudes, and the importance of speech. We've been learning vocabulary each day. Now let's see if we can use some of it." All eyes were focused on me. "We're going to make up our own skit. We'll use no prepared scripts. We won't rehearse. Do you know a word that describes doing something on the spur of the moment creatively?" We learned the words *spontaneous* and *improvise*. "We'll improvise and operate spontaneously."

In the general office clerk program, Wilbert asked, "How do we know what to say?"

"You'll react to each other depending on the situation. You'll respond to the other person. Let's work it out, and you'll see what I mean. We're going to pretend that this is an office." I pointed to my desk at the front of the room. "Make believe this is an IBM office." I wrote it on the blackboard: INTERNATIONAL BUSINESS MACHINES.

"Gee, I never knew it meant that," said Bailey.

"Now, our cast. We need a receptionist. Who wants to be the receptionist at IBM?"

Rosetta volunteered. "What must I do?" she asked. This gave me an opportunity to find out what these students being trained as general office clerks knew about duties of a receptionist.

"Answer the phone," said Susie.

"Smile," said Jim, the gang leader.

"Know the business," said Dick.

"Good. Let's begin with an applicant for a clerical job. Who wants to be the applicant?" Jim volunteered.

"While you're watching, be observing how Jim and Rosetta walk, listen to how they talk and how they answer the telephone if they do.

Jot notes down. Then we'll discuss your comments. Remember the criteria we use to come to our conclusions."

The Pacific Telephone Company, through its school department, had loaned us teletrainers. These consisted of a pair of colored telephones with a transmission box and amplifiers that could be operated by plugging in wires to ordinary wall outlets. There were buzzers to buzz the caller, busy-signal devices, and telephone bells. Here was an opportunity for action and speech improvement. I asked Dick, one of the shy members of the class, to be the teletrainer operator. I hoped to ease him into a more active role in subsequent sessions.

Prior to this we had learned the meaning of *criteria* and had discussed criteria that could affect job getting: poor posture, sloppy dress, bad manners, inaudibility, and unacceptable language, for example.

"What criteria will you set up?" This was a form of review.

"Poise and initiative," said Dick.

"Voice and words," said Jessie.

"Manners," said Belle.

"Good. Now we're ready. Curtain." There was still excitement and noise. I waited. They became impatient.

"Shut up. We want to start," said Rosetta.

"May I use your briefcase, Mrs. Dawson?" asked Jim.

"Certainly."

Jim swaggered in, swinging the briefcase. Snuggling up to Rosetta, the receptionist, he said, "Hello, babe, how about it?" Rosetta slapped his face.

"Mrs. Dawson, I was only fooling. Don't count this. Let's do it over."

He walked in again, using his natural gait, which combined the cakewalk with a shuffle. He spoke to the receptionist with his hat on.

"Dope, take off your hat. You're in a office." He quickly complied.

"Good afternoon, Miss Smith. I'm here for a job."

"What kind of a job?"

"A clerical job."

"Wait a minute, please. Do you have an appointment?"

"No."

"Sit down." Rosetta, the receptionist, picked up the phone before Dick had a chance to buzz it on the teletrainer. Laughter broke out. They corrected this. Rosetta continued on the phone. "Mr. Douglas, there's a fellow here for a clerk-typist job. Do we have an opening? OK. I'll give him one. . . ." Turning to Jim, she said, "I'm sorry. There are no openings now. Fill out this application and bring it in tomorrow at 2 P.M." Rosetta kept chewing bubble gum ferociously, while keeping her babushka tied around her head and her coat on.

When it came time to criticize, few said anything. This is the way it was at the beginning of each new program. Later they were able to criticize and accept criticism from each other. We talked generally about what was unacceptable without mentioning individuals. Chewing gum, wearing a coat, and manners were observed. We discussed ways of walking and sitting and how they revealed personality. I demonstrated slovenly sitting and poor posture when walking.

"The way you stand, sit, and walk shows someone observing you how you feel about yourself."

Rosetta's words were slurred, and this I mentioned, but without talking about her. I said that on a clerical job she might be asked to use the telephone. The impression she made on the hearer might have an effect on her employer's business.

"For the first time, you did very well," I told Jim and Rosetta. "It's always most difficult for the first ones. Those who follow learn from the beginners."

I noticed that throughout this first skit the rest had sat and listened attentively, no one even leaving for the rest rooms. When the bell rang, they were disappointed.

"Can we do this tomorrow?"

"We'll see." I didn't want to overdo any technique. It was much wiser not to allow them to become satiated. "Maybe at least once a week. We'll try various kinds of situations."

Role playing became one of the most pleasurable learning techniques in this first group. In subsequent groups, panels and group discussions were preferred. In role playing they had to listen to each other; they had to think, use their imagination, and plan.

ROLE PLAYING: LESSON FOR INTERRUPTERS

If I could get the students to understand what it feels like to be interrupted, maybe they would be more courteous to each other and, by extension, to a supervisor, an outsider, or to me. In each group of general office clerks, therefore I chose the flagrant interrupters for those to be interrupted in role playing, but they were not aware of my purpose.

"We're in the IBM office. I'll select the players today instead of asking for volunteers. Roberta, you will be the supervisor. Susie,[3] you will be the general office clerk. This time I need a few minutes to discuss the role with you privately.

"Roberta, I'll talk to you first." I took her aside. The rest watched interestedly. "Roberta, Susie has been a general office clerk in your department for only three weeks. For the first two, her work showed promise. She tried to do everything accurately. She came to work punctually. This past week, however, she seems to be slipping. Her work is sloppy. She has been late several times and has been spending too much time away from her desk. Call her in to discuss this with her. What you say and how you handle it will be up to you." Roberta, as usual, had still not been able to part with her coat or babushka in class. I was curious to see if she would do so in her role as supervisor.

I then called Susie aside, out of earshot of Roberta. "Susie, when Roberta calls you in, don't let her say a word. Interrupt her each time she opens her mouth. I don't care what you talk about. That will be up to you. OK?"

"Well, you know Roberta. She flies off the handle easily."

"I know you can manage. If you were in an office, you'd have to."

"All right," I told the class. "We're ready. Remember to watch for poise, speech, attitude, and manners. Then we'll discuss the presentation. Curtain."

Roberta picked up the telephone on her desk and said, "Miss Susie Smith, please. . . . Miss Smith, will you please come to my office? It's very important."

"Yes, Mrs. Wells," said Susie. Susie got up and went out the imaginary door, walked down the imaginary hall to Roberta's office, and knocked. She was told to come in.

[3] Susie was a match for Roberta. Throughout the course she was punctual, well groomed, and conscientious. Her voice was resonant. She always had a smile. As a result she was a scapegoat. Her reputation as a "brass polisher" made her the butt of daily attacks, but she was strong enough to withstand them. Her two small children came to school when no baby-sitter was available or when her husband went fishing. They were third-generation welfare recipients. She was most anxious to work and pay back the welfare department, however. Her husband didn't go along with her. He was unskilled but not interested in getting into job training as yet. She hoped to influence him. She wanted a home in the country.

"Roberta," said the supervisor, "You can sit do—"

"Oh, Mrs. Wells, what a lovely coiffeur! You . . ."

"Miss Smith, this is not what I . . ."

"Oh, Mrs. Wells, I like your dress. Is it new?"

"Miss Smith, I just to—"

"What, Mrs. Wells?"

"Miss Smith, I think you're . . ."

"Mrs. Wells, I saw your husband out last night at the dance with another woman." Susie spoke rapidly to get this out before she was interrupted.

"Now, I won't tolerate any more of this." Roberta's hair, still encased in a babushka, was showing as she shook her head in anger. Her dark expressive eyes flashed, and the group watched me to see what would happen. They knew how volatile Roberta was.

I looked at her and wondered whether to continue or to interrupt. I decided to let her continue, having complete confidence in her ability to handle the situation. It was a test, however. In previous situations she had never allowed anyone to get the better of her. It was fascinating to see what would happen.

Roberta picked up the phone and said angrily, "I want the Personnel Manager. Hello, is this the Personnel Manager? I have something to report . . . a hostile and belligerent employee." With that she slammed the phone down. Laughter.

In the discussion which followed, Roberta gasped, "Gee, Mrs. Dawson, now I get the feeling of what's it like to be interrupted. Is that the way you feel when I interrupt you?"

"Not quite. I don't get excited because I have had more experience in working with people. Roberta, you did admirably. So did you, Susie. They deserve a round of applause." The students applauded loudly for them.

"I thought for a moment Roberta would hit me. She got so mad," said Susie. "Knowing her, I was really afraid. But it worked out all right. Now I have a little more confidence in myself."

If I could change their tendency to attack someone who displeased them, we were making progress. Time would tell.

At this time in the first program, it was possible to criticize individuals without unpleasant repercussions. I asked Rosetta to go to the blackboard and conduct the evaluation of Roberta's and Susie's performances. Rosetta asked the class to give her criteria for their comments. These were reviewed and included manners, dress, posture, walk, use of the telephone, voice, speech, dialogue, ability to listen, and use of vocabulary from previous lessons.

The climax was reached when Roberta's best friend, Cindy, no model of propriety, yelled out, "Did you ever see a supervisor wear a head scarf and coat in a office? You was chewing gum, too. How you expect your employees to act when you don't set a example?"

"Look who's talking," said Roberta. "You always interrupting, so keep your mouth shut."

Progress was being made. Roberta was beginning to substitute verbal responses for violent reactions.

ROLE PLAYING: VEHICLE FOR CREATIVITY

At the end of the fourth month of the general office clerk program and a month after the office boys entered, there occurred a spontaneous outburst of self-expression and creativity. By this time I had introduced tours as a regular feature of Personal Development. On this day, however, there was a conflict. Only one class could go on tour, leaving another of my classes at school. At first there was disappointment. But I had told the students about this in advance. I tried never to disappoint them; they had suffered too much frustration in their short lives. I asked them if they wanted to have a joint session with another class or if they preferred to be on their own and see what they could do. I put this to a vote, and the decision was unanimous: "We want to be on our own and show you, Mrs. Dawson, what we can do." I was overjoyed. By this time I had given students opportunities to develop leadership and initiative by letting them conduct vocabulary reviews, chair discussions, and play roles.

When I entered school the next day, several students rushed down and asked, "Mrs. Dawson, have you heard what we did yesterday?" I had not heard. They wouldn't tell me. They wanted me to find out from other teachers first. This was another moment when enthusiasm, so slow in coming, was manifested.

I did hear later. I was told by the administrative staff and teachers that they put on a role-playing situation involving a murder, with a defense attorney, prosecutor, jury, and witnesses. It was so amusing that laughter reverberated to the office above.

They were so busily engaged they never heard the bell—a rare occurrence. This was the goal toward which we were striving: to become so involved that the whole person was called into action.

I began the session with the complimentary remarks I had heard. I let them know how proud I was that they were deriving some enjoyment from learning.

"Mrs. Dawson, we had a wonderful time. You see, we did learn something in this class."

"I would like to sit in the audience as an observer and watch you reenact the scene. How about it?"

"All right," said Jessie, "but Charles, the district attorney, is not here. He drove around again with a revoked license and is in jail. He'll be out tomorrow."

"Someone else can take his place."

Mahalia was chosen director by the group. She went into immediate action.[4]

Mahalia called the cast. Others set up chairs for the jury and placed a chair in front of the group for the judge. They were scurrying and buzzing. Jessie had unanimously been chosen to play the judge.

I sat in the room as an observer. I decided not to interrupt even when unacceptable language was used. This would disturb the creative interaction. Instead I noted what I saw and heard for discussion later.

The group listened to suggestions from each other. It was fascinating to watch them, in perfect freedom, play their roles as judge, defense attorney, plaintiff, defendant, witnesses, and jury so convincingly and so humorously. The way they responded to each other and anticipated actions was a study in behavioral science. They acted as if they had studied Method acting. This illustrated better than any textbook exercise or teacher-contrived situation what happens when creativity and freedom of expression are encouraged.

When they finished, several sighed; and Jessie, the judge, said, "Mrs. Dawson, we didn't do as well as yesterday. Yesterday it was funnier, and we had a better time."

That was an astute observation, I thought. It's difficult to recapture the enthusiasm created by novelty, an ingredient of any "first." Jessie's comment, echoed by the rest of the group, revealed something else

---

[4] This was one way of helping Mahalia, shy and inarticulate, become more involved. Heretofore she was afraid to participate. She was willowy and slim almost to the fragile point. Her reading ability surpassed that of the others. In my counseling sessions with her I discovered that she not only was a high school graduate, but had attended junior college for a year. She dropped out to have her first out-of-wedlock child. Her voice was soft and her diction good.

that was happening: continuing development of ability to criticize and to be criticized. Now they could evaluate themselves and not be afraid to say that they didn't do so well.

After praising each one individually and commenting favorably on specific actions or responses they had made, I asked if we could discuss improvements. This they were happy to do. The story was good; it was theirs. They had suspense and a surprise ending to keep the audience guessing. In fact, I told them that I thought it was so clever and interesting that the other students in the school would want to see it. How would it be, therefore, if they actually put it into better shape and were the first group to present an original offering to the entire student body? At first the actors hesitated. They were afraid they couldn't hold their friends' attention. Then others in the group supplied the moral support needed.

I set the date for a Friday, a month later, to give them the needed time, and said that they could work on the play in our Personal Development sessions.

We talked, and Belle acted as recorder, jotting down a checklist of steps:

1. Director and master of ceremonies
2. Cast
   a. District attorney
   b. Counsel for defendant
   c. Witnesses for defense
   d. Witnesses for prosecution
   e. Guard
   f. Jury (four actors to represent twelve jurors)
   g. Judge
3. Stage setting
4. Evidence — Exhibits A, B, C

I suggested the use of several levels for the performance: the stage for the judge and witnesses, downstairs in the auditorium for the audience, who unsuspectingly would be courtroom spectators, and the right front for the jury. In this way we could involve not only my students but the whole student body. The surprise element would add to the dramatic effect.

For the next three weeks we allotted a half-hour from each session for rehearsal. This gave the students added incentive to study vowel sounds and pronunciation and to improve language patterns, especially the defense attorney, who sprinkled his remarks with, "Man, I knows. He be's and I seen him." Such language patterns might not seem strange to their peers, but it would evoke laughter in the world outside.

The witnesses were very amusing, especially John, whose laconic remarks delighted us. When cross-examined and questioned about how long he had been a practicing physician, he said, "Fifteen years, seven months, six days, and four hours." Everyone laughed. They liked John and looked to him because of his clever repartee and impressive vocabulary.

We discussed the preparation of the program and how interesting it would be if the students typed it in their typing class and then mimeographed it themselves. They could appoint a committee to take charge of this. The typing teacher gave them permission to do it. Daily they showed me results which were not satisfactory. I made the corrections in spelling, design, and cast. Their perseverance and attention to details showed development.

The night before the big event we discussed wardrobe, props, and responsibilities. By this time they realized their own interdependence and cautioned those inclined to be late to be on time. "Show your initiative," said Belle.

I said that I would be the photographer, since I had a 35-mm still camera and would provide the color film. I also would bring in my black raincoat which could be worn backwards as the judge's robe; since Jessie was short and I so tall, it would reach the floor. I also would bring in long rhinestone earrings for Mahalia, a witness — the wife of the physician in the skit — who chose to be the fashion designer for *Ebony* magazine.

The day arrived, and there was great excitement and anticipation. I had invited many staff members from the Center and from the neighborhood community centers. I was anxious for them to see how the students were progressing and their tremendous potentialities. There was a full house. Although there had been rehearsals, there had never been a written script. This would have been contrary to the principle of spontaneity of expression and would have curtailed the flow of creativity.

The stage had been set during the lunch hour. The jury members, who had decided the type of persons they wanted to be, dressed accordingly. Belle was a dignified, conservatively dressed vocational nurse, Dick a telephone installer, and John a physician. Jim and Mahalia suggested the evidence: Exhibit A — a black dress; Exhibit

B — a drinking glass with lipstick imprint; and Exhibit C — a gun. When we discussed the gun, the students wanted to bring in a real one, loaded. I decided against such realism. I said it was good theater to allow the audience to use its imagination. They chose the title "Woman in Black."

Jim, the defense attorney, would not put on a collar and tie. He was adamant about this in rehearsals.

"I know, Mrs. Dawson, because I been in court enough times. Not every defense attorney wears a white shirt and tie, and I'm one of those that don't. I wears a sport shirt." He had had the experience he mentioned, and I didn't force the issue because he had figured out the kind of defense attorney he wanted to portray.

The skit went over beautifully. The members of the cast responded to each other's dialogue naturally, humorously, and almost professionally. There was little self-consciousness. The students were working as a team. Their remarks varied daily, as they did at the actual performance. The audience was so amused that there was constant laughter, sometimes uproarious, especially from me. I couldn't help it; I was tickled. Everyone was having such a good time. They had learned so much about themselves, and they projected their delight to the audience. The applause was resounding. I was only disappointed that the Center had not provided the press coverage I had asked for. Now, when the students were showing their capabilities, the bad press they had always received could have been countered.

William said, "Gee, Mrs. Dawson, why can't our class do a scene in a courtroom?"

"You can, but it doesn't necessarily have to be an imitation. Think of another interesting situation. Use your imagination. We'll talk about it later."

VOCABULARY DEVELOPMENT

Vocabulary was not taught from lists prepared in advance or taken from textbooks. It developed from discussions, from newspaper reading, or from my own inadvertent use of unfamiliar words. The problem with these students was their not having been taught to conceptualize. Therefore I tried not to assume that concepts familiar to the middle class would be familiar to these young people. I often stopped and asked them if they understood my words. Often they did. When anyone did not, I gave illustrations from their way of life to make the new terms meaningful. Their use of the words immediately indicated their interest. They loved vocabulary after they became accustomed to this method. In fact, I found vocabulary development a most effective tranquilizer.[5]

A few examples of vocabulary development follow.

"When you were talking at once, there's a word that describes the noise and confusion. Anyone know?"

Allen Williams answered, "I got it on the tip of my tongue, but I can't find it."

I wrote C H A O S on the blackboard. Then I pronounced it. I told them its Greek origin. By this time in the program they had become interested in origins of words and expressions. If I omitted to mention a word's origin, students brought it up and tried to guess. They were always pleased when they guessed correctly.

"Suppose you have a meeting of your social club. You're discussing plans for a dance. It's difficult to be heard because several fellows are beating their drum, which they brought for gigging later. Maybe a few others are singing at the same time, while others are carrying on private conversations. Everyone's doing what he wants to without considering anyone else. There is no order. There is great confusion. This is the idea of 'chaos.' Often there appears to be chaos right here." Laughter. " 'chaos' is a noun. 'Chaotic' is the adjective. There is chaos, but the situation is chaotic. Understand?" A few seemed doubtful. I continued. "After earthquakes, storms, or other disasters, transportation, electricity, and water may be cut off. Houses may be destroyed. The situation can be called chaotic. These disasters are beyond a human being's control. What happens in our classroom we can control."

Chaos proved to be a popular word with all the groups. In the first general office clerk program, when we were discussing what they liked most in Personal Development, Belle said, "Vocabulary. I use the word 'chaos' all the time when I'm home with the baby. 'Emma,' I say, 'don't make so much chaos. One day, Emma was playing with Sarah's baby. Sarah's child screamed and yelled because Emma didn't give her a piece of her candy. Emma said, 'You're making chaos. Stop it.' " We all laughed.

How the youths related their understanding of vocabulary to their way of life was illustrated early in the office boy program. William and

---

[5] Vocabulary was reviewed daily, but the methods used varied, as will be illustrated in Chapter 4.

Chops had been talking about how they worked together on a dance for their social club. They also entertained by playing drums.

"Do you know one word that can express 'work together'?" When no one answered, I said, "Let me give you another illustration. Then maybe you can guess the word. Suppose Curly and Chops write a song for the next dance. Curly writes the words, and Chops writes the music. We could say that they _____ on the song. Any idea?"

"No, give us a clue."

I put blanks on the blackboard and waited for someone to try to guess the word. Then I filled in several letters:

<u>C O __ __ __ __ __ R __ __ __</u>

When no one knew, I filled in the blanks:

<u>C O L L A B O R A T E</u>

Then I broke it down into prefix, root and suffix.

COL LABOR ATE

Col was the same as *con*, meaning "with." *Labor* they knew, of course. And the meaning is "to work with" or "to work together."

"Do you understand, or do you want more illustrations?"

"We got it," said Chops. "Me and Curly collaborated to jump Nick." [6]

"Good. You used it correctly, but why always react violently? Can't you think of a more peaceful illustration?" Laughter.

As I said earlier, there was resistance to my methods at the beginning of each Personal Development course. Students equated learning with memorizing, and I was trying to break that identification. They were too impatient to wait for explanations.

During the first two weeks of the framemen program, Wiz frequently said, "You're a good teacher, but your explanations are too long. Give us definitions. That's what other teachers do."

Duke expressed this sentiment, too: "Aw, shee-it, you talk too much. Quit the explanations. Give me the definitions. I'll copy them. Then test me like you wrote them, and I'll know them."

"I will not give you definitions for you to copy. I told you when we began that my methods were different from what you had experienced.

---

[6] Nick, one of the docile members of this group, was eager to learn. The only one without a police record, he was the butt of many practical jokes.

I'm more interested in your getting the ideas and feelings expressed by a word. These are different for each one of us, depending on our association with that word. When you understand the idea or the concept, then you can look up the word in the dictionary. It will mean more. Have you noticed how many words you are using to express yourselves in discussions? In this class you have to think, not memorize."

"Yeah, we got a list in high school," said Edward Emile Edlow. "The teacher never explained with so many illustrations. We looked them up in the dictionary, but that still didn't help. Maybe that's why I didn't like to read. I didn't know the words, huh?"

Demo, another member of this frameman group, was as resistant as Duke. When I sensed undercurrents, I said, "Some of you seem unhappy with the way I introduce vocabulary and explain." Oohs and aahs sounded around the room. "All right. I said on the first day that nothing was taboo for discussion. I mean it. I can accept criticism. Let's discuss it."

We gave Demo the floor. [7] Sprawled out in his seat, he said from the the side of his mouth, "What's so wonderful about vocabulary?"

I sat in the circle as an observer. Ali-Tees was moderator.

"What I need vocabulary for?" continued Demo. "All I want to be is the biggest pimp in the world!"

"He means it, too," said Edward Emile Edlow.[8]

"Don't interrupt me," said Demo. "Vocabulary ain't help me get a job."

"How could it?" said Coolsann. "You ain't around enough. You here to learn. Give yourself a chance." [9]

[7] Demo was tall and handsome, with long sideburns and large, dark eyes with very long lashes. He was not well groomed like Duke. His attendance was poor. He attended once a week to sign his weekly allotment form. He seldom was punctual when he did come, but he was quick to pick up information. He was hustling nightly and told me after class that he was too tired to get up in the morning.

[8] Edward, now approaching twenty-three, had spent the years from age sixteen to twenty in an assortment of correctional institutions. His record was full of felony charges, some reduced to misdemeanors. When he entered my class, he had been hostile and had refused to participate. He said that over a period of time he had checked me out, liked the way I operated, and so become one of my unsolicited publicity agents.

[9] Coolsann, twenty-two, with two out-of-wedlock children, was one of the few who had been gainfully employed, in spite of a long arrest record. He worked in a large department store by day while he pimped by night.

"So, wise guy, where's it get you? You're still here. You ain't got a high job?" This came from Stanford,[10] who was a pal of Demo's and among the four in this class to whom we referred as the perennial resisters or "the opposition." They didn't approve of anything we talked about or the methods we used.

Coolsann answered Stanford, "I don't expect a job yet. I got to finish this course first. But I'm developing myself. Like Mrs. Dawson said, she's helping us to develop our potentialities. That's a word I learned, and now I can say things in different ways."

"Man, you fronting, that's what," said Demo. "I'm satisfied with myself, and I sure don't need no vocabulary."

"Yeah," said Stanford "I know a guy who's deaf and dumb. Vocabulary never helped him. But he's the wealthiest man around. Peoples in the country that never left the country and ain't ever had those big words we getting, knows more than the scientists about the country, see. Vocabulary ain't never help them!"

"You know what else," said Coolsann. "When you're not used to using correct words, but only 'in' language, you may forget on a job and say, 'Yeah, man, I went with a slick broad last night. Sure, plenty of cats around, but we bagging' !"

Now the resisters ganged up on Coolsann. Demo, his eyes flashing, said, "You stupid, man. Don't you think we got more sense than that? We know not to use that 'in' language outside. We'd never use it on a job."

"I still don't see the sense of vocabulary helping me, that's all," said Stanford.

"Let me give you an example," said Coolsann. "Suppose I have to send a telegram some day. You know you pay by the word. So take one of the words we learned. Take 'improvise.' If I remember right without consulting my notes, it means to make something up from the top of your head with no rehearsing. Think of all those words and what it would cost me if I didn't know one word that could say all that — 'improvise.' "

"I ain't never send no telegram," said Demo "and I ain't never gonna. I writes a letter. It's cheaper, see." Laughter.

[10] Stanford, twenty, also attended once a week, coming on the day to sign for his weekly stipend. I had talked to him frequently after class as I did with Demo, explaining that this was maybe a last chance for a new life. To throw it away wasn't using the intelligence he had. For a few days this had an effect. Then he went back to the old pattern.

"Let me say a word," said Stewart.[11] "I had a good job in a hospital all through high school. I couldn't have kept it if I didn't understand the vocabulary. I'm learning more here than I ever did!"

"Hospital? Who cares about no medicine job? That's for doctors," said Stanford.

"What kind of a job do you plan to get?" asked Stewart.

"Pipefitter," said Stanford.

"Man, that's a technical job. You need learning for that," said his friend, Demo.

"Hell, you don't. My father is a pipefitter, and he can't even count to ten," said Stanford.

"I knows what I wants to be," said another resister. "I wants to be a gangster, but the biggest."

"You can't be that stupid," said Coolsann. "I ain't even answering that!"

"Let's get serious, guys," said Deacon. He usually waited in the discussions until the antagonists were at each other's throats; then he entered cooly and collectedly. "Yeah, let's be serious," others said as each tried to outshout the others, the noise rose wildly.

Stanford said, "Hey, fellows, cool it. This is plain chaos. I can't even be heard."

"It's friendly chaos, anyway," said Deacon calmly. "Stanford, did you hear yourself? You used a word you learned right here, 'chaos.' " Everyone laughed, including Stanford.

The next morning, Deacon met me before class and said, "You know, Mrs. Dawson, after all that heated discussion yesterday on vocabulary . . . well, in the Reading class, Stanford spoke about something and used five words he had here. I almost fainted. I knew you'd be interested."

Stanford's and Demo's attendance never improved. Stanford was being "kept" by an older woman who let him drive her Cadillac. Neither one made any attempt to change his habit patterns even after being counseled. I understood that not every youth could be reached. I was sorry for Stanford and Demo because they were very bright. If they could only transfer to learning their acumen in hustling!

[11] He had been cooperative from the beginning and tried to influence the others. He was twenty-one, was married and had two small children, and was concerned about supporting his family. He was having marital difficulties, however, because, he told me, his wife listened to her aunt instead of to him.

DISCUSSION METHOD

Coolsann commented in our weekly evaluation sessions on the effectiveness of Personal Development content, "I like to discuss the way we been doing. We never did this in school before. No one cared what we thought. I think it's conducive to my learning!" (He beamed with pleasure at his new-found facility for using vocabulary.)

The discussion method was a very effective tool in getting the students involved, in encouraging interaction, in developing self-confidence, and in improving communication skills. I used it regularly throughout each program as the setting or springboard for our mutual learning. Each group, like each individual, is unique, however. The time for introducing discussion, therefore, depends on the group's mood and the situation.

In about the second month of the general office clerk program, I looked over at Bailey and saw a sad expression on his usually smiling face. He had deep rings under his eyes, and his hair was uncombed, his shirt soiled, and his pants unpressed. I was disturbed. By this time my students and I were communicating. They felt comfortable and free to bring out anything troubling them.

"Bailey," I said, "why do you look so sad? You look as if the roof had fallen in on you."

"It sort of did. My mom threw me out of the house last night, and so I slept in a car. I couldn't wash or anything. I'm sorry, but I can't think much today."

Everyone else seemed equally disturbed.

"Tell us why," asked Belle.

"Yeah," said Sarah. "That's terrible. You must of done something bad?"

Bailey's situation gave me the opportunity to use this as an educational experience with discussion as the technique. I was pleasantly surprised to find that although the students were on Bailey's side, they understood that his mother's action must have been precipitated by something "terrible" on Bailey's part. They were beginning to see more than one side to a problem. The discussion flowed freely to a related topic brought up by Jessie.

"What do you think about raising children? My daughter is now two and a half, but when she gets to be Bailey's age, would I put her out of the house?"

The women agreed that, no matter what, it would be dangerous to throw girls out. They only got into trouble. Soon, the discussion grew more heated. The bell rang.

"Aw, gee," could be heard throughout the room.

"Can we continue tomorrow?"

"If you want to, certainly."

I spoke to Bailey after class and said I would like to discuss this with the principal if it were agreeable to him. He agreed. The principal, an older black man, with a background of elementary school teaching in the South and over twenty years' experience in business with youths from low-income areas in San Francisco, immediately went to work. He called Bailey's mother to find out her side of the story. She said that recently Bailey had been staying out all night, drinking, and "acting bad." She couldn't control him any more, and so she told him to leave, but she was sorry and wanted him home. Bailey got the message quickly and ran home.

In the office boy group, discussion first arose from vocabulary introduced by Chops to test my reactions to something "dirty." As the class started in the second week of their program, Chops, with a twinkle in his voice, said, "Yeah, you, too, are a nym— . . ."

"A what?" asked Curly.

"I don't know. It sounds bad, don't it?"

I heard it and said, "Is this what you're trying to say?" I wrote on the blackboard: NYMPHOMANIAC.

"Geez, I never heard it like this. Wow." Everyone laughed.

"Let's talk about it. It's much better that way. There's nothing dirty about this word. It does have to do with sex. Chops, you could never be a nymphomaniac. Do you know why?"

The attention was intense. No one knew. "Only a woman can be referred to in this way. A nymph is a woman. A mermaid is a sea nymph, for example. In Greek mythology there were nymphs." I realized that I had used the word *mythology* inadvertently. "Do you know what 'mythology' means?"

Several knew it had to do with stories or legends. John had heard about Hercules. That was Roman mythology. Venus was also known in myths as the goddess of love.

"Many myths in both Greek and Roman mythology concerned gods and how they changed themselves into different shapes or animals to win the women they loved." Attention was riveted. "I'm off on a trip. Let's get back to 'nymphomaniac.' Some people are driven by compulsions. They have to do things. They have no control over their actions. I'm no psychiatrist, but these people may need professional help. Some people overeat because they have to. Some wealthy people have a compulsion to shoplift. They are known as 'kleptomaniacs.' Others are compelled to indulge in sexual relations excessively and with anyone who pleases their fancy. The woman who has this disease, according to a doctor, may be referred to as 'nymphomaniac.' The disease from which she suffers is 'nymphomania.' Both words come from the Greek. A man cannot be called a nymphomaniac. A man suffering from this illness is referred to as a 'satyr,' also a word from Greek mythology. In mythology satyrs were represented with a tail and horses' ears but with the body of a man. There is no scientific evidence that any creature like this ever lived on this earth at any time. No one in this class has this disease. Neither do any of your girl friends." Laughter. "Who is interested in reading other myths? I'll bring a book in." William volunteered to do some reading and later reported on the story of Achilles for the significance of the phrase "Achilles' heel."

From this explanation, the topic skipped to treatment of diseases. The students were interested in the close relationship between mind and body. Such words as *promiscuous* and *psychosomatic* were introduced and illustrations given. Several expressed worry about their own sexual indulgences and the effect on their bodies. Could they become ill? We discussed the possible effects of excessiveness in any area—smoking, eating, and drinking. Our session ended with, "What we gonna talk about tomorrow? Geez, things is interesting here."

It was from such elementary beginnings that discussions developed. Discussions gave me an opportunity to listen and learn more about the students. I tried to speak little, allowing them to bounce the conversation back and forth in free association. I interspersed a comment, an opinion, an explanation when necessary. Discussing instead of accepting statements became a practice in personal development. Our sessions were filled with vitality and suspense.

When we first began to discuss, I acted as moderator. But as soon as the group was ready—and this point varied with each group—the students took turns acting as moderator. Discussion sometimes followed a film showing or an unexpected incident—a guest's visit, a tour, a newspaper or magazine article, or an experience in a student's life. The lecture method was not used. Guests were so advised: they were participants, not lecturers.

It took weeks for students to learn to listen to each other. Often it seemed, from the continuous interrupting, that discussions would never be able to be conducted effectively. I was confident, however, of the long-range efficacy of this approach. I shared my feelings with the students. We were communicating.

"Wow! I know today is a bad day, but I think I've had it." Either it was a Friday or their weekly allowances had been delayed. Delay in receiving weekly Manpower Development Training allowances happened too frequently throughout each program.[12] It was understandable that inability to meet rent payments, inadequate food, and other effects of lack of money would affect behavior and motivation in the classroom.

Randy said, "Hang on, Mrs. Dawson. You're doing fine. We didn't get our checks and we figuring out how to pay the rent. My landlord don't believe me when I tell him the truth. Anyway, we want you to remember us. This way you sure will. We're giving you good experience. After us, you would teach anyone, huh?" Everyone laughed.

"Randy, I'll hang on. I've tried to be patient and understand why you act up."

"You sure have. I wondered when you'd break," said Monster.

"I'm not breaking. Anyone who is trying to break me, give up. I know you've had difficulties. I think you're wonderful, and I have the greatest respect for you. You are in school, and haven't collapsed in the face of overwhelming problems. I don't know if I would have been able to do as well under similar circumstances."

"So, don't worry. We'll be ready to work on Monday. This is the best class we got."

Discussion could be a motivating factor. At one session in the frameman's group, we were discussing narcotics when a heated controversy arose on whether or not brain damage could develop from injection of heroin. Randy, who had part-time work after school in the medical center library at the University of California in San Francisco, asked, "Mrs. Dawson, how about me looking it up in medical books?"

"Wonderful, and you know what? We'll use the tape recorder for the first time, too. We'll play it back so you can hear yourself." He gave an excellent report; the students liked it so much that they made him repeat it for two consecutive sessions. The tape recorder was used almost daily thereafter. Guests were taped, as were comments from our feedback sessions.

[12] In the framemen program we took action. See Chapter 6.

Often it was difficult for me not to satisfy the urge to interrupt. I did control myself, however. If things seemed to be getting too chaotic, I would say, "May I have the floor, please?" In the beginning I was sometimes unable to be heard above the din.

"Mrs. Dawson wants to say something. Let's venerate. She deserves it. OK, Mrs. Dawson, you can talk now, but make it short." This was their way of teasing. I advised students to try to express themselves briefly.

It took time, but slowly moderators began to learn how to moderate and keep the discussions rolling smoothly with almost full student participation.

In every group there is a scapegoat. He is usually meek and weak. He is attacked verbally and sometimes threatened physically. In the frameman group it was Lionel. He was an epileptic. At first the students did not realize how this disease could affect personality. Lionel, the youngest in this group, was eighteen. He had had a concussion when he was fifteen which resulted in epilepsy. From the first day of this program, he had already informed each teacher so that he could be excused frequently to take pills. He was extremely self-centered and always complained about being "picked on" by his peers as well as by the teachers. He was afraid to speak out in class at first. Later he developed more courage. He never learned to take the teasing. He reacted the way his peers intended. Once he stalked out of the room. This gave me the opportunity to discuss behavior with the rest of the class. The discussion focused on treating people who are different, especially the handicapped, with understanding, tolerance, and respect.

"Do you think it's fair to pick on people with weaknesses or handicaps?" I said. This started a heated discussion. Edward Emile Edlow wanted to be moderator.

The meeting ended with such statements as, "Only bullies do that. Remember, Lionel is epileptic. Let's be tolerant."

Lionel was clever in mathematics. He was especially skilled in solving square roots, which, as Edward Emile Edlow said, "he can do in his head, geez." I tried to use his skill in math to buoy up his spirits in personal development.

Several weeks later after we had had the word *protégé* Edward Emile Edlow, increasingly interested in reading and vocabulary, said, "You know what, Mrs. Dawson? Lionel is my protégé. Right?"

"Yes. I'm pleased to hear you say so."

At another time in the frameman group, discussion was on maturing and self-discipline. The controversy became so heated that I asked to say a word and got the floor.

"You talked about maturing. As we develop, there's one thing we have to do ourselves. We have to be able to exert self-discipline. It's difficult. We all want things, especially if others around us have them. We have to develop values for ourselves and our children. Even if we want certain things, we may have to put the brakes on and do without them."

"People who get ahead, that's what they do," said Ali-Tees.

"They only benefit themselves."

"No, they can benefit others."

Wiz said, "You were speaking of self-discipline. Take a narcotics addict. He's on the stuff. He breaks aways. His friends say, 'Come on, Pat, have a fix.' He may try to exert self-discipline. But if every time he's with friends and they shooting this stuff into their arms, his self-resistance is going to end. People get emotionally upset sometimes. There might just be one day when he's had it bad, everything's gone wrong, and they say, 'Come on, have some of this smack.' He knows it's wrong and bad for him, the same with alcohol. . . ."

"It's like this," said Allen Williams, a friend and close rival of Ali-Tees since childhood. Ali-Tees graduated from high school, but Allen dropped out in the tenth grade. Allen was able to reason and had courage to oppose others in class even when they threatened to jump him. He continued, "I smoked stuff myself. I ain't ashamed of it. When I quit, that was when I was maturing. I figured this wasn't getting me nowhere. I started trying to work and doing odd jobs. My friends came back to me. They said, 'Let's do this, let's do that.' When they saw my resistance was that high, and how much I was maturing and how better off I was, gradually they come from it, too. If you can hold up that self-discipline . . ."

Someone else said, "First of all, you're talking about a touchy subject, which is to keep away from friends who use narcotics . . ."

"You don't understand . . ."

"I do, but you're confused."

"I have friends from all categories. People who do things I don't approve of . . . I socialize with them, but . . ."

"Because you don't have enough inside of you to resist," said Allen Williams, pointing to his head.

Coolsann said, "People I know who shoot the needle, I go up to their house sometimes. But I have never took a fix, even when they say, 'Come on, have some.' Some days I go up there and they say, 'We have such a nice time.' I'm feeling bad, maybe my check ain't come, or my car not running, maybe we don't have no food in the house, I'm depressed and all upset. I might say, 'OK, man, put it there."

"I was getting loaded for four years, but I stopped. I don't get loaded no more even when I'm with the same fellows," said Edward Emile Edlow.

"Wait, man," said Deacon. "You contradicted yourself. You said that people did this, you wouldn't associate with them. Yet, you'd go to their house. If you smoke, why expose yourself to temptations?"

There was a pause. I said, "I feel happy that you feel free to express yourselves. No one is going to be looked down at because he thinks in a certain way. Each one of us has a certain limit to what he can take. Nobody can tell you your limits. You have to find this out for youself. If someone says you're wrong, you have to be convinced. This is where an open mind comes in. If your mind is closed, you won't learn. You have to be open to new ideas. Keep a question mark in your head. You always talk about getting out of the bag you're in. It's difficult to get out all at once. Try punching a hole in it daily so that you can breathe— mentally. This is mental ventilation. If you think you know everything, you're tying the knot more tightly. It's up to you. . . ."

Discussions served many purposes. I could observe quiet ones being brought in subtly by some of the more sensitive moderators. To sustain interest, however, I varied the conduct of discussions. Sometimes we had panels or a team of speakers followed by discussion. Our panels on work habits, good health practices, and appropriate office attire served as reviews.

We set up criteria by which we evaluated each other:

1. Organization
   a. Was the presentation well planned?
   b. What were the sources of information?
   c. Was it timely?
   d. Was there a beginning, a middle, and an end?
   e. Was the material specific?
   f. Were the facts checked?
   g. Were the *who, what, where, when* and *why* covered?

2. Presentation
   a. Did the speaker have poise?
   b. How was his posture?
   c. Did he use new vocabulary correctly?
   d. How was his speech?
   e. How was his language? Was any "in" language used?

Susie and Belle were among the first in the general office clerk program to volunteer for a team presentation on proper diet. This followed an explanation of metabolism. The students reviewed their notes and supplemented these with reference books. Susie talked about proper food and Belle about the digestive process. This breakdown was their own decision. They did so well that others followed, speaking on office attire and office etiquette.

Another variation to stimulate discussion were students' five-minute talks on subjects of their choice, which were taped. I conducted it this way. "Tomorrow, we're going to introduce individual talks. These will give you the experience of getting up before a group and expressing yourself. Now we're not afraid. We've been working together for many weeks. You choose your topic. It can be anything you have read or thought about, or an interesting experience. Whatever you choose, we're interested in how well you plan, your choice of language, and your ability to think. Don't memorize. Put notes down to look at. Our criticism will be given in a friendly way. We're here for the same purpose — to improve our ability to communicate. I'll give you several days to prepare. Volunteers? If not, like the army, I'll assign you." Laughter. Several volunteered. The others I assigned.

Discussions covered many topics. The common expression was, "Let's discuss. I don't agree."

"That's controversial," Lionel said proudly.

"In this class what ain't?" said Duke.

LANGUAGE HABITS

Language patterns of young people from poverty areas or ghettoes differ greatly from what the middle-class ear finds familiar. Their "in" language is descriptive and should not be laughed at or ridiculed. Their language patterns may be disturbing. The following examples are typical of their English usage:

1. Double negatives in profusion: "It don't make no difference."
2. Lack of agreement of verb with subject: "He do the work." "I does it that way."
3. Incorrect use of verb tense: "What if he has it did up nice?"
4. Incorrect use of adverbs and adjectives: "He got it quick."
5. Different concept of word meaning: "I was on a job messing with solvents and come home with nasty clothes."

Accept these language patterns as part of their culture. When you and your students are able to communicate with each other, you will find them deeply interested in learning middle-class English if it is taught as a second language. In this way you begin where they are. You bring to their attention better ways or more acceptable ways of expressing ideas.[13] You should not be shocked by their constant use of profanity. Whenever Duke and Wiz used profanity, others told them to hold it and remember where they were. As the course progressed, I never scolded about the use of four-letter words, but I noticed that the students' control over such expletives gradually increased.

As I said earlier, these youths have to be more than bilingual. In many cases they have to be multilingual. I wonder how many of us would fare under such conditions. Whenever they used their own language to express themselves in class, I made notes. I made it a point never to interrupt them in a discussion. This would only have intensified their feelings of insecurity, stupidity, and hopelessness, feelings which I was trying to dispel. They had enough problems to cope with in their environment. I waited until they had finished. Then I called their language to their attention and, phrase by phrase or expression by expression, we examined it and translated it into more acceptable English. They were soon able to correct themselves whenever they heard "in" language. They were also cognizant of language appropriateness.

One of the criteria for evaluating students who participated in discussions or role playing was their languge patterns. The tape recorder was an excellent tool for such evaluation. The students' attention span and listening ability increased. They beamed with self-confidence whenever they were able to select more appropriate language structure. No longer were they afraid to criticize each other openly.

[13] Chapter 4 goes into this in more detail.

"Gee," Ruby said in the duplicating machine class one day. She had just given us her comments on the book *Black Like Me*. We were listening to the tape. "I didn't speak good, huh?" She shook her head and continued. "I sure got to be more alert, huh?"

Other Practices

GUESTS

As the course in Personal Development progressed, we tried other practices. Variety and suspense were essential elements in this class. In our weekly evaluation sessions, I asked the students if they were interested in having outsiders visit—as participants, not lecturers. Perhaps some students knew men and women from slum backgrounds who had made successes of their lives. If so, we would be delighted to have these people as discussion participants. We were open to suggestions. While they were investigating possibilities, I said I could invite people from the community, staff members from the state department of employment, prospective employers, and others with whom they could discuss what they wished. I felt that their feelings of hopelessness could be further assuaged by exchanging ideas with other guests. I always put my ideas to their vote.

"You have great initiative," said Edward Emile Edlow.

Our relationship was definitely improving. To get to this point had taken time. I stress this because too few people realize the importance of the time factor in the teaching-learning process.[14]

SPECIAL PRESENTATIONS

The students' interest reached a climax on Wednesdays and then took a sharp turn downward. How to sustain attention and interest through Fridays posed a problem. In thinking about this I wondered about the value of experimenting with special programs that would reflect the students' problems. They needed exposure to contemporaries who were realizing their goals. If I could locate such young adults, men and women, from similar environmental backgrounds with whom they could identify, maybe this would help change these youths' self-fulfilling prophecies of failure.

---

[14] Our visits with guests appear in subsequent chapters.

From our class discussions and the feedback from our tours, I became aware of their unrealistic concepts of what to expect on a job, including salaries. On our tours some remarked, "Gee, that's a low salary, $100 a week. I wouldn't work for less than $150. I can make more than that one night, hustling." It was possible. "He's a nut to work so hard for so little," they would say.

Another objective in such contemplated programs, therefore, was to help students understand that an employer pays for skills; that they need skills and that skills are developed through hard work. I called it learning to face reality.

Early in the general office clerk program I began to discuss my objectives with a representative of the Boys' Clubs stationed at the Youth Opportunity Center. This young man, twenty-four years old, had originally asked me to help him improve his communication skills. He had grown up in a similar environment in an area adjacent to San Francisco. The students liked him because he spoke their language and because he was "blood," no Uncle Tom.

I told him my plans for a special program for which he would provide three young people who had suffered hardships but who were now employed. They could be dropouts who had returned to school and were still pursuing learning. If the students could hear how these people attained success, this might help change their hopelessness to hopefulness. The presentations were to be autobiographical. This Boys' Club worker was to be moderator and a participant. He liked the idea, and our plans were set in operation.

We allowed one month for planning and preparation. During this time I thought of a title that would call attention to itself. I came up with "Tomorrow May Be a Porcupine." As was my practice, I shared this with my students in the general office clerk program. They were amazed.

"What does it mean?" asked Bailey.

"That sounds way out," said John.

"Do you want to hear why I chose this?" Unanimous yesses. "What does a porcupine do if he thinks he's being attacked?"

"Sticks his needles out," said Jessie.

"That's the idea. This is his defense. The future can be full of problems, but to react in a defensive way like a porcupine accomplishes nothing. We have to face reality in a more mature way. What do you think? Do you like the title?"

"We can't think of anything better now, so go ahead and use it. It'll attract attention, anyhow."

Daily for a month I announced the date of this special presentation. In Personal Development we set up committees to prepare leaflets which the students later mimeographed for distribution. By this time we had a bulletin board, which we also used. A bulletin board committee was responsible for arranging notices attractively, rather than with the usual jumbled effect. There was also a deadline for removal of obsolete information. The use of bulletin boards, therefore, became an important adjunct of the communication process.

The three young participants were a young woman who was the secretary to the director of the Youth Opportunity Center, a young man who was the art instructor at the Boy's Club in the area, and the young Boys' Club worker who had made the arrangements.

The guests arrived on time and were shown to the front of the auditorium. All the gas heaters were on in full force. Several coat-clad students were bunched in front of them. Two men had their backs so close I thought their rears would get singed. A few office boys slept through the program; a few others giggled and pinched each other. No attempts were made to single them out in the presence of their peers. This would have accomplished nothing except to arouse their hostility. I spoke to them later, however. We used this for a topic in our Personal Development session, too.

The young woman spoke first, kept to her five minutes, and displayed great poise. She was attractively dressed, and her hair and make-up were in the best taste. She was a native of Seattle. She had not been interested in school, but had failed and dropped out. On her first job, she was so influenced by her boss that she returned to school, got her high school diploma, and then attended junior college. She was taking courses and hoped to finish college. Coincidentally, when she came to San Francisco, her first job was with this same boss.

The art instructor held the students' attention. He was informal and the most enthusiastic of the three speakers. He had brought various illustrations of what he discussed: oils, lithographs, and photographs. These he had placed in the front of the auditorium. For many of our students, this was their first exposure to these mediums. The artist remarked that doodling had always fascinated him; money was not his goal, but enjoying his work was. (As he said this, I noticed one of our students doodling. I had seen this student's caricatures, thought them good, and urged him to study art at this Boys' Club.) This young man continued. His doodling came to the attention of his teacher when he was twelve. Instead of a reprimand, he got praise. This teacher also arranged for him to attend art classes. He has been studying since and maintains a studio in his home. He said he loved to paint, sculpture, and do lithographs. He explained lithographs briefly. He was so full of enthusiasm that it affected even the sleepers.

The Boys' Club worker was on last. My students listened as he told about his background. He grew up in an environment similar to that of our students. He was a gang member and went along with whatever the gang decided. He loved football and aspired to be a professional player, but he fooled around so much in high school that he was almost dropped. He did graduate, and he received an offer of a football scholarship to college. He did not want to take it because it would mean leaving the gang and the fellows he knew so well. And he was afraid. For a while he did nothing. He joined the gang's program: crap shooting, card playing, and crashing parties. Then he began to think about his future. He entered San Francisco State College. But the first year he cut classes, loafed, talked back, and finally got himself kicked out of school. Now he realized that he was fighting fear and was afraid of failure.

He decided to work and got a job in an ice cream factory. He got a good salary, but he knew this was not for him. He quit his job and became a counselor at the same Boys' Club where the art instructor was located. He returned to San Francisco State College. His grades improved, and he completed his requirements for a bachelor's degree.

After the panelists finished their five-minute presentations, the floor was thrown open for discussion. It was interesting to note that no one asked questions of the young lady or the moderator. The art instructor was the center of attention. Students wondered how he worked, where he worked and why he still liked art when his earnings were so small. Later they surrounded him, asking questions about the paintings.[15]

I thought about the students' reactions and their apparent interest in art and wondered why they disregarded two of the speakers. Were the other two touching upon problems with which these youths identified too closely and from which they were trying to escape? On the other hand, art was far removed. It afforded them a refuge.

[15] See Chapter 5 for students' reactions to visits to art museums.

FILMS, SLIDES, AND FILMSTRIPS AS EDUCATIONAL TOOLS

To vary the learning experiences films were frequently used. Unfortunately, however, there are still too few with multiracial representation, just as there are too few textbooks with contributions of diverse ethnic groups. But educational film producers are now producing films to correct this omission.[16]

Films, or any other audiovisual materials, do not substitute for the teacher. Students have to be prepared for what they will see, and there has to be discussion afterwards. The students' comments will provide ideas for future programs.

I previewed many films in the audiovisual department of the board of education. In spite of the weakness mentioned, I decided to select several and experiment with them. The first film, *Feeling of Hostility*, was introduced when we were discussing what it means to act in a mature manner. This had followed discussion of attitudes and behavior, especially hostility and belligerence. The protagonists in the film were younger than our students, and their clothing dated the film (which was *c.* 1940), but the behavior problems were applicable to our students' situation. A high school baseball player misses a pitched ball. He gets so angry that he throws his bat down and stamps on the ground. Our students laughed. Later, in the feedback, they said they recognized themselves—often they acted like children, too. This was progress in self-criticism.

Another film, *Habit Patterns*, focused on planning wardrobes and stressed punctuality and setting schedules for study. These were controversial points and stirred up vehement reaction. Rosetta said she came home too late to set out clothing for the next day. Wilbert said he had no trouble planning his wardrobe because his clothes were always in the cleaners. Dick said he just fell into his clothes because he never opened his eyes fully until after morning coffee break. On the other hand, Belle, Sarah, and Susie washed, ironed, and set out their clothes, and prepared their lunches before they went to bed. They looked it, too—they were neatly coiffed and attired.

How to Concentrate was another appropriate film because it dramatized a problem close to home.

"Sitting in class for seven hours a day is too long. I can't concentrate that much," said Bailey.

[16] See Appendixes, pp. 309–317.

"I got to learn to concentrate more," said Jessie. By this time their period of concentration had increased from seconds to minutes — at least fifteen minutes.

TEXTBOOKS, NEWSPAPERS, MAGAZINES, AND OTHER INSTRUCTIONAL MATERIALS

Reading is an essential part of the communication process. With few exceptions, most young people from poverty areas and ghettoes read little. Many are poor readers with problems of communication. The reading habit is not instilled in them from early childhood as it is in many middle-class homes. The fact that these youths have poor communication skills does not imply stupidity or mental retardation; it stems from their environment. Their parents have had to work and have had little time to read to the children, or even to read themselves. I have seen the effect this MDTA youth program has had on many parents. In the early stages of the program parents were suspicious of the program's objectives. They thought that jobs were the main objective and that job training only delayed job getting. As the program continued to develop, however, the parents' attitude toward education changed: they were the willing liaisons between their sons and daughters and the MDTA school, and they cooperated with the school in helping to reduce students' absences and tardiness.

Something else happened. Many parents became so interested in educating themselves that they began to attend evening adult education classes in their neighborhood. The newspaper was now read daily, and interest in community problems increased. Later several parents developed such leadership in community affairs that they were able to obtain paid jobs as community action aides in the anti-poverty program and could dispense with domestic jobs and manual labor. Some parents have learned how to write news articles for their neighborhood newspaper. As a result, students find themselves competing with their parents in improving themselves.

Materials are only part of the reading problem. The teacher's awareness of these MDTA students' backgrounds is important. Trying to survive in a hostile environment has occupied these youths' time and energy and affected their attitude toward intellectual pursuits like reading — they consider such activities "square." This has been brought out in discussions in Personal Development; but it may be only a surface expression. Underlying this attitude is their fear of failure and of being called stupid. Calling those who read "squares" is part of their defense.

I have found from my experiences that these youths can be motivated to read if they are given a favorable set of circumstances. My students' delight with their ability to recognize and comprehend vocabulary they had met in our sessions was encouraging. They were beginning to realize the importance of reading as entertainment, mental stimulation, and an aid in job getting. This interest came about gradually through our discussions, films, tours, special programs, and guest participants.

Textbooks were not followed as daily guides in Personal Development as I conceived it. Content that was pertinent to the needs of the students was evolved. For our purposes I supplemented our reading with editorials or news items I culled from a variety of sources and reproduced. Later, the students also contributed selections. When we were discussing anthropology, I brought in Theodora Kroeber's book *Ishi*[17] and Robert Ardrey's *African Genesis*.[18] The students actually vied with each other to borrow them. I did not expect them to read these books in their entirety; instead, several students volunteered to read a chapter and then report on it. The rest of the class listened intently to the reports.

I kept a running file of newspaper clippings on housing, consumer education, law enforcement, narcotics, health, fashions, employment, civil rights, and other relevant topics. These included the Watts-Los Angeles situation in the summer of 1965, on which we had heated discussions. To develop the student's critical attitude was an important objective. Exposure to an assortment of points of view alerted them to the need for becoming critical. Their comments indicated they were thinking, not memorizing.

Brick, a member of the office boy group, was especially stimulated to read. He was so excited that one day he met me before class with three books in his hand.

"I want to take up social work in college, so I asked the psychiatric social worker at the Center for books. He brought me these. I tried reading one last night, and you know what? It took me three hours to read three pages. Gee, I must be awful stupid, huh?"

[17] Theodora Kroeber, *Ishi*, University of California Press, Berkeley, California, 1961.

[18] Robert Ardrey, *African Genesis*, Dell Publishing Co., Inc., New York, 1963.

I assured him this was not the case — these books presupposed knowledge in sociology and in behavioral sciences. Furthermore, they were written in traditional textbook style. I suggested he visit the librarian in the public library and ask for a novel on social work as an introduction to the more advanced treatment of the subject.

We did use textbooks in Personal Development, but not regularly and not in chapter sequence. We referred to them when the occasion arose. The following were pertinent: *Personality and Human Relations,*[19] *Business Behavior,*[20] *Consumer Economics,*[21] *You and the Law,*[22] *Clerical and Civil Service Training,*[23] *A Pictorial History of the Negro in America,*[24] *English Fundamentals,*[25] and various pamphlets published by the Telephone Company.

One day late in the framemen's program, Duke came in with a paperback book under his arm. He said, "You won't believe it, but I been reading *Black Like Me* evenings before I meet the fellows. It's interesting. Want me to talk about it?"

He did, to the group's delight. His comments were recorded.

Those students whose reading ability was below high school level were referred for tutorial services provided by the San Francisco Unified School District. This program was set up at our Center and supervised by an English teacher in the city schools. There was still a problem in getting those who needed remedial reading most to attend. Students felt there was a stigma of stupidity. Saul, whose reading level was only fifth-grade, was ashamed to apply for remedial sessions.

I also made myself accessible for tutorial service during coffee breaks and lunch hours. At least five students in the framemen group came three times a week.

[19] Sferra, Wright, Rice, *Personality and Human Relations*, McGraw-Hill Book Company, New York, 1953.

[20] Allien R. Russon, *Business Behavior*, South-Western Publishing Company, Cincinnati, Ohio, 1964.

[21] Heimerl Wilhelms, *Consumer Economics*, McGraw-Hill Book Company, New York, 1959.

[22] Arthur P. Crabtree, *You and the Law*, Holt, Rinehart and Winston, Inc., New York, 1964.

[23] Robert Fisher, *Clerical and Civil Service Training*, South-Western Publishing Company, Cincinnati, Ohio, 1959.

[24] Langston Hughes and Milton Meltzer, *A Pictorial History of the Negro in America*, rev. ed., Crown Publishers, Inc., New York, 1963.

[25] Emergy and Kierzek, *English Fundamentals*, Form B-4 ed., The Macmillan Company, New York, 1959.

It took time for students to realize the importance of reading to their understanding of other subjects — mathematics problems, basic electricity, and typing. Their speed in typing was noticeably increased as their reading comprehension improved.

Reading was stressed in their regular English class. Mechanical devices such as the Tachistoscope were used daily to develop speed in comprehending phrases. But the students' reactions to these machines ran counter to the enthusiastic endorsement of some teachers and administrators.

"Gee, it's boring. Every day the same thing," was a typical student response.

California Achievement Tests were given students before they entered the program, at least twice during the program, and at the end of each program. Comparison of each student's scores in reading comprehension showed marked increases on the whole. Some rose from a fifth-grade reading level to an eighth-grade level; while others rose from tenth-grade to over fourteenth-grade. In my opinion, however, tests of this sort are not always accurate measuring devices. Students are quick to become accustomed to formats. In addition, fear of failure often compels them to cheat.

There are advantages to such tests, however. They test comprehension and ability to follow directions. The students also learn to sit and concentrate for longer periods. To pass pre-employment tests requires a long span of concentration. But no one test is adequate. The students have to be exposed daily to interesting material. If good material is provided, reading habits will soon develop.[26]

TOURS

One of the teacher's most effective tools is the judicious use of tours. At first we visited potential employers, usually large companies employing thousands of people. Such companies afforded greater opportunities for members of minority groups. The choice of industrial establishments depended on the particular training program — general office clerks were taken to insurance and utility companies, while framemen were taken to such companies as Pacific Telephone, Pacific Gas and Electric, IBM, National Cash Register, and Otis Elevator.

The purpose of the tours was to give students an opportunity to

[26] In Chapter 7 I discuss further my attitude toward tests.

get outside of their close-knit environments, broaden their outlook, apply what they learned in class, and increase their hopefulness. I was especially concerned with having the students introduced to the new automated world of computers and other electronic devices. They were also able to talk to personnel directors directly, to see how employees act and dress, and to observe working conditions and employer-employee relations.

THE FIRST TOUR — METROPOLITAN LIFE INSURANCE COMPANY

The first tour with the students in the general office clerk program was a momentous occasion. It was like a holiday. I had the students meet me at the plant rather than follow the traditional system of chaperoning students. Students cannot develop a sense of responsibility and time unless they are given opportunities to establish a pattern of independence. I was happy that the students met me on time and that none were absent.

The students looked wonderful; their appearance was a measurement of success. The women had their hair attractively arranged — there were no extreme styles. Makeup was just right. Skirts were not too tight or too short. Even Cindy's skirt amply covered her. I was proud of their appearance and told them so. The men who had worn hats in class at first now removed them indoors. The sunglasses had disappeared. Each man wore a tie and shined shoes. High hairdos had been lowered, and a few men even dyed the bleached ends dark brown or black for the occasion. Sideburns were more normal in length. Only Bailey wore white sneakers and a sweater, and the rest objected to this. They made him return home and change.

Before the company tour began, the women went to the rest rooms. They stayed so long that I had to go in after them. I discovered that their concern was more than a matter of grooming. They were afraid — this was their first tour to the world of work. The rest room was a temporary escape from the unknown.

Their fears were melted, however, by the warmth of the director and the hostess. After a substantial lunch we were taken through the company by the guides. There was one guide for each five students. The students were free to make comments and ask questions.

It was amusing and satisfying to note the students' concentration and excitement. At one point, Rosetta gasped as an employee passed by, "Ooh, ah, look at her! She rushed by with no stockings."

"Her heels were run down, too. That's not right," said Mahalia.

"Oh, Mrs. Dawson!" yelled Jessie. Then she put her hand over her mouth and said in a lower tone, "Isn't the clerk sleeping at her desk?" She appeared to be.

"Jessie, it may be her coffee break. Why don't you bring this up later?"

"Watch her. She's chewing gum and making noise. That ain't—I mean, isn't—right," said Belle.

The IBM system of computers—"memory machines," as the students referred to them—captured their attention. The students would have liked to spend more time on this.

After the tour the personnel director asked for comments. The friendly atmosphere had so relaxed the students that they felt free to talk.

"Well," said the director, in reply to their comments on employees' dress and behavior, "we have over two thousand employees working here, and often there are slip-ups. When the girls come for their job interviews, they are impeccably dressed. After a few months, however, if their supervisor falls down on her job, sloppiness results. This carries over to the work as well. Often we have had to call this to the attention of the supervisor. When I distribute the evaluation sheets we use in considering promotions, you will see how important we rate appearance."

"Employees were smoking while they worked. How come?" asked Jim. "We are not allowed to do this in our training."

"I'm glad you asked that," said the director. "You're too young to remember the period immediately after World War II. At that time we had been enforcing a no-smoking policy. We noticed that the returned veterans, older than many of our employees, left their desks frequently and spent more than fifteen minutes each time in the rest room to finish a smoke. This was bad. Much time was wasted. So after several meetings we changed our policy, and now we permit smoking at the desk."

The director concluded the program by outlining the company's hiring policy; he stressed attendance and punctuality. When he mentioned pre-employment tests, I noticed the students' discomfort. Their anxiety lessened, however, when the director stated that the tests were geared to high school level. During his talk, both the length and the depth of the students' attention were greater than ever before. No one left for the rest rooms. No one chewed gum.

The director then distributed evaluation sheets which the Company used when considering employees for promotion. The students asked how many absences were permitted, what the beginning salary was, how often salary increases were given, how much vacation time there was, etc.

FEEDBACK

It is important to provide opportunities for students to express their reactions: this is necessary to the development of communication. The following day, as I had previously planned with their English teacher, the students wrote their comments on the tour. These comments were then given to me for our feedback session that afternoon. The refrain was their delight with the way they had been received. I was not upset by their inability to express their ideas in acceptable English; in fact their written tidbits gave me enough ammunition for exercises in communication for the rest of the general office clerk program. We had fun working to improve their ability to communicate. As Belle said later, "We be's interested in developing our potentialities."

Feedback should be introduced early in each program. In a friendly atmosphere, students feel free to express themselves. Not only will they be pleased by your willingness to listen to them, but you, too, will learn more about them. Allow time for feedback, therefore, after each guest appearance, tour, or film.

PRAISE

Praise each change for the better. Notice how frequently throughout our daily contacts I stopped to encourage or praise. Students who have met nothing but failure and who expect to continue to fail need such reinforcement. This does not imply that you assume a patronizing or hypocritical manner and hand out praises arbitrarily. You should give praise only when the situation warrants it.

Summary

The antisocial attitudes and uninhibited behavior of young people from slum areas or ghettoes present great problems to educators and others unfamiliar with their background. These problems must be understood in an environmental frame of reference before teaching and learning in the more formal sense can take place. These young people have to be accepted as they are, not be judged by middle-class standards. They are in a difficult situation, but so are you. Both they and you have to learn to live in two different worlds simultaneously. When you can accomplish this, you are communicating. More socially acceptable habit patterns will then develop, and discipline problems will lessen.

It is your responsibility as the more mature person to pierce the surface of hostility and defiance with which you are initially confronted and look beneath this hard shell. Each youth expects to be treated like an adult in spite of his frequent displays of deliberately infantile behavior; such displays are meant to provoke you and test your acceptance of him.

Your effectiveness in communicating can be measured by your capacity to withstand attacks and provocations and to convert them into educative experiences. When you bring this about, the students' apparent apathy to learning is sloughed off. Defensive tactics are abandoned, and highly intelligent, perceptive, and motivated students are revealed. This takes time, patience, warmth, sincere interest, imagination, and know-how. Sooner or later friendly responses will indicate that a more compatible relationship is developing. The concept of "I and they" is becoming a concept of "we." The walls of separation are coming down, and you are on the way to being accepted.

Their acceptance of you has to be earned. Your professional status means nothing to them in the beginning. They see you as a symbol of authority and therefore an enemy, and your being an outsider intensifies their mistrust. You have to prove that you are free from prejudice. You are constantly being observed and tested to see if your actions match your words. Gestures, inflections of the voice, and other forms of nonverbal communication may to these youths seem to have overtones of superiority. Much depends on your sincerity and your ability to relate to people with cultural differences.

The comfortable atmosphere you create in the classroom is of great importance. Anyone with sensitivity to human relationships can sense the mutual acceptance and respect for individual differences that is nurtured by such an atmosphere. It is permeated with good-naturedness. It is up to you to make your students feel that they are being reached—not as things to be manipulated, but as human beings with individuality. In the right atmosphere, interaction is encouraged, and both students and teacher can accept criticism and grow in the process.

To the uninitiated or to the traditional-minded observer, however, such an atmosphere may seem too permissive, only perpetuating these youths' erratic behavior. This is not so. What the inexperienced observer may fail to see is that the lively interaction is a manifestation of the youths' feelings of being accepted. Learning is occurring at various levels in a frame of reference understood and evolved by the students, not imposed authoritatively by the teacher. You, the teacher, are involved every moment — physically, emotionally, and intellectually. You listen more than you talk, waiting for the opportune moment to interject your own contribution.

When you become aware of the problems of attitudes and behavior, you realize that traditional methods and approches will not achieve the desired goals. You are also aware that job training in itself is too narrow a concept. Job training has to take place in wider educational framework. It has to be part of a larger goal — learning for living. You have to help your students broaden their concepts of learning to extend beyond the classroom into every facet of life. This goal demands innovative approaches. You must experiment and try various techniques, always remembering to evaluate them honestly and discard those that prove ineffective. You have to understand that each group, like each individual, is unique. Therefore your approach and techniques will have to be adapted to each group. With some groups role playing may work, and with others it may fail, for example. You have to be flexible and perceptive.

The classroom cannot be divorced from the students' daily lives. Examples used in developing concepts of unfamiliar words for instance, have to be based on the students' experiences. Vocabulary means more when it is introduced in a familiar context. The more vocabulary is developed naturally in discussions, the better. You will be amazed at the rapidity with which your students will assimilate new vocabulary. There is one caution: Listen to yourself and guard against using vocabulary which these youths may not understand. Whenever you do use unfamiliar terms, stop and explain; unless you explain, you will fail to communicate.

For these young people, language patterns which constitute English in a middle-class sense have to be developed as part of a second language. When you approach the subject in this way, you are not depriving your students of their "in" language, which furnishes security. In a sense they are learning English as a foreign language. They soon become aware of when it is appropriate to use this "new" language, and you should give them continual opportunities to use it. When they fully realize its importance, even gang leadership will exert constructive influence. Their speech will also improve if you permit them to listen to tapes of their talks and discussions. Allowing them to conduct discussions and assume responsibilities will get them involved and increase their span of attention.

These youths will be encouraged to read if their imagination and interest are aroused by references to literature in terms which they can understand.

Tours and special programs are important adjuncts to regular classroom procedures. These help your students develop a better understanding of their relationship to the community. Daily crises and outbursts of capricious behavior can also be used for teaching-learning experiences.

If you listen, accept, experiment, and evaluate, you will be communicating with your students; and you will be helping them not only to become employable, but also to throw off the yoke of poverty.

4 • Evolving Content and Structure

WHAT SUBJECT MATTER IS INCLUDED in a course on personal development for job training of youths from low-income areas who are culturally different? What criteria are used in selecting subject matter? Must a daily plan be followed?

In Manpower Development Training programs, state departments of employment and vocational training schools cooperate. The state departments of employment, after surveys of the labor market are made, determine the jobs for which youths are to be trained and recruit the trainees. The school heads prepare the curricula for the specific jobs and provide the training personnel. I received the following prescribed curriculum for Personal Development for the office boys program:

OFFICE BOY (HIGH SCHOOL DROPOUT)

UNIT 5: PERSONAL DEVELOPMENT AND HUMAN RELATIONS

a. Learning good grooming: hair care and styles, appropriate clothing for office wear, cleanliness, planning of wardrobe, shaving and skin care, fingernail grooming, weight control, and the cleaning of teeth

b. Learning to get along with fellow employees and supervisors

c. Training for situations similar to those that will be faced in an office boy type of contact. Examples: relationship with immediate supervisor, fellow employees, vendors, and customers

Textbooks are selected in advance by the educational administration. How much leeway each teacher has in determining course content then depends on how the principal interprets his role and the role of the teacher. If the principal is authoritarian and fearful of innovation, the teacher and students are doomed. The students' needs and interests will not be met by a processed package preconceived and presented by persons who have never established a growing relationship with impoverished youths from minority groups. Fortunately I was allowed to supplement the prescribed content with material the students needed. The content my students and I evolved was never questioned so long as it contributed to the students' preparation for employment. Preparation for employment is too narrow a goal, however. It is not realistic because it does not consider such related problems as the effects of arrest records on chances for employment, effects of poverty on health, effects of racial discrimination on housing, and effects of gang influence on the habit patterns and value systems of the individual.

The students' needs determine your focus. Therefore the textbook cannot be your sole guide. You have to be able to listen to the students and to translate their needs into meaningful content. The outward semblance of apathy created by sleeping, restlessness, tardiness, and absence is often misinterpreted as laziness, stupidity, and lack of motivation. It is really the students' way of communicating feelings of rejection.

Most textbooks are prepared for the middle-class youth. Reading materials that do not relate to impoverished youths' daily living problems intensify their feelings of being left out. Because their cultural backgrounds differ so markedly from those of middle-class youths, young people from poverty areas need material that begins where they are. To be of educational value in getting culturally different youths from where they are to where they have to go, material has to be carefully selected to narrow the cultural gap.

You are on the spot. It's up to you to create an atmosphere of acceptance and friendship in which freedom of expression and free association of ideas will be encouraged. Academic subjects can be introduced and pursued with interest once the atmosphere is established. Under such circumstances the students' motivation for learning will emerge, and their self-confidence and hopefulness will increase. This takes time, patience, and ingenuity. Approach and content have to be dynamic and creative. You begin with their world. You have to improvise like a musician until you strike a chord they will respond to. For example, eating habits of students may spark discussions of diet, food purchases, and meal planning. Your ability to select subjects that affect your students' welfare and your method of using this material will help develop their latent talents.

Your attitude, which comes across in subtle ways, is immediately filtered through their nervous systems. If you are sensitive to people, you will know how they feel about you. How they feel about you determines your relationship. To disregard this factor is to perpetuate their hostility. When my classes were switched and the original teacher of the office boys was told how "bossy" her students felt she was, she remarked, "What do I care about what my students think? I couldn't care less. I know what I must do, and they will have to do what I say, or else. . . . I would never have taken this job if I had to be evaluated by my students." [1]

No subject will penetrate these youths' initial hostility and destroy their defenses until rapport has been established between you and them. The authoritarian approach, therefore, is out. Traditional concepts of teaching consider the student a recipient rather than a partner. But if teaching and learning are conceived as separate entities, teacher and students will not learn from each other, and no meaningful relationship will ever develop. Teaching and learning are a process, and a process implies change. Learning results in change: nothing remains exactly the same. Changing, or becoming, is a concomitant of living; it is also a concomitant of learning.

Don't be disturbed, however, if the students seem to demand demonstrations of authority from you. There is reason for their ambivalence. They resent authority, and yet this is all they have experienced. Development of rapport, therefore, between you and these young people proceeds at a very slow pace at first. It is made slower by their consuming hatred and mistrust of whites. This is understandable, because few if any youths from ghettoes or low-income areas have ever had pleasant and continuing social relationships with white people.

As Edward Emile Edlow said months later in our discussion on prejudice, "I used to blame whites for everything bad. This was real, because it weren't a brown man who dropped me from school; it weren't a brown man who arrested me; and it weren't a brown man who hired my father and made him sweep floors. Now in this class I learned. I don't lump all whites. I see them as individuals and I check them out as individuals. There are good and bad in all groups, even in mine."

The approach I use in Personal Development gives the students opportunities to vent their wrath verbally. Both the students and I are direct and honest with each other. We don't pretend racial preju-

[1] This teacher changed her ideas as she stayed on. It was even more difficult for her to work with these students in a traditional frame of reference because they expected more from her. She was black.

dice has disappeared. Because it is so important, it is woven into almost every topic included in the course. The students' strong anti-white feelings cannot be disregarded; they have to be understood and accepted. The effects of racial prejudice on the students' world and on their outlook on life have to be faced frankly. "The Man," their term for white society, is their enemy. To help them think of whites, and of other minorities, as individual human beings rather than undifferentiated enemies is a goal underlying the content and approach in this course.

Rapport is made more difficult to achieve by many things the sensitive ears of these young people pick up. This is real and not imagined. Too often in public places, in faculty lunchrooms, and at social gatherings have I heard such things as—

"Why don't they respect people? I have degrees and would never tolerate attitudes like this in the parochial school where I used to teach. I demand respect from my students."

"The nerve!—They tell me they don't like what I do and that they're bored. I don't listen to them. I don't have to. They have to listen to me. They have to take orders from me."

"It's impossible to teach them. They don't want to learn. They're lazy."

"She said her baby was sick and she had to stay home. I don't believe it. You know, they always lie."

"If they don't measure up to standards, drop them. We are not equipped to play around. We don't have the time. They just don't belong."

"They're getting so much. Why don't they face up to reality? We never got paid to go to school!"

Reality has many faces. When we listen to middle-class people who have experienced neither hunger nor racial prejudice speak this way, we are dismayed by their indifference and smugness. Their conception of reality appears shallow. What is reality to these young people?

"Jobs? We ain't getting no jobs. The Man is just trying to keep us quiet by throwing us a few crumbs."

"Who's going to hire us with arrest records?"

"I'm staying here because I got to eat."

"The white man rules this society. I can only go as far as he lets me."

"Suppose he is blood and got a good job? He'll be fronting soon and be another Uncle Tom."

To middle-class minds, these youths' views of reality may seem out of focus. But we must examine their world more closely. They are told that a high school diploma will help them enter the world of work. Daily they see their friends who have earned such diplomas standing around on corners, unemployed. They know what it means when they hear, "Blacks are the last to be hired and the first to be fired." Although conditions have changed for blacks since World War II, there is still far to go before equal opportunity is achieved.

Reality is a word and, like other words, means something different for each individual. The word is not the thing, but only a symbol. What *reality* means for these young people is a function of their experiences in a particular environment. Similarly, others—employers, teachers, social workers, administrators, the police—have their own concepts of reality. The problem is this: how to educate these youths to contend with a world of ambiguities and reconcile these varying concepts of reality. Pat answers or formulas will not suffice.

I feel that educators have a responsibility of honestly admitting the existence of racial prejudice and proceeding from there to help reduce the anti-white feelings of their students. This happens when these youths begin to see their friends getting jobs in capacities for which they received training. It happens when students get jobs in spite of arrest records. It happens when they can move where they wish, where they no longer hear the usual answer from the landlord: "Oh, I'm sorry, but the apartment was just rented." It happens when they begin to see that community action and political involvement can bring about changes. It happens when they can develop a meaningful relationship with a white person—a teacher, a social worker, a community relations officer of the police department, or anyone else who accepts people as people regardless of cultural differences.

Whatever our world of reality may be, it involves people. To get along with each other, we must be able to relate to each other. These young people, when they become employed, will have to be able to relate to others, both white and non-white. Therefore, the world of relationships must be seen as part of the world of reality. Accepting another person as an individual in his own right, without concealing his humanness in a sea of stereotypes—this must be practiced by you and your students. This is difficult, because these young people think of stereotypes as going only one way. They think that people outside their environment categorize all youths from ghettoes or poverty areas as delinquents, no-goods, and potential rapists, but are shocked to learn that they are committing the same offense when they refer to all whites as devils.

Content

I have discussed my students' participation in and reactions to a variety of experiences designed to improve their communication skills and open up new vistas to themselves, their friends, and their families. It was a panoramic treatment, however, to acquaint you with these youths' world and our need as educators to accept this, understand it, and incorporate it into the curriculum.

In this chapter I will dwell on evolving subject matter and the ways in which topics can be used to generate students' interest and enthusiasm and to effect changes in their attitude and behavior. Whatever the subject matter, I found that vocabulary could be developed from it, listening techniques could be devised, and language structure could be improved. The following topics, in differing sequences, were developed in each group: language, appearance, wardrobe planning, health, work habits and attitudes, prejudice, consumer education, office etiquette, black history, community action, arrest records, citizens' rights, and preparation for employment interviews and pre-employment tests.

Certain topics exposed the students to different value systems and set them thinking in new ways. They asked personal questions and expected honest answers.

Rosetta asked, "Mrs. Dawson, do you love your husband?" This arose from our discussion on love and marriage.

"Yes, Rosetta, I do love my husband," I said, and I went on to explain what love meant to me.

"Well, if love means mutual respect and mutual everything, I guess I ain't never been in love!" [2]

In the initial stages of the office boy program, various extracurricular activities were utilized to whet the students' interest and obtain their involvement. Among these were karate and judo. Adolph, who was a karate enthusiast, volunteered to demonstrate the holds in karate with his friend Frank, another student. First, Adolph drew a diagram of

[2] Rosetta was eighteen and had one out-of-wedlock child. Currently she was living with an older man who was employed, but the legal nature of his employment was dubious.

a man's anatomy on the blackboard, pointing out vulnerable points of contact. The rest of the group immediately shifted from their languorous attitudes to more attentive ones, and an exciting class session ensued. They watched Adolph and Frank closely. After each hold, Adolph and Frank explained their actions, emphasizing the need to predict an opponent's response. Then other students volunteered to see if they could apply what they had learned.[3]

This karate session stimulated the students to read more about this art. Adolph promised to bring in literature. He did, and we spent the next lesson reading silently and aloud. Interest had risen to such a point that I was happily astounded by students' vying with each other to read aloud. They wanted to test their ability to pronounce new words correctly. From this karate discussion much new vocabulary developed: *vulnerable, defensive, alert, aware, opponent, opposition, feint, faint, anatomy, achilles' heel*, etc.

It may be asked, "What does karate have to do with preparation for employment?" There is a connection. Planning is involved in karate, as well as knowledge and understanding of human behavior. On any job, of course, ability to plan is essential. It must be remembered that learning goes on at different levels. When learning situations contain analogies like this, the students' concepts become broader. The teacher, therefore, has to be concerned with the way subject matter can be related by extension and analogy. If you follow exactly what is in the book or in the curriculum statement, neither you nor your students will be developing potentialities fully.

Many educators may question my focus on communication skills. "That's English. They get this in their English class. You should stick

---

[3] Adolph, before he entered this program, had had a forestry job in which he had become a supervisor of 100 men. He liked the work, but it had no future. When he heard about this training program, he left his job. After class he and I often evaluated the content and wondered how we could reach his classmates. He said he was thoroughly disgusted with their infantile ways, but he wasn't going to interfere. He had never been in trouble. He lived with his parents and was planning to be married. His leisure time was never spent hanging around the corner. Instead he studied karate. Adolph was exerting a favorable influence on Frank, who had a long police record. Frank was now an expert weight-lifter, winning the title of "Mr. Hunters Point." Since this program's inception, Frank had done nothing to violate his probation. For the first time, too, he was showing interest in learning. A high school dropout, he had now decided to work for his high school diploma.

to personal development." This is a very narrow concept of education. What is more important to personal development than being able to communicate? I think that more interrelatedness is needed, and more thinking in analogies. The whole world has to be brought into the classroom. Communication is especially important to these young people who have had little opportunity for communication in their environment. I have found how much they can learn about language and how important they feel it is to their welfare when it touches their lives. They cannot get enough practice.

There is never a dearth of subject matter for the educator with imagination and perception — karate, love and marriage, and new scientific discoveries are some examples. I found the students fascinated by uses of the Laser beam. They first saw it as a torture instrument in a spy movie, and their introduction to its uses in medicine spurred their interest in reading. To see them become enthusiastic about anything was encouraging. No matter how unusual the subject matter seemed by traditional standards of education, it served to draw the students into reading and thus to increase their general understanding — which implies their understanding of mathematics problems, typing material, employers' instructions, and questions on application blanks.

LANGUAGE

Each session's content included attention to language in some form. The students' written comments on tours, films, and visitors' presentations, and written problem-solving exercises, provided ample sources of misspellings and unacceptable language patterns. Their language habits as recorded on tape during impromptu discussions, also served as introductory material to learning English as a second language.

For more effective communication, listening is an important habit to cultivate. This applies to teachers and students. Students will have to listen to supervisors, or they will run the danger of losing their jobs. Learning to listen becomes a challenge. Having them listen to themselves on tape was one technique I found effective. There were others, too, with which I experimented. Among them was listening to telephone messages. I introduced this early in the general office clerk program. I took the role of a supervisor's secretary from an outside company; my students were clerks receiving simultaneously the same message telephoned by me. I distributed printed blanks for telephone messages and, we read them to note kinds of information required. This exercise gave the students practice in learning how to get the gist of messages. I dictated by phrases. At first, the students kept asking me to repeat. The first message was simple, but as we progressed I introduced new vocabulary to give them practice in hearing the word and in spelling it. For example, a message might be:

Hello, I'm Miss Ryan calling for Mr. Owens, Personnel Manager of Reynolds Aluminum Company. Please tell Mr. Cook that Mr. Owens had to attend an industrial conference and will not be able to keep his appointment.

In one session, Rosetta said, "Mrs. Dawson, can I be the supervisor and make up a message?" This is the direction each activity was designed to take. Rosetta improvised, as did others. Later messages included such things as customers' complaints on receipt of defective merchandise. It was becoming apparent after several sessions that more students were beginning to listen. I corrected each student's message, noting errors in spelling and in language.

For practice in written communication, I presented them with this situation: Each student was to play the role of an office clerk. He had been on the job only three weeks. On this particular day his supervisor was called away from the building. In his haste, the supervisor had neglected to leave word where he could be reached. There was no one else around when the clerk received an urgent call to return home. Each student was to write a note that the clerk would leave on the supervisor's desk to explain the emergency. He had to create a reasonable explanation. This sounds simple, but it wasn't. When I went over the students' notes in class immediately after they had finished, it was obvious that they didn't know how to write the body of a note, how to address a supervisor, or how to conclude. Their spelling was poor. Punctuation was nonexistent. Past tenses were seldom used, and when they were, only past participles appeared.

"Someone in my family pass away."

"I miss the work yesarday."

"About the forms I did it."

"My dota has the mez." (My daughter has the measles.)

There was one verb that was regularly misused: *to be.* Belle and Sarah said, for example, "We be's cold. He be running. We be's studying." Other commonly misused regular verbs also provided material for daily sessions.

It was apparent that there were common language characteristics to be considered in working with these students. For example:

Peculiar pronunciations can be noted: *ax* for *ask*, *stastistic* for *statistic*, *pacific* for *specific*, *credick* for *credit*, and *chilerns* for *children*.

The letter *s* is often added to form plurals of words which do not take *s* in the plural: *mens*, *womens*. ("The mens was there." "He told the womens.")

The irregular verbs we began with were *begin*, *ring*, and *see*. Bailey said, "Gee, that sounds wrong. 'Has the bell rung?' 'Has the bell rang?' sounds better."

"Correct me when I say it wrong," said Mahalia. "I got to get used to. I don't hear no different."

The focus on speech also helped in spelling. When the students began to understand words in context, they began to differentiate between *their* and *there*; *two*, *too*, and *to*. When they slurred endings or failed to place accents correctly—as *inFLUence* for *INfluence*—they criticized themselves. The use of teletrainers, mentioned earlier, gave them added opportunities to listen to themselves. Mispronunciations evoked laughter; but pointing them out no longer gave offense.

Spelling was included in class sessions at least twice a week. It arose naturally from errors in filling out job applications and in writing telephone messages, notes and letters, written comments, and reviews. Each review consisted of no more than ten words; this lessened the chance of failure.

Students were exposed to a variety of methods for reviewing spelling, language structure, and vocabulary: these included oral, written, and pantomine exercises. When we were reviewing the words *perceptive* and *nonchalant* in the basic electricity group, Coolsann volunteered with illustrations.

"If I saw Deacon come into class one morning with his tie over to one side, his shirt collar open, and his eyes half closed, with a sad look on his face, I'd be perceptive enough to know that he had had a bad night." Laughter. "I wouldn't have to ask him. His appearance and gestures would communicate how he felt."

"That's good," I said. "Now what about 'nonchalant'?"

"I want to act this out. May I go out the door and come in?"

"Certainly."

Coolsann's long, lithesome body slowly ambled in through the half-opened door. He looked around as he shuffled his alligator-suede, highly styled, gray-and-black shoes, puffed on a cigarette, blew smoke rings and then, portraying indifference, sat down very slowly.

"That was excellent."

The students were no longer equating learning with memorizing. They were learning how to conceptualize and liking it. Without trepidation they used new vocabulary at unexpected moments.

Duke, always too restless to listen to explanations of any kind, demonstrated his understanding of vocabulary in a spectacular way. One morning, just as our class was to begin, the door slowly opened; a disheveled head appeared first, and then an apparently independent body followed it almost as if the feet were on rollers. The students laughed, but I gasped. It was Duke. I had never seen him this way. He was always well groomed, but this day his eyelids were so swollen they were almost shut. His speech was slurred: "Shorry I'm late." He bumped into the nearest chair and slumped down with his head on his desk. I could understand such behavior on Mondays or Fridays; but this was the middle of the week. I assumed he was high on narcotics. He sat there quietly for a few moments. Suddenly he stood up shakily, put his right hand to his stomach, grimaced, and tried to bow. "Mrs. Dawson, I'd like to use a euphemism. If you don't mind, may I please have your permission to go to the latrine?" The class roared.

"By all means, and get there as quickly as possible. Do you want anyone to accompany you, or can you make it on your own steam?"

He sailed out the door. I talked to him the next day privately. He had been high on marijuana. Fortunately, he never appeared in class like that again.

Malapropisms provided opportunities to introduce additional vocabulary. We were discussing business behavior in the duplicating machine operators group. Our attention was focused on how to conduct oneself on an interview.

If the interviewer asks you what kind of work you did before you entered this program, what would you reply?"

"I'd say what's for real. I had a good job pacifying milk." Several laughed.

Elizabeth said, "You mean pasteurize."

"Well, whatever you call it, that's what I did."

We discussed the difference between these two words after pronouncing and syllabicating them.

In a newspaper article we were reading in the office boy group, Sam thought *zephyr* was a kind of cow. He also confused *typhoon* with *tycoon.* Brick corrected him and explained that a *tycoon* is "a big blow with dough" and a *typhoon* is like a hurricane.

"No," said Chops, "That ain't right. A 'tycoon' is a animal before something else."

"Stupid," said Curly. "That's a 'cocoon.'"

Written vocabulary reviews took place at least twice weekly. Sometimes the students were asked to write sentences using newly acquired vocabulary. At other times they were given phrases whose meanings they would have to match to words. To vary the practice, I made up a vocabulary game. "I'll give you a phrase that expresses the idea of a word, but I won't tell you the word. You write the word you think it is. If your word differs from mine, it might still be considered correct as a synonym. All right. Listen to the sample, which will not count. If there's confusion and noise in this room, what's a word that expresses this idea?"

Their reply was immediate: "Chaos." This was simple, because the situation usually applied.

Don't be disturbed by the students' slow pace in the beginning. They have to become accustomed to new practices. They will prefer to memorize at first. "Quit the talk. Just give us the definition. Write it on the board so we can copy it." You may become impatient, but don't give in. Don't give definitions. Instead, give illustrations using concrete situations. Be sure to reinforce learning by praising each indication of progress. Before the first month had ended, my students asked for a complete list of the vocabulary we had jointly developed.[4]

HEALTH HABITS

These youths' health habits were understandably poor. Health education, therefore, was essential to their personal development. If they were to be prepared for employment in offices or large industrial plants, they had to conform to lunch-hour regulations. They couldn't eat whenever they pleased. Frequent absences because of headaches, colds, all-night partying, and inadequate diet had to be reduced. Fried potatoes, hamburgers, and soft drinks had to be supplemented and then replaced by more healthful regimens. Stress on preventive medicine had to result in change. Students needed information on family planning and venereal disease.

[4] See Appendixes, pp. 291–296, 300–306.

Early in each program I distributed a health questionnaire I had devised and asked students to fill it out in class. The pattern in each group was about the same. The students' answers confirmed my assumptions and observations about their lack of information on what constitutes good health habits. For example, the following facts emerged:

Only those who are married or live with a family understand what is healthful food.

Most eat rich desserts, drink alcoholic beverages daily, and sleep only two to three hours nightly during the week and often not at all on weekends.

Few go in for active sports. Most are spectators.

Men seldom go for annual checkups, and only a few women do. Most wait until medical emergencies arise.

A few have had ear infections.

A few visit the dentist regularly; the rest wait until they have toothaches.

A few wear glasses; the rest never visit eye doctors. School eye examinations, however, reveal that they have good vision in spite of their poor health habits.

Discussions of proper diet arose in many ways. In the first general office clerk program, Bailey and Wilbert furnished the opportunity. Bailey decided on his nineteenth birthday to assert his independence and move out of his family's home. He and Wilbert shared an apartment in the public housing project.

"Who does the cooking?"

"I do," said Bailey. "Wilbert keeps me company."

"What do you cook?"

"Spaghetti and meat balls, enough for the week."

Spaghetti and meat balls were good food, but I suggested supplementing this dish with raw vegetables, and milk instead of soft drinks.

When asked if they went home for a regular dinner hour each evening, Bailey said, "Gee, Mrs. Dawson, soon as we leave school, we go to the street and stay there. Sometimes we don't eat dinner until eleven o'clock at night."

"That's right," said Jimmie, who was married and at twenty had two infants, but seemed never to spend any time at home. "I go out popping with the guys." By this time I knew that "popping" involves shooting craps, meeting women, perhaps smoking marijuana, and driving around aimlessly.

"When do you stay home with your family, Jim?"

"I don't have time to. My wife takes care of the kids. She knows she can't keep me at home. I'm restless. I got to be moving."

Several weeks later Bailey said, "Mrs. Dawson, know what? Wilbert and me ain't had headaches for a week." His eyes sparkled, and he let out his usual gurgling laugh. "Honestly, maybe this diet stuff is OK. We been getting to sleep more regular, too. Now we partying only weekends."

"Bailey, this sounds good; but — in your language — are you putting me on?"

"Aw, no, Mrs. Dawson — no sense fooling you. You'd find out."

Lack of planning, lack of education on essential daily food intake, low income, and environmental influences accounted for their poor diet. Healthful diet had to be emphasized in Personal Development. We spent several sessions on balanced diets. Not only did we list essential foods, but we discussed why they were essential — how they were converted into minerals, blood, etc. This led to more new vocabulary, such as *physiology, biochemistry, genetics.*

Later in the program, the students began to see that those who ate properly had stamina while those who didn't were listless. Marietta refused to change her eating habits, however. "Mrs. Dawson, I just can't eat. I don't care about food. I gets cramps all the time. I don't know. My mother worry, too. I got no appetite." Marietta was very slender. In class she slumped in her seat, and she seemed continuously lethargic. She entered the room like a somnambulist. (At a mention of "gigging" she was metamorphosed! She would jump and run around in the gyrations of the monkey dance, which demanded a great expenditure of energy.)

To set an example, I brought in my lunch. In the general office clerk program, which was held in the old church, I had to eat in full view of the students. They looked at my cheese sandwich on rye bread and my cucumber or celery and carrots with amazement. "Is that all you eat? Geez, cheese? No hamburger or hot dog?"

"Want to taste this cheese? It's imported from Greece and made with goat's milk."

"Hell, no," was the consensus.

As we worked together and their feeling of freedom to express their feelings became more pronounced, Edward Emile Edlow said, "Is that why you have so much pep?"

"You ain't sick like us or other teachers. You ain't never out?"

"Your mother must have been related to a rabbit," said Bailey, chuckling.

"Know what we first thought until we check you out? She must be on bennies, huh? No one could be that peppy every day."

When we discussed the need for annual physical checkups, the men said they were a waste of time. Who wanted to wait around all day in clinics? The women were more health-conscious.

"Maybe that's why men die before women . . . . Mens is afraid of doctors, huh?" said Mahalia.

"That ain't true, neither. Women don't live longer. I know," said Duke with authority. "I got proof. My uncle, he'll live forever. He's pickled in alcohol." Laughter.

Students were now developing the courage to oppose Duke openly. "Hey, man, that's only your opinion. What about getting the whole picture first before jumping to conclusions?"

After discussions on health, I was always surrounded by students who had personal health problems to discuss with me. "I'm not a doctor. I can't diagnose your symptoms." I suggested proper referrals and then followed them up.

Because many students didn't have proper rest, their eyes were often bloodshot. I talked about the beauty of eyes and their importance in communication. Several women spontaneously demonstrated the emotions of surprise, hostility, and tenderness. This evoked laughter.

"Bloodshot eyes ain't very attract, huh?" said Rosetta.

"No. What if you have a cold?"

"Of course, that may do it. It could be from other things, too." More laughter.

We discussed the difference between *ophthalmologist* and *optometrist*. I talked about the need to be wary of optometrists who advertised on radio or television, or in busses or newspapers. The students had to be protected against malpractice. I suggested that they telephone the State Association of Optometrists, who would give them three duly accredited optometrists from whom they could select one. This same principle applied to medical doctors, dentists, and chiropodists.

This discussion of eyes also provided material for pronunciation: *pitcher* for *picture*; *attract* for *attractive*.

Few of the students went to the dentist regularly; they went only when they had a toothache. Visiting the dentist twice a year would give them more protection. Only a few still had all their own teeth. Those with missing teeth had never had them replaced. We talked about the importance of immediate replacements, daily brushing, and regular visits to a dentist. I demonstrated correct brushing and gum massage. This led to my explaining high-speed drilling equipment and how it reduces drilling time and pain.

The harmful effects of soft drinks and sweets in excess were stressed.

Only a few students engaged in any form of active sports. Those who did were men. A few went in for weight-lifting, karate, basketball, boxing, and football. But most were spectators, especially of baseball; there were many avid supporters of the home team, the San Francisco Giants. Because of this interest the students would read about sports and become acquainted with vocabulary in that field.

Exercise, even among those who participated in sports, rarely included walking. Whenever we planned to go on tours, if getting there meant walking several blocks, the students lost interest.

In our discussion on the need for exercise to maintain body tone and good health, we used analogies. Disuse of an automobile caused the battery to go dead; a parallel situation could be imagined for the body. Daily exercise and fresh air were essential for good health. Fresh air was no problem for the students because they spent most of their free hours on the street. When indoors, however, they were afraid to open windows. It took months to accustom them to working in a class-room heated to 70 degrees. They preferred temperatures in the eighties.

Our discussion on exercise led to the effects on posture of daily exercise, proper rest, and adequate food. How posture reflects one's inner feelings was also emphasized. Most of the students had poor posture. Their heads preceded the rest of their bodies when they walked. They dragged their feet or walked in a half-crouched position. They rarely sat with their hips in the chair, but slouched or lay back in a lounging position. To a large degree, this poor posture was the reflection of a negative self-image. We worked on posture in our role-playing situations, and posture became one of the criteria used in the students' evaluations of each other after each role-playing experience. The students became aware of the importance of posture to an employment interviewer. As they gained self-confidence and a feeling of self-worth, improvement in their posture naturally followed.

Discussions on health encompassed new discoveries in medical science. One of these special areas was endocrinology. Before introducing this topic I asked, "Do you know what affects your height, the length of your fingernails, your hair, eyelashes, eyebrows, and sexual

characteristics? For example, men in circuses who are seven feet tall —
why are they that way?"

"They got Watusi in them, that's why," said Duke. Laughter.

"That's a good answer. It shows you're thinking. There is that
possibility," I said laughingly, "but it's usually caused by something
else. The study of this has now become of especial concern to medical
science. I'll give you a clue: it has to do with glands."

Since no one knew I put on the blackboard ENDOCRINOLOGY and
ENDOCRINOLOGIST. We learned to differentiate between the specialty
and the specialist by the suffixes. It was the pituitary gland that controlled height. I drew a rough sketch of the head, showing the size and
location of the pituitary gland. Then we discussed experiments now
in progress to treat glandular malfunctions. This led to discussion of
other glands, which added new vocabulary, such as *adrenal, thyroid,
lymph,* and *salivary.* We had already had the words *congenital* and
hereditary.

NARCOTICS

The problem of marijuana smoking is not confined only to impoverished youth. Experimenting with marijuana, LSD, hashish, heroin,
and other drugs has also become prevalent among youths from high-
income areas. From the discussions which arose on this subject,
it was apparent that many of the students knew too much about heroin
not to have had personal experience. Several, having engaged in pushing narcotics to make extra money, had become users. This was a
dangerous way of hustling. As a five-minute taped presentation, each
group chose to discuss narcotics; this fact revealed their concern.

In the general office group, Bailey opened a session with, "Did
you see the papers today? There's a big column on narcotics. I brought
it. Let's talk about it?"

We put it to a vote, and the class was unanimous in favor of discussing narcotics.

"Tell us about the article," said Jessie.

"Well, it was about several hundred white teen-agers in New York
whose parents just found out that while they were out of town, their sons
and daughters fooled around with heroin and later became addicted."

Everyone sat up, intensely interested. "See, they can't blame such
things only on blacks. Usually they mean us. This time they weren't
poor, either."

"Why do you think these teenagers became addicted?"

"For kicks," said Bailey. "I knows many who do, you know."

We then talked about what happens to the body when a person becomes addicted. This led to a discussion of doing what friends do just to be "in." Several young women said they had been to parties where others urged them to smoke marijuana, or take other drugs, but they couldn't be persuaded. Belle and Sarah were among these.

"If I went to a party and someone knocked me on the head and, when I was unconscious, give me a fix, would I be a addict?" said Jessie.

"I'm not an expert, Jessie," I said, "but I think you'd have to become accustomed to it by regular use to develop the habit. By this time your body would require it, and then you could become addicted."

In the discussions on narcotics in subsequent groups, students centered attention not on addiction, but on the effects of laws on narcotics and addiction, and on citizens' rights. Several students who were or had been on probation for possession of narcotics vehemently protested against the enforcement of narcotics laws.

One discussion, moderated by Ali-Tees, stirred up such controversy that it had to be continued the next day.

"Yeah, laws are all wrong on narcotics. I think it's more or less a bunch of nonsense myself," said Wiz. "There wouldn't be no trouble if there wasn't such laws. In fact today the average person thinks for himself. He thinks whether he's going to be an alcoholic or he thinks whether he's going to be a drug addict. If he wants to go that way, he's going to do that way anyway, regardless of the law or not.

"It still goes back to the same thing. There's alcoholics out there right now . . . there's addicts out there right now . . . so that go to show you, they thinking for their own selves, regardless of what the law says."

"I go along with that, too," said Simon. "I always feel that by their striving so hard to say that this is such a hangup that self-consciously or not, laws influence people. Millions say: 'I'm not supposed to have this, I'll test it.' You shouldn't let this become an everyday bag. You should do it when you feel like or when you're partying. Don't take pills, they bad for you. They get you hung up. The next thing you be loaded all your life."

"You get addicted to cigarettes, too. They ain't good for you. They ain't no law against that."

"Why don't they do what they do in England—allow doctors to give drugs if a person needs them?"

"This is supposed to be a free country. We supposed to be striving for uh, individuality. If we have individuality we have free choice."

"Do you think that if narcotics were allowed, this would do away with the black market?"

"It would get rid of a lot of detrimental things."

"I hate to disagree with you," said Allen Williams. "You can't put drugs on the free market. You got brothers and sisters . . . they ain't got a mind of their own. Maybe they start smoking and taking pills and there you go. . . ."

"You have to keep it out of your chilern's hands. You worry about your problem, everybody worry about theirs. . . ."

"I didn't finish yet. . . . You try to tell me you'd keep it out of their hands. You know what'd happen if that stuff were on sale, any kind could get it through someone. You know that at fifteen, most kids smoke that stuff. That age has dropped down even lower—pills and everything. See what I mean?"

". . . That's a very controversial subject. See, if he's going to come under the influence, he going to come. What you got to do is to be ready and have them prepared for the worst."

". . . Could I ask a question?" said Allen Williams. "Have you guys been with barbiturates and all that stuff? Do you know they're habit-forming?"

"Do you necessarily become a alcoholic from alcohol?"

"To excess, yes."

"Just like you try to keep your kids away from cigarettes and alcohol, you got to tell them while they're young, 'Don't mess with this.' "

"That's all you have to say . . .?"

"Man, you can't do it that way. You have to explain. You have to say why so he can understand."

"Wait a minute. Do you understand what I'm trying to say? If you tell them—say a fourteen-year-old—and you give them five dollar a week, that's his allowance . . . you don't know if he's taking them or not. Then he's sitting around shaking, and he's only fifteen years old. Then what?"

"So then all you have to do is explain how the drug works, how bad it is, as if you were a record player." Laughter.

"So if my child at five see me smoking weed, I tell him, 'Don't worry, you can do this when you get older.' Maybe I'd drop a bennie in his milk?" Laughter.

"Don't interrupt me. I'm not finished yet."

"You're looking at the bad parts of it. . . . Gentlemen, may I make this closing statement. . . . Gentlemen, gentlemen—less chaos, please. Actually, we didn't come to any conclusions. So we'll have to carry it on another time. You can combat problems with intelligence. That's all it takes. I'm going to close this right now," said Ali-Tees, the moderator.

This series of discussions occurred late in the Personal Development course. Changes were becoming evident. Students were less afraid to disagree with their peers. They were thinking in analogies. They were using new vocabulary unconsciously because it had now become part of their own vocabulary. They were listening to each other, although still interrupting. Our stress on seeing things in more than "either-or" ways had left question marks in their heads—as I had planned early in each program. Their open-mindedness was beginning to show. I was very much encouraged. We still had far to go, however; and we knew this.

Instead of interrupting the discussions to give the students my opinions, I listened and decided to introduce films and reading material on the harmful effects of narcotics to broaden their perspective. As one of the sources, I used the services of the Narcotic Educational Foundation of America. This nonprofit organization, based in Los Angeles, has leaflets and films for rental at nominal cost. The films are produced with actors and actresses from the University of California's dramatic department, who portray addicts realistically. The sequences that depicted the agonies of withdrawal had such an impact on the students that they requested more than one showing. Two groups asked to see the film three times and then were anxious for their friends to see it. I couldn't arrange this, but I did distribute literature for their friends. The films *Narcotics* and *Assasin of Youth* are recommended. The leaflets "Youth and Narcotics," "Glue Sniffing," "Drug Addiction," and "Living Death" are also available by the hundred-lot from this same agency.[5]

VENEREAL DISEASE

A newspaper article on the increase in the incidence of venereal disease among teen-agers and young adults gave impetus to our including this in our discussions on health. I explained my plans to the

[5] See Appendixes, pp. 309–317, for audiovisual materials and sources.

principal before making the necessary arrangements and was given the "go" sign. I contacted both state and local health departments and readily obtained their cooperation. I experimented with a team of health educators — a man and a woman — for the first program of general office clerks and office boys, whose reactions differed from those of later groups.

I prepared the students for the sessions. When I mentioned venereal disease, Chops, in the office boy group, said "Mrs. Dawson, we know all about it, Muriel disease."

He wasn't being funny this time. This is what it sounded like to him. I tried to refrain from laughing out loud. "Muriel may have started the chain reaction, Chops, but it's properly referred to as 'venereal disease.'" Laughter. I wrote it on the blackboard.

We discussed the importance of knowing more about venereal diseases. Such information would be helpful not only to the young men, but also to their wives, girl friends, or prospective wives. I also added that their attendance at such sessions in no way indicated any lack of masculinity or sophistication.

On the day of the first session on venereal disease, the health educators arrived early, with their literature. Both were young enough to be considered contemporaries of the students. The man was tall and handsome, and the girl was attractive. Her long, blond hair fell below her shoulders, unlike what we considered appropriate office coiffure. I knew that the women would be quick to notice this — and they were.

I planned two sessions, one a week, to cover the various aspects of the subject. On the afternoon of the first program there was a roomful of women — no men. I looked outside, and there were the men, giggling and huddled together as if they were discussing something *verboten*. Finally, Sam, the ex-New Yorker and self-styled sophisticate, said, "Just looking around. I don't know if I'll stay. I know these things, you see." He smiled, came in, and sat down sheepishly. Two more men tiptoed in and sat in the back.

We began. I introduced the health educators. The man conducted this session, and his female partner gave the second session the following week. His manner was friendly, and immediately he got the group's attention. He had paid attention to my suggestion that he shouldn't talk too much, but should put his points across in response to students' questions after he had introduced the topic. First he asked, "What does venereal disease mean to you?" While several women were answering in a vague way, Chops entered and walked up to the front of the room bravely. Now there were four men out of a possible twenty-six.

The health educator explained what *venereal disease* meant and asked if anyone knew the specific diseases the term usually referred to. Few knew. He proceeded to discuss syphilis and gonorrhea, allowing himself to be interrupted by questions as he went along. Chops and the women asked questions throughout.

In his discussion on syphilis, some of the students' questions were: "Will the sores disappear?" "Do they hurt?" A few students were familiar with some of the symptoms of the second and third stages of the disease. They knew about possible blindness; but they didn't know about the possibility of insanity, other crippling effects, or death. They were particularly concerned with the subject of damage to unborn babies.

He then discussed gonorrhea similarly. He asked for the colloquial name and got it from Rosetta — "clap." He told of its effects: sterility in men and women, arthritis and blindness in children. Some of the students' questions were:

"How do you get these diseases?"

"Why are people ashamed to admit that they have the disease or think they have?"

"How did the first person get it?"

"What if you're treated today — would you get it again on contact?"

"Are there more veneral diseases than these two?"

"If a man is in the third stage of syphilis, can he pass it on?"

During these questions, Chops ran back to me and whispered, "Mrs. Dawson, I want to ask another question, but I want to use the right word. What do you call for protection?"

"Prophylactics."

He asked his question and stunned the audience with his vocabulary.

A film followed the discussion and served as a review of what had been discussed.

The students' reactions in our regular feedback session indicated that they had learned something useful for their own and their families' protection. I asked why so few men had attended, but got no answers. The office boys said they would attend the second session. This session was devoted to discussion of treatment and available treatment centers, and literature was distributed.

In subsequent groups, the health educators were able to speak more frankly, and the students, too, were less self-conscious. It was interesting, but natural, that after the session the men consulted the male educator about personal health problems.

Several men told me they were visiting the city clinic to check on suspicions of VD. Stewart said, "I may not be to class today because I got to get a blood test. I'll try to be back, though." I said I hoped he would return because I was interested in the findings.

"Negative, Mrs. Dawson. Geez, am I glad. I don't know what my wife would say. I been fooling around when we were separated. I remembered what you say about quacks. I telephoned the medical society and got names of three doctors and chose one. He only charged me $2.50, and I saved time."

Vocabulary developed from our discussions on health: *hemoglobin, hemorrhage, hemophilia, hemophiliac.* We learned the Greek origins of these words; the common root, they understood, meant "blood." The students were now very interested in word derivations. In discussing *hemoglobin,* we talked about the different kinds of anemia and reviewed the importance of a balanced diet. In discussing *hemorrhage,* we included mention of the clotting element in the blood and what *coagulate* meant. This led to *hemophilia,* which in turn led to discussion of the white blood cells and their function, to *gamma globulin,* and to the many research studies in *hematology.* The *RH factor,* and what it meant to a pregnant woman, was brought up. *Genetics* and the *genetic code* concluded these sessions on health. Other words that developed were: *addiction, venereal, susceptible, chronic, acute, congenital, endocrinology, ophthalmologist, oculist, optometrist, mastication, podiatrist, pediatrician, biochemistry, gynecology, gynecologist, nutrition, malnutrition, obesity, coronary, circulatory.*

GROOMING

The students were interested in attire and hair styles, but they were unaware of the appropriate styles for office work. Eva, in the general office clerk group, arranged her hair down to one side and wore a pair of capris partially covered by a paneled skirt. She was overly made up, with eyeliner, eye shadow, and mascara.

"Let's talk about what to wear in an office," said Jessie. Eva had unknowingly stimulated a discussion on appearance and grooming.

In spite of their unwillingness to conform to the rules and regulations set up by the principal, they did conform to their gangs' or peers' styles — women's extremely high hairdos and overly made up eyes;

men's long sideburns and high front locks with bleached ends, ruffled shirts, vivid jackets, small-brimmed hats, and sunglasses.

The need to spend some time on learning appropriate styles for office work was obvious from the first day. Since this involves changing attitudes, the approach is important. If you begin by criticizing and telling what you think, the students' hostility will only become more intense and the establishment of a receptive atmosphere delayed. To tell them how wrong their styles are is the same as telling them how incorrect their language is, how bad their habits are, and how poor their communication skills are. They don't need any more negative feelings about themselves.

We agreed that at home or partying they could wear what they wanted, but that at an office they had to dress more conservatively. Extreme makeup called attention to itself.

"Yeah, it makes you look too unnatural," said Wilbert. "Grotesque, too."

The women took umbrage at this. Rosetta blurted, "You like to see your wives or sisters looking like sick ones—ugly, too—or don't you think makeup improves them?"

"Yeah," Bailey said. "It improves them if they know how to use it. My girl knows, and she looks glamorous, but she's good-looking to begin with." Laughter.

Ebony magazine had helpful hints, which the women were urged to follow. Makeup should vary for different occasions. It should be as appropriate as the attire. Artificial eyelashes and too-heavy makeup are taboo for office work.

Wilbert complained about the girls' habit of overdoing it, and Jim said, "Some look as if they stuck their faces in coal bins. Sometimes they got a Halloween look."

Both men and women students were extremely fussy and sensitive about their hair. Prior to the emergence of the "Black is Beautiful" period, processed hair was fashionable. Towards the end of the sixties when pride in African heritage assumed major importance, the majority of blacks both male and female, especially the young, shifted to the Afro or natural hairdo. In fact Afro wigs made of synthetic fibers have also become popular, even among whites.

"How often should we shampoo our hair?"

"This varies with the individual. Only you can determine the frequency. Use common sense. If you're often in dusty places, or if you perspire doing something like weight-lifting, a shampoo may be needed frequently. Shampoos that don't contain detergents are preferred. Chemicals have a tendency to destroy the hair or make the ends brittle. As in everything else, don't overdo it."

The men were now wearing sport shirts and sometimes ties, but no more ruffles; but they were more resistant to changing hair styles than attire. The bleached ends were dyed, however, or cut shorter, as were the sideburns. Both men and women were becoming much more aware and critical of inappropriate apparel. Coolsann, for example, was continually chided by his classmates for his outlandish clothes. He wore several shades of red—his red shirt was a different red from his socks or tie—and did the same thing with yellows. Sometimes he varied these colors with costumes of somber hues—dark grey suit, black shirt, and black hat. On these days, Duke—and others—said, "You look like what you are—a pimp." [6]

Their criticism extended to people outside of the class. At our invitation the head of a teen-age grooming clinic from a San Francisco department store visited the class to discuss suitable clothes for office work. She arrived very enthusiastic about her talk. Her clinic at the store had attracted both boys and girls aged thirteen to sixteen, but she was a little apprehensive about addressing our age group—eighteen to twenty-three. Her manner was warm and friendly. Her hair, worn short, was not carefully groomed, but looked disheveled. A dark green three-piece knit suit hung loosely on her petite frame. Her shoes, of dark green suede, listed to one side, and her heels were worn down. Her stockings hung in folds around her ankles, and she slid in and out of her shoes as she talked. I watched the students. Their eyes were fixed on her movements. Both men and women were taking notes.

When the question period arrived, there were few questions. This disturbed the speaker. Rosetta rose and said, "Miss G., there are no questions because you spoke so well you covered all the material." Rosetta volunteered similar tactful remarks to each of our visitors.

At the feedback session the next day, Marietta said, "You know, Mrs. Dawson, she looked like what we're trying not to."

"That's right," said Jessie. "She looked sloppy. Did you notice her stockings and wrinkles? She even had a hole in the toes. I don't think she knew it, but—wow! She's supposed to set an example of grooming for us?"

---

[6] He was. Coolsann had told me. He had two out-of-wedlock children to support, and this was his way of supplementing his weekly MDTA allowance. He hoped to be able to dispense with this work as soon as he successfully completed this course and got a job.

At another time, after we had had the word *comely*, Wiz said, "Why does Mr. Y., the English teacher, be so uncomely? His pants cover his shoes and the jacket is always too big and too long." I was glad he was observant, but I didn't want to encourage discussion that could be construed as a verbal attack. This led to our discussion on office etiquette. The students' comments demonstrated their increased attention to appearance. They were quick to see flaws and inappropriateness in dress. This was encouraging evidence of their personal development.

To set an example, I dressed in ensembles, wearing basic clothes with a touch of color in earrings, scarf, or other accessories. I believe it is important for the teacher to apply what he professes. Do not underestimate your students' powers of perception. They have had much exposure to hypocrisy and they are quick to cut through false facades. They expect you to set an example, and they are not afraid to call your attention to any failure to live up to what you recommend.

Students, on the whole, were also attentive to personal hygiene. They used deodorants daily. Daily baths were not always easy to come by, because some students lived in apartments where bathrooms were in the outside hall, to be shared by other tenants.

These discussions gave us the more new vocabulary: *appropriate, inappropriate, suitable, unsuitable, ensemble, attire, apparel, accessories.*

CONSUMER EDUCATION

By observing, listening, and counseling, I learned how important consumer education was to the Personal Development course. The students considered planning and budgeting unnecessary. "Mrs. Dawson, you talking about planning for tomorrow. We don't know what's going to happen tomorrow. Why should we worry? Today's important—I don't care about tomorrow."[7] To develop the students' awareness of the importance of budgeting and planning—not only of essentials such as food, clothing, rent, and transportation, but also of time—was another step in preparing them for living.

---

[7] This attitude could have had something to do with their inability to use the past tense. They spoke and wrote of past and future events in the present tense.

To stimulate discussion on planning and budgeting, I asked for volunteers to go to the blackboard and show us how they budgeted their weekly MDTA allowance. Wilbert, who had lived alone before sharing an apartment with Bailey, dictated his budget to Belle, the recorder.

WILBERT'S WEEKLY BUDGET

EXPENSES		INCOME
Rent	$10.00	$20.00 (MDTA, allowance)
Clothing	8.00	DEFICIT
Food	4.00	$8.00
Laundry	4.00	
Total	$28.00	

"We can do better than that."

"How do you figure the $8 you don't have?"

"You can't keep that up, Wilbert. Soon you'd have to steal and hustle to make up the difference."

"Why do you have to spend so much for clothing and for laundry?"

"Because I like to be sharp. I dress good when I'm partying. I'm no slob!"

I indicated that I understood how difficult it was to live on $20 a week. However, it would be helpful to acquire the habit of figuring out how to provide for essentials, even on so small an allowance. To be able to think in wholes instead of fragments applied to budgeting as much as it did to any other daily problem. What the students considered essentials generated much controversy.

"Whenever I get a check, I run for a shortneck. That's more essential to me than anything," said Deacon, who had a wife and infant.

"What does your wife do about the rent if you spend it for alcohol?" asked Randy, who was single.

"Let the landlord worry about that. I got to have some fun."

"If your wife works, do you combine your incomes?" I asked.

"My wife," said Wiz, "wants her income for herself, but when I work she expects me to support her. Some nerve, huh?" [8]

---

[8] Wiz was an operator who was adept at hustling. He had told me that his wife didn't know how much he earned.

"We pool our money. We budget all the time," said Simon.[9]

Some students agreed to try to budget weekly to prepare themselves for budgeting when they got employment. We talked about the need for assuming responsibility by not having to borrow. Several students showed how they managed to survive on $20 a week.

Two young men who lived alone tried to help Wilbert think differently. "What do you do about paying back the fellas?"

"I don't worry. It's their problem," Wilbert said smilingly.

Wilbert's attitude brought up the problem of impulsive buying. "That's immature, ain't it," asked Sarah, "when you can't wait, but have to get it now? My daughter acts that way, but she's only two and a half."

This led to the importance of watching for sales in food, clothing, and appliances. In most newspapers, food sales appeared weekly. In San Francisco there were also special outlets like the dented-can company, where large cans of fruit juice cost a fraction of the retail price in supermarkets. The dents affected esthetics, but not the contents.

"I guess I'm impulsive, then," said Jessie. "I watch for sales, but I still can't control myself. Each time I go to a dance, I want to buy something new. Many times I spend a lot of money. After I have a dress cleaned, it shrinks and I got to get a new one."

"I did something impulsive, too," said Mahalia. "I bought a long white knit coat for $40, and then I couldn't eat much for a week." (Two weeks later she came in wearing the coat. She had washed it, and it drooped unevenly. As the program progressed, she learned how to sew and made her own clothes as well as her infant's.)

We talked about what to look for when purchasing men's suits and how to evaluate material, lining, etc. From some knowledgeable community guests, we learned about purchasing second hand expensive suits for little cost through legitimate pawn shops.

"Wilbert, how would you like to be responsible for keeping us posted on sales of men's clothing?" He assented.

Maintenance of wardrobes was also an important factor to consider in our discussions. Proper maintenance implied planning and saved

[9] He entered the program on his arrival in San Francisco from Texas. He was a hard worker, motivated and anxious to succeed. He was disturbed by the attitude of his classmates who were born and brought up in northern cities.

money in the same way proper maintenance of a car did. Coin-operated dry-cleaning machines had proved effective and less expensive than store dry-cleaning; but unfortunately, there were none in this neighborhood. We located a few which could be reached by car, and the students arranged to pool car rides for this purpose.

Wardrobe planning and purchasing took up several sessions. To get student involvement, I had the group select a chairman who asked questions about the principles of wardrobe planning and the kinds of clothing to be bought for office wear. This served as review. The importance of reading labels to understand fiber content was new for many students. The students were asked to submit clothing budgets for their families on a weekly and monthly basis, and these were discussed. By the end of the program, planning and budgeting habits were still being developed. To become familiar with various budget forms, we referred to *Consumer Economics*.[10]

"What do you do about purchasing expensive items like cars?"

"I go to a dealer and buy for cash," said Coolsann.

"Before you do, it might be to your advantage to check on used cars to find out what makes are more functional and more safely designed than others. There are two magazines that can be very helpful if you want to buy cars, refrigerators, television sets, transistor radios, or any other appliances. These are *Consumers' Guide* and *Consumers' Union*. You don't have to buy them, but you can consult them in a public library. They have research departments to test the various products on the market to find out whether they measure up to standards of safety, function, and durability. Because they do not accept advertising, their findings are unbiased."

I brought in copies of the magazines devoted to evaluations of cars —new and used, domestic and foreign. Students were allowed to keep them overnight and then pass them on. None of the young men was interested in foreign or compact cars. Coolsann explained that they were too small for his purposes: he had to transport at least four women a night for prostitution.

"To be a wise consumer, you have to be able to evaluate and be critical. That's where the word 'criteria' really comes in," said Ali-Tees.

"You can't be fooled by advertising. You have to be perceptive,"

---

[10] Fred T. Wilhelms and Ramon P. Heimerl, *Consumer Economics*, 2d ed., McGraw-Hill Book Company, New York, 1959, chap. 2.

said Coolsann. These were just words, it turned out; shortly thereafter Duke said Coolsann would be a little late because he couldn't get his new car started. When Coolsann arrived, we opened the discussion on his purchase. He hemmed and hawed and said he hadn't had time to check on used cars, but had bought one for cash. After he signed the papers, he found that the car couldn't start without being pushed.

This led to talk about credit buying and discriminatory practices. Reporters who have investigated have found that supermarkets in poor black neighborhoods were charging higher prices for poor-quality food and clothing than stores of the same chain in more affluent neighborhoods.

"Why aren't there more blacks in the commercials?" asked Stewart. "They want to sell to us, but we don't count in commercials, huh?"

"There are some more blacks in newspaper commercials and even on TV now," said Allen Williams.

"Yeah, where?"

"You got to have quick eyes, because they flash by, but they're there more than before," said Allen Williams.

"If you wink, you're going to miss them. That's what's not fair. they're not in there long enough to be recognized," said Wiz.

Marketing research has shown that the average black spends more than his white counterpart on cosmetics, appliances, stockings, soft drinks, hair preparations, phonograph records, and movies. You'd never think so from the black's invisibility in advertisements. If these young people and their families saw greater representation of blacks in advertising, their morale and sense of dignity would receive a much-needed boost.

Because minority groups are often exploited by unethical credit stores, we discussed the services of the Better Business Bureau. The students were urged to contact the Bureau if they thought they were victims of unfair practices, such as bait-and-switch games, phony credit certificates, health quackery, or work-at-home schemes. The bait-and-switch game, for example, is a retailing racket in which an advertisement entices customers into a store with "bait" of a great bargain in a well-known product. In the store, the salesman attempts to switch the customer to a higher-priced inferior item. Films demonstrating such schemes were shown at later sessions.[11]

---

[11] See Appendix, pp. 309–317.

COMMUNITY INTERESTS

Community interests were made part of the content of Personal Development. I believe that school and community have to be brought more closely together; there still exists too much separation between them. Related to our discussion on consumer economics were efforts of the Hunters Point community to establish a neighborhood co-op. I therefore invited men and women from the community who had spearheaded this venture to visit our class to discuss the benefits of co-ops.

One man and two women came and gave us a team presentation on the purpose of the co-op, the membership cost, the credit union, and future plans. The credit union was a much-needed service; many of my students were still paying high interest on loans from finance companies.

The reaction of the students in our feedback sessions was interesting.

Deacon said, "Why should I pay $5 a share if I'm not going to get any profit? I can go over to any other supermarket and save money. What am I gaining by this?"

"Deacon," said Edward Emile Edlow, "you got a negative approach. You don't have to buy brand names, you know, as you do in a supermarket. You can still get quality at lower prices and save money. Then you can really budget. It'll mean something."

"You know," said Stewart, "if you go into a supermarket, the owners can increase the prices. . . . You're not sure of the packaging. You don't know how much you're getting. It's difficult to distinguish between 'economy' and 'king size.' "

Joining the co-op was up to the individual. However, as consumers they at least became acquainted with such community resources.

HOUSING

Inadequate housing affects young people as much in Hunters Point, San Francisco, as in any other poverty area in the world. The students' seeming indifference in the beginning was another way of communicating their feelings of hopelessness.

"Why talk about housing? It's been this way for years, and nothing's been done. Cockroaches and rats are fighting for space, too. Walls are so thin you can hear everything." Laughter.

"If whites lived in these housing projects surrounded by garbage dumps, there'd have been action long ago!"

"Yeah, so what's the use? No one's going to listen to us. Most of us ain't old enough to vote yet!"

Gradually, as each program progressed and the students improved their communication skills and gained self-confidence, they became more concerned about what was happening in their community and in the world.

The students' attention was aroused at one point by a newspaper account of plans to raze the public housing project in Hunters Point in which most of them lived. According to the article, Federal and local agencies had conflicting points of view on philosophy and procedure. One agency preferred to wait for a master plan, while the other did not.

"What's going to happen to us when the buildings are torn down?"

"When they're replaced, are the rentals going to be higher than we can afford?"

I couldn't answer the questions. We needed to see the agency heads responsible for the plans.

"How would you like it if I could arrange for the two directors of the agencies involved to visit and discuss their plans with us? You can then ask them the questions you just asked me. Newspapers may distort views."

"Go ahead, but we know they won't come here. We're not important enough."

"Nothing happens unless we try. I'll call this afternoon and keep you informed of progress."

The San Francisco Redevelopment Agency and the San Francisco Housing Authority agreed to the meeting. Men and women active in the community were also delighted to attend. When I extended invitations to the rest of the student body, my own students immediately reacted.

"This is our program. Why should they be included? They don't invite us anywhere. We always inviting other classes on tours, too. Why don't their teachers show initiative?"

This possessiveness had appeared whenever I invited students from other classes to special programs. I used such occasions for discussion of the purpose of our program and the common objectives of all the classes, hoping to see a gradual change from competitiveness to cooperation.

When I consulted the principal for permission to hold the meeting, he immediately assented. However, when I asked him to publicize the meeting, he refused. I pointed out the importance of bringing the community into closer relationship with the school. "There's nothing unusual about this program," he said. "We have to get permission from higher-ups at the board of education." I didn't pursue the matter of publicity further.

There was a great deal of bustling the morning of the meeting, because chairs had to be brought in from other rooms. Several students volunteered to move them; this was a change, because these students had never volunteered to do anything before.

The students were told that this was their meeting and that they would have ample time to question the guests. The meeting began. The directors of the agencies emphasized their complete compatibility on housing redevelopment plans, contrary to the newspapers' implicatins. One director illustrated his talk with slides showing housing in another area of San Francisco which had been redeveloped. The houses were attractive and had individual gardens. From the outside they were modern and not as boxlike as much low-cost housing. The tenants were permitted to use their creativity in designing their gardens. Those with carpentry skills were encouraged to use them in the maintenance of their apartments. A two-bedroom apartment could be rented for $130 a month, including utilities and carport. A wave of resentment went through the audience when this price was mentioned.

By this time there were no longer any lulls after speakers' presentations. The students were becoming articulate, and these meetings showed their ability to apply what they were learning from our discussion methods.

Edward Emile Edlow opened up the question period. "You mentioned $130 a month for an apartment. What about women who have no husbands, but have eight children and an income under $3,000 a year? Are they eligible?" There was applause. Women from the citizens' council of Hunters Point nodded their heads in agreement. No acceptable answer was forthcoming, although one director said that such a family would be considered for permanent public housing.

Other students wanted to know if unmarried mothers were eligible for such dwellings. The answer was in the negative, and this caused a terrific uproar. It was at this point that several women asked to speak. The women from the citizens' council urged the students to come to the regular weekly housing meetings and get involved in community problems.

"What plans are being made to relocate people while redevelopment takes place?" Both gentlemen indicated that the plan was to raze the buildings gradually, relocating tenants as they went along.

Another woman student said she noticed the slow rate of housing improvement in certain areas which were inhabited by minority groups. "Mr. Speaker, when are we going to have action instead of talk? How long will it take for these houses you mention to be completed?" When he said it would take two years, again the audience reacted angrily.

One of the women from the citizens' council said, "You claim to be our friend. Maybe, but we watches you very closely and take nothing for granted. We fights you when we has to."

In feedback session the following day, the students were highly critical and suspicious of the agencies' underlying motives. The weather and view in Hunters Point were so attractive that the students were afraid that the usual high-rise, high-rent apartments would replace their present housing project. High rents would automatically exclude them. In spite of this negative reaction, they expressed pleasure with the "big" people's willingness to visit and to listen to them. They were now going to become active in the community. A few said they would attend the housing meeting the women on the citizens' council had spoken about.

The meeting was another way of boosting the students' morale. Perhaps, if they took an interest in community problems, they could see action instead of talk. Their questions were so numerous that they wanted a follow-up meeting. The directors agreed, but their particular program ended before a second meeting was possible. This was unfortunate, because the students were now aroused, and another meeting could have given them an opportunity to discuss the problems in depth.

SCHOOL MOVING EPISODE

A school's failure to consider community reaction to plans affecting the community can have serious repercussions. An episode at our school is an example. The black community in Hunters Point was aware of the existence of the new job training program in their area, but unaware that the program suffered from certain disadvantages: location, and obsolescence of facilities. The community did not realize that to institute a vocational training program in a ghetto results in de-facto segregation. In such a situation, the students cannot be properly prepared for multiracial living. In addition, the proximity of nonstudent friends who hang around outside the school, or who drive by honking horns to attract attention, increases the difficulties of developing acceptable attitudes and behavior. It also seemed essential for such a program to be located outside the ghetto so as to recruit students on a citywide basis. Our obsolete physical plant made it difficult to train the students adequately for employment in technologically modern offices. Early in the Youth MDTA program the faculty requested more modern facilities, but no other buildings were available. Alterations in our old building, made at considerable cost, improved the situation only slightly. We still had to operate under substandard conditions in a segregated community.

After a few months we were told that plans were under way to move our training school to a regular vocational institute in another part of the city. Again there was failure in communication: the community was neither brought into the plans nor apprised of the reasons for moving. Students were not to be told about moving until it was a reality.

Parents of the students had developed pride in this first Manpower Development Training school focused on young people in their neighborhood. It gave them a feeling of possession. It was the first time something constructive was actually being done to alleviate unemployment in this poverty area. Ironically enough, parents' views on moving were never considered.

At a special faculty meeting we were told that we would begin at the new quarters the following week. The principal would notify the students; teachers were ordered to remain silent. Despite the efforts at secrecy, word about moving immediately spread throughout the community. Reaction was immediate; the community was annoyed and insulted that it had been bypassed in the decision making.

The students, too, were similarly aroused. As a moving van was transferring the typewriters and other equipment, William jumped out of a car and dashed over to me. "Mrs. Dawson, I need your advice."

Before I could find out what he wanted I was surrounded by five young men, not students, who had been sitting in the car. They, too, seemed interested. William continued. "About this move we were told about today. What do you think? I've been wondering whether to go along with it. Suppose you were a lawyer, what would you do?"

I laughed. "I don't want to misrepresent myself, William. I'm not a lawyer. Please don't spread any rumors to that effect. You know how obsolete the facilities are in this church. It's very difficult for you to imagine these as office facilities in this electronic age. In the new quarters there will be offices, signs, modern equipment, and rules and regulations similar to those you will have to follow in an industrial plant or large company. Let's face it honestly. You won't be able to run home at lunchtime for liquid refreshments. You'll have to develop more self-discipline than is possible in these antiquated surroundings."

"See, fellows, that makes sense. At least we get reasons. OK, I'll go. Do I have to buy new clothes? I don't have the money."

"No, I wouldn't. Just wear a shirt and tie. Take your hat off indoors and cut your sideburns a little shorter. You'll still make it with the girls." The men laughed.

I was very pleased with William's change in behavior. Now he was voluntarily asking for my advice, although he had been most hostile at the beginning of the course. I was encouraged by his progress.

Roberta and Frank disagreed with each other as to the advantages of the move. Roberta tried to persuade the students that the move was to their advantage, while Frank worked feverishly on the opposing side. He lined up petitions to cancel the move, organized committees to make signs and threatened to put picket lines in front of the church and to notify the press. Only Belle and Sarah refused to sign the petition; the other students were afraid not to. Most of the students in this first program had not yet developed to the point where they were strong enough to withstand their peer group's disapproval. Regular class sessions had been suspended for a few days before the move; therefore there was no opportunity to discuss the reasons for moving or to take the students and members of the community to the new location to show them its advantages.

The community called emergency meetings at which they demanded the presence of the principal and the Center officials. At this citizens' council meeting, emotions overwhelmed reason. To maintain the program in operation, the moving plans had to be cancelled. This decision was disadvantageous to the students and the community. There had been ineffective communication between community and school. Morale was at a new low. Typewriters and other necessary equipment could not be returned for at least a week. Attendance fell, and student committees voluntarily went into action only after we discussed in Personal Development what could have been and why. Then the students telephoned absentees, and things began to return to normal. Even Frank's reversal amazed us. Without asking permission, he had posted the following statement, which he had formulated and typed, on the bulletin board of the assembly room. It appears unedited.

THE YOUTH OPPORTUNITY SCHOOL PROGRAM (STUDENTS) I DON'T KNOW WHY IT IS THAT MY FELLOW STUDENTS DON'T SHOW UP FOR SCHOOL LIKE THEY ARE SUPOST TO, I GUESS IT IS BECAUSE WE ARE NOT YET READY TO HANDLE THINGS IN OUR OWN WAY, I CAN'T SAY THAT FOR SURE BUT IT IS MY OPINION ON THE MATTER, THE ATTENDANCE HAVE NEVER BEEN LIKE THIS . . . OBSOLETE BEFORE ALL THIS STUFF ABOUT TRANSFAIRING OUT OF HUNTERSPOINT, IN A WAY I THINK THAT THAT WOULD HAVE BEEN BEST, DON'T THINK THAT I'M TRYING TO GO BACK ON WHAT I BELIEVE IN OR FOUGHT FOR BECAUSE I'M NOT. I'M JUST EXPRESSING MY OPINION ON THE MATTER LIKE I SAID BEFORE, BECAUSE MYSELF I KNOW THAT I'M CAPABLE OF HANDLING ANYTHING THAT COMES MY WAY I CAN NOT SPECK FOR THE WHOLE SCHOOL, THEY THEMSELVES MUST ANSWER THE QUESTION ON WEATHER THEY CAN HANDEL THEMSELVES IN ANY <u>POSITION</u>: BECAUSE I FEEL LIKE THIS, <u>YOU HAVE TO HELP YOURSELVES BEFORE YOU CAN HELP ANYONE ELSE</u>: THAT'S JUST A SHORT WAY OF SAYING, "<u>YOU HAVE TO CRAWL, BEFORE YOU CAN WALK: YOU HAVE TO HAVE A HIGH SCHOOL DEPLOMIA BEFORE YOU CAN GET A DECENT JOB, YOU HAVE TO GO TO SCHOOL BEFORE YOU CAN GET A HIGH SCHOOL DEPLOMIA, YOUR NOT CHEATING ANYBODY BUT YOUR-SELVES BY NOT GETTING YOUR EDUCATION WHILE IT'S AVELIBLE TO YOU.</u>

Frank's statement provided material for discussing spelling and standard usage for the duration of the program.

In evaluating this unexpected incident as a learning experience, I was encouraged by the students' attempts to solve problems by reasonable actions rather than reacting violently. They still had to learn that effective problem solving depended on more complete information. It was apparent, however, that their feelings of self-worth were increasing and that they were beginning to assume responsibility for their actions. What better evidence of change in attitude!

ATTITUDES

Those who set up training programs and develop curricula for young people from poverty areas have not shown enough understanding of the effects of poverty and rejection on attitude. They are not aware of how daily frustrations and sordid surroundings create negative attitudes toward school, law enforcement agencies, employment, and church. Planners—and many teachers, too—fail to perceive these youths in their "wholeness." For example, toward the end of the basic electricity program several students were sent by the state employment service to take pre-employment tests. The rest of the group anxiously awaited their return. Duke, the first to appear, seemed dejected.

"You look bad, man. Tests too heavy for you, huh?"

"Of course not. I knew every answer—so what?"

"Let's hear, then. Give us the questions and see if we can answer."

"Yeah, all right." Duke went to the blackboard, wrote several questions, and gave his fellow students a chance to reply. None knew the answer. Duke willingly explained with diagrams.

"Gee, you smart. How come you look that way, then?"

"Because I am smart. I know they ain't giving me no job because of my arrest record."

To overlook the effects of arrest records on chances for employment is to perpetuate frustration and feelings of hopelessness. This is part of a larger and crucial problem. Fulfilling training and pre-employment requirements—as Duke did—is not enough if the major problem is left untouched—attitudes. And even elimination of the problem of arrest records from job getting will not solve this major problem of changing attitudes. Why not? Because the problem has not been grasped as a whole. Why does Duke have such a record? How can he be made aware of his need to change his attitude unless planners and teachers become aware of the need to change theirs? To change attitudes—to work on the complex of difficulties as a whole—the student must be given unbroken daily exposure to experiences which challenge his ingenuity, broaden his perspective, and enable him to cope with ambiguities.

Throughout the Personal Development course every topic that arises is perceived in its relationship to attitudes. Role playing and discussions were used to help the students see themselves as others see them. At the start they see themselves with a distorted view caused by conditions of poverty. The fundamental purpose of educating these young people is to develop their inner resources so that they can break this distorted mirror and become wholly functioning individuals in the mainstream of society. The struggle against their resistance to change continues throughout each program.

POSITIVE ATTITUDES OF YOUTHS FROM POVERTY AREAS

Too many educators, sociologists, psychologists, and employers see slum youths only negatively. This thinking is reflected in their negative approach, and it stimulates negative responses from these young people. As a result, these youths do not reveal their inner selves, and both sides suffer blind spots and perpetuate stereotypes. It is true that the negative effects of ghetto living outweigh the positive, but just being able to survive slum conditions indicates the existence of some positive factors. Some positive attitudes, then, can be observed.

Toward children: "Mrs. Dawson, I got to hustle at night. I can't let my two children suffer just because I didn't marry their mother. I have to pay $40 a week for their support. That's no chicken feed, and until I finish this course and get a good job, I got to continue. Nothing's more precious than my children," said Coolsann.

"That's right," said Edward Emile Edlow. "My son has asthma, and whenever he has a bad attack, I told his mother to call me. I spend many nights staying up all night to comfort him until he gets over it. I'm studying now to get a job so that my son won't have to suffer from lack of education the way I did."

In our discussion on how unmarried expectant mothers approached the question of adoption, Marietta echoed these sentiments. "We love our children and would never think of giving them up for adoption like the white girl usually does. Our parents don't encourage it, either. They don't throw us out. They take care of us and still love us and our children. There is always a way to take care of them. If parents work, grandparents or aunts and uncles — even cousins — are there."

Toward hypocrisy: These young people are extremely sensitive to hypocrisy and quick to discern whether a person means what he says. They separate the sincere from those who pretend to be sincere. They recognize condescending and patronizing approaches. They prefer directness in speech rather than elaboration and platitudes to conceal prejudices.

"He never touched the nitty gritty," said Duke in his evaluation of a government agency representative's remarks on chances for employment. "He thinks he fooled us by his evasiveness, but he didn't. We see through him."

They are also less inhibited in expressing their emotions than their middle-class counterparts.

Toward slum living: The fact that they have developed a culture that helps them survive, even though it is a culture alien to the middle class, shows strength. There is growing militant leadership in ghettoes resulting from the inhabitants' desire to help themselves.

In spite of sordid conditions, they have an ability to see the humor in themselves. Often it is "in" humor, understood only within their group. They create their own brand of entertainment, showing remarkable creativity. I have heard a locally formed vocal quartet, "The Impressions"; their leader is versatile, composing and conducting the lyrics and music as well as playing various instruments. This group, in my opinion, ranks with the well-known female group "The Supremes," though they are not known to the general public.

If these positive characteristics were known and considered, what changes in educational practices might take place! We should stop trying to make the black a carbon copy of the middle-class white.

NEGATIVE ATTITUDES OF YOUTHS FROM POVERTY AREAS

Toward employment: "We're not getting jobs, nohow. This is to make it look good for the agencies."

"This is a white man's society. He rules it. You can only go so far as he lets you."

"If the foreman don't talk right to me, I quit."

"I ain't getting no job with my arrest record. Who they fooling?"

"I won't work for less than $150 a week. I'd be a fool to work for that for eight hours a day. I can earn that much in three hours hustling at night."

To counter these attitudes we discussed the students' feelings and opinions on employment. I listened to their complaints and, with their approval, arranged for field trips, films, and visits by policy-making personnel of large industrial plants and state employment representatives. These activities provided the students with opportunities for communicating in face-to-face contact how they felt about their chances for employment and how they viewed employers' attitudes toward them. The students complaints were followed up in feedback sessions, and then appropriate constructive action was taken.

Toward school: "It's boring, always the same thing. Teachers don't like us. In high school I told the teacher I didn't understand, but he went ahead and never heard me."

"Teachers talk too much. They think they know it all."

"I don't have time for studying or reading. I got to hustle after school. Think $20 a week is anything?" (This was the minimum weekly allowance students received from the Manpower Development Training Act.)

Toward themselves: "What's the use, I'll never make it."

"I'm no good. I'll never amount to nothing."

Our daily discussions on an assortment of topics enabled the students to hear themselves. Acquisition of new vocabulary and improvement in ability to communicate increased their self-confidence. Any success, no matter how small, received immediate reinforcement. Very slowly the students' self-concept changed.

"I'm going to make it."

"I studied last night and the night before."

"I'm determined to pass the pre-employment tests."

"Now that I know so much vocabulary, I'm reading a newspaper regularly."

After we had been working together for a while, the students no longer responded so vehemently to labels: "culturally deprived," "dropout," "delinquent."

Toward their families: Attitudes toward their families are ambivalent. They used to blame their parents for not understanding them, but now they are more concerned about preventing their younger sisters and brothers and their own children from learning about life the way they did.

In the matter of attitudes, work habits were also stressed daily. Years of living "on the street" result in poor work habits. To expect definite changes in a predetermined number of weeks is psychologically unsound.

Frequent absences and chronic lateness present continuous problems. My students were absent for legitimate reasons very often. Women with out-of-wedlock children, extremely concerned at a sneeze or cough, became panicky and took their infants immediately to the city clinic, where they had to spend the day waiting their turn. At other times baby-sitters were unavailable. Often students were ill because of inadequate diet and lack of sleep, particularly the young men. They were not always partying at night. More frequently they were hustling to survive when weekly Manpower Development Training allowances were delayed or out-of-wedlock children had to be supported.

Our introduction to attitudes and habits began like this in the general office clerk group. "Here we are at the beginning of the third week, and people are still straggling in long after the bell has rung. If you were on a job and appeared at your desk a half hour or more after lunch, what would this reflect about your attitude?"

"Not much interested," said James, who had been present but silent the first two weeks. His appearance had already undergone changes. His highly coiffed hair with bleached ends had been closely cropped.

"That's right. The way you act tells others what you think or feel. No words have to be exchanged, either. If you're always late on a job, if you're sloppy about your work, if you're always ready for a fight or give that impression — what are your chances for success?"

"Not much," said Bailey.

Their usual excuses for lateness also led to discussions on habits and attitudes.

"I didn't have a clock."

"My alarm didn't go off."

"I had a headache."

"We try to understand that work habits have to begin to be developed in this course. Whatever we do here, we'll relate to an office. Habits take time to develop. To wait until you get employment is too late."

"But we're not in a office. In a office I'd act different."

"You have a point. It is difficult in these surroundings, but we have to make the best of it."

Discussions on attitudes led to discussions on self-respect. Many said they had never associated acting badly to others with not respecting themselves. We pursued this for a while: the relationship of self-respect and respect for others. I said that each person was important as a human being, but he had to feel this importance. I let them know that I understood what their suffering and environment had done to their feelings about themselves and others. However, I pointed out that they also had to consider the effect of their actions on others.

In talking about consideration for others, we brought in office etiquette and how it, too, reflected attitudes. Students listened in on conversations not meant for them, derided others, and attacked verbally whenever they felt like it. They didn't understand the meaning of tact. Role-playing situations and films gave them practice in applying principles of office etiquette. Those who never prefaced requests with *please* or showed appreciation by *thank you* were beginning to change. Students now became highly critical of each other whenever anyone omitted essentials of courtesy. *Personality and Human Relations.* (Chapter 14) is a satisfactory reference for office etiquette.[12]

---

[12] Adam Sferra, Mary Elizabeth Wright, Louis A. Rice, "Personality and Human Relations," McGraw-Hill Book Company, New York, 1961.

The attitude we were trying to establish includes tolerance of others who talk, dress, or act differently. Students have to understand that those whose cultural backgrounds are different than their own are not "nuts."

"Remember when you called me a 'nut' the first day because I reacted in ways unfamiliar to you?"

"Yeah. We sure gave you a bad time."

"We know different now. You ain't like other teachers. You never yell. You got good attitudes."

"Yeah, why are you so good to us?" asked Rosetta.

"Because I like you. It's as simple as that. I think each one of you is wonderful and unique." I explained what *unique* meant, noting the root *unus*, "one." They quickly understood that every individual is different from every other individual.

"We all got a lot to learn about working with other people," said Ali-Tees. "We got to be more tolerant of other ethnic groups. They got problems, too. They're discriminated against, too, you know. I mean the Mexican-Americans, American Indians, and Chinese."

To focus the students' attention on attitudes and behavior I devised the self-evaluation sheet. I distribute this at the beginning of each program to find out what the students think about themselves and then again at the end to find out if they feel they have changed. I am amazed at the honesty of their self-evaluations. Some underrate themselves, but only one has ever overrated herself. Florence in the duplicating machine operator's groups said, "I'm high in everything. I can't help it if I be's perfect." (It was interesting to note the derisive reaction of her classmates.) A few admitted that they were below average in "willingness to admit mistakes," "willingness to accept criticism," and "willingness to listen to ideas with an open mind."

The criteria an employer uses to evaluate the effectiveness of an employee are closely related to points in the self-evaluation sheet. I distribute examples of employers' evaluations to stimulate discussion.

What it means to be mature is also discussed in each group because this question is so closely related to attitudes and behavior. It can serve as review.

Belle told what maturity meant to her. "Since I be's in this school, I be's more mature. I use to yell and hit someone when I didn't like what he said. Now I wait, think about what he say, and I answer back." I didn't interrupt her to correct her language, but later used it as an example to teach English as a second language.

To illustrate the characteristics of maturity, I asked for volunteers to devise role-playing situations in teams. The students were exceedingly creative and were beginning to improve in posture, pronunciation, and diction.

Several young men had this to say about maturity:

"To have an open mind requires a certain amount of maturity."

"Have the ability to face problems you face in everyday life."

"Say you get kicked out of school. You go to the liquor store and get drunk. Therefore, you become nothing but an alcoholic. You're immature. You can't face life. Life doesn't mean anything to you."

I said, "Let's see if we understand each other. We're not talking about doing anything once and being considered immature. It's when something is repeated and becomes a pattern. Alcoholics are sick people. Some physicians are alcoholics. Some business executives are, too. Alcoholics are usually people who have a very low level of tolerance under pressure or stress. No one is ever completely mature. There are degrees of maturity. Some people are more mature than others."

Many times after our discussions the students' unexpected comments indicated their increasing awareness and understanding of what it means to be mature and how attitudes and behavior reflect growth in maturity.

By basing the course content on what the students need, by giving them limitless opportunities for self-expression, and by introducing them to a variety of activities, I have seen their attitudes toward school, employment, themselves, and others change.[13]

YOUTHS AND THE LAW

Young people who have grown up in ghettoes or in poverty areas look upon the police not as protection but as another arm of oppression. Changes in these youths' attitudes occur when they feel that their complaints about police brutality and police harassment are heard. The high incidence of arrest records in poverty areas has to be seen in perspective. It is so intermeshed with unemployment, poor housing, lack of education, and racial conflict that it cannot be considered apart from these social ills. Violations of the law cannot be condoned, but they

---

[13] See Appendixes, pp. 295 and 298 for self-evaluation sheet, employers' criteria for evaluating effectiveness of employees, and characteristics of a mature person.

can be reduced if more effective communication is set up between law enforcement agencies, educators, the public, and the young people who live in ghettoes or poverty areas. In many urban areas community relations divisions of the police department are being established to accomplish this.

Arrest records are as prestigious to gang members in a ghetto environment as doctoral degrees are to the middle class. A youth is considered "chicken" unless he has had at least one confrontation with the law. He finds difficulty in being accepted by his peers if he does not conform to gang standards, and only youths with strong self-concepts are able to do without their peers' approval. About two out of fifty students entered our program without police records.

My students aired their grievances about their treatment by the police after rapport had been established between us.

"The police is always on us," said Jim.

"If I stand on the corner minding my own business, they comes up and talks nasty. You talking about aggressive and hostile, what we're supposed to be. The police sure acts that way. We hate them."

"If they want to obey the law, then why the discrimination against us? Whites aren't treated bad for the same things."

Allen Williams said, "Well, I can tell you an experience I had with the police. They drug me down the stairs — I was handcuffed from behind. They knock out my friend's two teeth. We got picked up for defending ourselves against a gang. A gang of boys jumped on us. They beat up my friend. They got me, and we were walking back down the street trying to get home. We hollered at the police, and they stopped us and put us in the car and said everything was going to be all right, and that's when they took us down there and did that. 'Hey, black boy, we're going to send all of you back to Mississippi,' they added."

"Yeah," said Ali-Tees. "I think most police is prejudiced. When they stop you, they yell, 'Hey, boy, what you doing?' I don't look like a criminal. I'm no boy. I think I'm a man just as much as he, you know."

Feelings such as these generated many discussions which centered on the students' responsibilities as citizens to obey the law. "If they want us to obey the law, then why the discrimination against us? Whites aren't treated as bad for the same things."

Many lawyers, both black and white, have concurred in the belief that no area of the legal system is free from prejudice. An impoverished black, according to them, is usually detained longer without bail than his white counterpart. Blacks are kept under surveillance more than any other group. Offenses go on their police records, which would be handled less formally if committed by middle-class whites. Even descriptive terms attest to practices of discrimination: black youths on a corner are immediately suspected of loitering, but a group of white youths are considered as just passing the time of day. Criminal activity may be much more evenly distributed throughout the population than superficial statistics would indicate.

A special meeting with representatives of the police department naturally suggested itself. Both the students and the law enforcement agents could benefit. I presented my idea to the students, who at first expressed negative attitudes. "Nothing will happen to change, you'll see. The police won't listen to us."

"Go ahead with the meeting. We'll be there, but it won't do any good."

The principal gave me leeway to experiment. The community relations representative of the police department was the liaison. He arranged for the presence of his superior, the head of police community relations, and a neighborhood youth group working closely with the police. The title I came up with was "Why Me?" This reflected the students' attitude — "Why pick on me?" — as well as that of the police.

As had been our practice, the students were prepared for the approaching event weeks in advance. Personal Development sessions were used to plan their questions. I shared my thinking with them and explained that instead of talking among themselves, they would now have the opportunity of talking to those who could hear their complaints and take action. They asked if they would get into trouble if they spoke their mind. "Absolutely not," I said.

On the afternoon of this meeting, not only did the head of the community relations division of the police department arrive, but he brought four associates with him, among them a tall, handsome black. All wore civilian clothes. They cam a half hour early to get oriented.

The community relations officer of the San Francisco police department was designated as moderator. This was an auspicious beginning, because he was known and respected. He was always wrestling with the problem of how to reach the youth *before* the youth got into trouble. His outgoing personality generated warmth and a friendly response. The students agreed that he was no phony. He was most concerned about the effect of these youths' police records on their chances for employment.

This was Friday, and as I looked around I noticed that several in the office boys group had lunched on wine or vodka. I hoped that nothing unseemly would happen as a result.

The head of the police community relations department opened by giving an account of the history of his division, the reason for its having been established, and its functions. When he finished, the floor was thrown open for questions.

Wilbert was among the first questioners. "If you want us to like you, how come the police is always after us? Even if I'm standing on the corner, doing nothing, the police car stops and the guy gets out and says, 'Move on or show me your driver's license.' He speaks like we was criminals. It ain't right. We don't like it."

The lieutenant meekly asked, "Can you give me any specific instances so that I can check on them?"

"Sure, we all can," said Jim. "For example, last Friday night we came out of the recreation center at 9:30 P.M. when it closed. We were sitting in a car talking to another guy standing outside at the front of the car. Suddenly for no reason, the police car cruising Hunters Point stopped and the police got out and came to where we were. 'What are you doing here?' he said in a nasty tone. 'Nothing, just talking. Why?' 'Move on before you get into trouble.' We moved, but why did he think we were going to do something? We have as much right as anyone else in another part of town to stand on the corner and talk if we want to."

"All right. I'll look into this. Any other questions or comments?"

"Yeah," said Dick. "There's supposed to be no discrimination in the police department, right? Well, how come I see only white policemen in the better sections of San Francisco? Why should black policemen be sent to black areas?"

"You could have been right if you said this a year ago. Now, however, things are changing. We are sending black policemen into any area, as we do non-black policemen. We will be doing more of this as we go on. I'll look into it, however."

"Why do you put police dogs on us? We're not animals. They do it in the South. But up here I thought things were different," said Wilbert. He was articulating the sentiments of his fellow students, some of whom were more timid and less fortified with alcohol.

This question caused murmurs throughout the room, and it was obvious that Wilbert had touched an area of intense resentment. The walls seemed to expand with the tension generated. The police community relations officer was calm. He said he had never ordered dogs into action; but he would investigate these charges and set up in-service training sessions on where and when to use police dogs. He admitted that policemen represent a cross section of the population and suffer from prejudice, too. He could not condone police brutality, however.

Wilbert was not satisfied with his reply and told him so. So did others; some of the women also broke in in high-pitched voices.

It was at this point, when the atmosphere was so tense, that Marietta asked sweetly, "Could I take the civil service test for police-women?"

"Certainly. We need policewomen, and any woman who meets the requirements—including a strenuous physical exam—can qualify. The salary is good, and the fringe benefits are many. When you finish this course, if you're still interested, see the moderator."

The meeting was over. It had lasted an hour and a half and it had been exciting. The visitors were amazed at the students' fearlessness and their ability to express themselves. The next day in the feedback session, the students expressed mixed feelings about the effect of their complaints, but all were happy at the opportunity for direct contact.

The police community relations officer and I were anxious for a series of meetings, but so many other daily crises arose that this was not possible. This was unfortunate, because I believe that one-shot programs accomplish little. We had to get off the volcano we were sitting on.

In each group the problem of arrest records and discussions of the police and the law occupied several Personal Development sessions. At one time an excellent program concerned with the Bill of Rights appeared on a national television network. Short scenes were presented, each ending with a problem to be answered by the viewers. I noted the problems and the following day I asked the students if they were interested in discussing them. Of course they were; but instead of telling them the problems, I suggested that they dramatize the situations.

One scene opened in a kitchen, with a mother and a son about twenty years old sitting on a couch. The doorbell rings. The mother opens it. A police-man asks, "Mrs. Smith?"

"Yes."

"I have a warrant to search your house for jewels just stolen from the corner jewelry store."

Question: Does the policeman have the right to search Mrs. Smith's house?

The next scene showed the policeman in the home questioning Tom Smith, the youth involved. "Tom, tell me how you stole the jewels." Young Mr. Smith refuses to answer.

Question: Was he legally right or wrong in refusing to answer?

Another scene showed Tom Smith in jail. He is pounding on the bars of his cell because he has been there for forty-eight hours. While he pounds, he yells, "Get me out of here. Tell me why I'm here. If you have no charges, get me out."

Question: Was he legally right in demanding to know the charges?

Question: Was he legally right in demanding his release?

The last scene involved three men and an observer. The three men are the center of attention while an observer is on a bus caught in traffic at the time of the incident. The scene opens with the bus bogged down in traffic and proceeding very slowly. As the bus approaches a jewelry store, two men emerge, dragging a third man out to the street in front of the jewelry store. One beats this man with a weapon. Then both get into a large car and speed away, leaving their victim limp and helpless on the sidewalk.

Questions: 1. Should you get off the bus when you see what happened?
2. Should you summon the police first or go to the man's aid?
3. How many men were involved in the crime?
4. Did they wear hats?
5. What kind of weapon did they use?
6. What kind of car did they ride away in?

Questions 3, 4, 5, and 6 tested perception.

While each group performed, the attention of the spectators was intense. At times the discussion became so heated that it was obvious a criminal lawyer or a law enforcement agent was needed to acquaint us with the legal implications of these situations. The students recognized our limitations after I said, "I'm sorry, but I can't answer your questions. I'm not a lawyer, and I just don't know. How about my trying to get a criminal lawyer?"

"Can't we have the guy from the community relations of the police department? He must know."

"All right, I'll talk to him. Then, if necessary, we'll contact a criminal lawyer."

Before making final arrangements, we prepared for our guest's visit. The students were now becoming accustomed to planning agendas. In addition to settling the controversies that arose from our dramatizations, they wanted answers to other questions:

1. What rights do the police have to stop you on the street?
2. How many telephone calls are you allowed to make if you are arrested?
3. How long can you be kept in a cell when you are first arrested?
4. What about sealing of records?
5. What is a ward of the court?
6. Isn't everyone who is put on probation as a juvenile a ward of the court?
7. How long can you be held in jail without being allowed to consult a lawyer?
8. How do you apply for a driver's license in another state if your parents live outside the state?
9. How much of your arrest record should be put on an employment application?

The community relations officer of the police department came willingly to answer the students' questions. In answer to question 9, he proposed a meeting with executives from three major companies who determined personnel policy and who could tell the students directly about their attitude toward hiring applicants with arrest records.

I am not including the answers my students received to their other questions, as state laws differ and interpretations of law vary with different law enforcement agents. The answers given by San Francisco's police department may differ from those of departments in other cities. I suggest that you contact your local police department and criminal lawyers for answers to similar questions raised by your students.

Such discussions generated interest in reading about the law. We referred to *You and the Law*,[14] but the general information in this book has to be supplemented if the students' respect for the law and understanding of their rights are to develop.

ARREST RECORDS AND EMPLOYMENT

Before we arranged our meeting with the employers' representatives, we discussed the problem of arrest records with the police community relations officer at a Personal Development session. Each group was concerned about how to record arrest records on job applications.

[14] Arthur P. Crabtree, *You and the Law*, Holt, Rinehart, and Winston, Inc., New York, 1964, pp. 204-216.

"Be honest," the police officer said. "If you have a record, don't deny it." He cited instances where several youths with police records from this area had obtained jobs, answering "no" when asked if they had ever been arrested. As soon as the security division investigated and uncovered the discrepancy, however, these youths were fired.

Discussion on this point became intense. "That's the trouble," said Edward Emile Edlow, who had two pages of felony charges to present to any prospective employer. "What about me? You know my situation. If I'm honest and show the interviewer the sheet, before he even listens to me to learn how some felonies were reduced to misdemeanors or to how since I'm going to school I'm clean, he says 'no.' So it's hell if I do and hell if I don't. They got us either way."

His sentiments were echoed throughout the groups. The police officer said he realized their dilemma and was trying to do something about it. He was engaged in a campaign to educate employers about how to interpret arrest records. Employers had to understand the difference between a charge and an arrest, between a felony and a misdemeanor. The young people, too, had to know the difference. Often out of ignorance they indicated on an application blank that they had been arrested, when in fact they had only been charged on suspicion of an offense. If the charges were dropped for insufficient evidence, it was honest and legal for these youths to answer "no" to the question of arrest.

To help our students still further, this same officer volunteered to supply applications from large industrial plants so that the students could get practice in filling out such forms. He would then compare each answer on arrests with the actual arrest history of the individual student. Any variances would be discussed confidentially. In this way each student could be prepared for the reality of job applications.

An unexpected incident increased the importance of our meeting with the employers' representatives. Randy, one of the brightest students in the basic electricity group, had been sent to take job tests at a branch of a large industrial electrical plant. He passed these tests with a very high score. He was then called for the interview. Well groomed and soft-spoken, he seemed to be making a favorable impression until they came to his "yes" answer on arrests. Randy didn't know at the time that what he thought was an arrest was only a juvenile charge, which was never substantiated and therefore had been dropped. Legally, therefore, he had not been arrested and could answer "no" to the question on arrests. The interviewer didn't know the difference between a charge and an arrest, either. Randy did not get the job. When I heard his story, I advised him to see the police officer, whom he had neglected to familiarize with his problem. Randy did this, and negotiations were in progress when these employers' representatives arrived for our meeting.

Each personnel official presented a brief description of his company's product, the types of jobs open to our students, the requirements for these jobs, the competition for the jobs, and finally the company's policies on hiring applicants with arrest records. "The aptitude tests are not to screen you, but to know whether or not you're capable of using your hands. They aren't hard to pass. Now, as to policies. We only check on previous employment to find out what your attitude was toward the job — whether you enjoyed working or didn't like that type of work. Then we go to police records. These are taken into consideration only as to gravity of the offense if there's an offense indicated. Outside of this, we don't go any deeper. We do hire people who have had a record. We've hired some students from your school who are doing very well with us. Their attitude and what they've learned here has helped them."

The students were allowed to ask questions as the speaker went along. Their questions were intelligent and pertinent. Since this representative came from the company that had rejected Randy, the students were anxious to put him on the spot.

"What's the depth of your record?" asked Allen Williams. "What's allowed when you're screening?"

"We take each case on its merits. We try to find out circumstances and what brought them about. If the degree of guilt wasn't high, then we would tend to hire that person."

"What if a person took your aptitude test and passed it. Then they screened him and found out he had a juvenile delinquency record, not a regular police record. Whay would you do then?" asked Edward Emile Edlow.

"We would hire him."

"Then why didn't you?" asked Randy. "That's what happened to me. I had one juvenile offense, but I didn't falsify it on the application when they asked if I ever was arrested. I didn't know at the time that the charge was dismissed and that therefore I could have answered 'no' to the arrest question. So what are you going to do?"

"Yeah," the rest chimed in. "You ain't playing fair. You got to give Randy a job. He passed the tests high, too."

The students' eyes were on this guest as they awaited his reply. He hemmed and hawed and was ambiguous, but Randy had the support of his peers. Finally the representative said he would talk to Randy after this meeting, get the details, and investigate.[15]

Randy's situation prompted the police community relations officer to discuss the sealing of juvenile police records. This information was helpful to all of us, including the representatives from the utility companies. Before a youth could request that his record be sealed, he had to meet specific requirements:

1. The arrest had to occur while he was a juvenile.
2. There had to be indication of no further offenses.
3. Five years had to elapse from the end of the last probationary period.

When the record was sealed by court order, it was forever closed and kept in a vault. For all purposes, therefore, a person with a sealed record could answer "no" to the question, "Have you ever been arrested?"

The next personnel official continued where his colleague had left off. His description of the company's operation was already familiar to the students because we had toured the plant several times. He stressed the competitive factor more than his colleague, however. "You've got 60,000 people looking for 4,000 jobs. So you do two things to try to determine who should get these 4,000 jobs. You give tests. These tests are not difficult. One test does nothing more than determine what you know about words. I don't know how much reading you people do, and I'm talking about reading newspapers and books. The more reading you do, the more you can build your vocabulary, and this will get through any part of this one basic test. The other part of this test has to do with simple fractions. It's easy. Then there's the aptitude test. The other form, which is similar to other companies', goes to the point of arrest records. We want to know about your driving violations and any other arrests. Here's some advice. If you have an arrest record, or if a driver's license was suspended or revoked, or if you have had moving violations, indicate it. I might say that most people in their lifetime have been in fights. These are minor sorts of offenses. When we look at arrest records, we take these things into account."

---

[15] This was done, and Randy's story was corroborated, which resulted in his being hired. This action served to bolster the morale of the rest of the group and put another dent in the students' original wall of hoplessness.

He then cited examples of applicants with arrest records and his company's evaluation of their employability. The interviewer was trained to consider the frequency and recency of the offenses. If an applicant had been arrested only as a juvenile and his record had been clear since, his chances for being hired were good. If, on the other hand, he had been arrested every six months in a continuing pattern, he would be considered a poor risk and be rejected. The personnel official stressed security clearance, especially with government contracts. Many employers required bonding, and this meant considering the nature of an applicant's offenses. His next comment aroused anger. "If an applicant's record indicates charges of rape, the question comes up of whether we hire him to install telephones in people's homes." He concluded, "Regardless of whether you've got a job at our company or somewhere else, you've got to bear in mind that this is a law-abiding system. We've got to conform to the laws. If we don't, we have chaos."

The question of arrest records and job applications was then introduced by the police community relations officer. He said that he had checked the sample applications the students had filled out and was astounded by what he found. "You really don't know what you've been involved in, and you don't know what to put down on your job applications. Employers and their personnel don't know how to interpret arrest records. It's a problem of educating everyone."

We were anxious to give the employers' representatives firsthand knowledge of the reasons for many of these young people's arrests and let them see how the students' attitudes toward the law were changing.

Edward Emile Edlow said, "Most of my crimes was committed because I was narrow-minded. I didn't know any better."

The police officer interjected. "Everything fine at home? No problems?"

Edward's answer revealed a broken home and the absence of both parents. In reply to a question on what he wanted to be, he said, "I'm not quite sure, but I know it's not a nobody or a nothing. But it's hard for me to get a job. I don't have a high school diploma. I have an arrest record. I'm a thief. I'm a burglar, you know. They say, 'We don't want him, he might be a bad influence.' They don't realize that if you didn't want a job, you wouldn't be there. They don't realize you going to school to improve yourself."

Several others recited their problems with interviewers on account of arrest records. Then someone brought up the pre-employment tests and said they were unfair because only applicants with middle-class backgrounds could understand the quotations and literary references on some tests. Others pursued this topic with complaints that potential employers did not tell an applicant of his weaknesses when he failed.

Wiz said, "You don't know if you pass or not. If he really wants to help me, he should show me where I failed. Anybody, I don't care who it is, if he don't have money and he's hungry, cold, and raggedy, naturally become depressed. He says, 'Why can't I get it?' He does, and then there goes more on his record."

"It's a two-way street," said Edward Emile Edlow. "If companies expect us to be honest, they got to be honest, too, and give us a chance. They got to do this before they automatically say 'no.'"

Coolsann added, "The only problem today is that most of the employers are old coots. They're up there in age. You've got to say, 'I'll show you how you can make money.' Then the old coot will go for it."

"People have to begin to realize that people do change," I said. "It's most difficult to change human behavior, but it happens. What about in-service training programs in your companies for personnel to learn the various legal implications of arrests so that they can evaluate an applicant's arrest record?" The employers' representatives said that no such programs were in operation yet.

Stewart interrupted with, "Let employers know that most problems were when we were younger—when we didn't have enough brains. We want them to more or less overlook things, because with the black it's more or less a thing of eating and surviving."

"Why do you hire an applicant as janitor and expect him to want to be manager?" asked Duke. "Suppose the guy don't want to go higher? Maybe he likes being janitor. You have to have one, and if he's good, so what?"

One representative answered, "People on the job must show us that they continue to learn and want to advance themselves. The guy who starts in where the other guy leaves off gets a little further ahead."

The meeting concluded with the police officer's plea to the employers' representatives for more understanding of the many problems facing these youths. "What these young people are asking for is a chance to explain, a chance to make employers understand what they are attempting to do and the various obstacles that confront them."

At the feedback session the following day, the students' reactions were interesting.

"They're just giving us the usual whammy test," said Stewart. "They got us in a dilemma. They's not giving us jobs."

"That one guy sure laid it on about the competition, like we was so dumb we'd never make it with the other dudes competing," said Deacon.

"We talked about it after the meeting, and you know what? They're phonies. They'll find excuses not to hire us with the records. You think they'll really give Edward a chance with his long sheet?" asked Randy.

"Another thing," said Edward Emile Edlow, "The deal with the rapes. There the white man goes again, always pointing to us on rapes. That's an insult. You know what else? His ideas, as we discussed many times, are based on stereotypes. Right, Mrs. Dawson?"

"Possibly, but I didn't get the same impression as you did from the meeting. Certainly it may be that these gentlemen are still a little prejudiced. We don't know. At least they came to talk and listen to you. This is the first time they came out to you at your request for better understanding. They showed their interest. Can't we begin to credit them with even a tiny bit of sincerity? You're near the end of the program. Soon we'll be able to test their sincerity. If you pass the employment tests and are rejected on account of your arrest record, then the police community relations officer and the state employment department can be notified and an investigation conducted. Doesn't this seem fair?"

"Now, watch it, Mrs. Dawson. Don't you fall for the employers' soft soap."

"I won't, and you should know that by now. You do have to face reality. Figure out how you would act if you were in business. Try to put yourself in the other fellow's place."

"That's right," said Randy. "Sometimes it's hard, but I think we're improving. You often said, Mrs. Dawson, changing attitudes takes a long time. Be patient with us; we're coming along."

PRE-EMPLOYMENT TESTS

The students' feelings of futility were intensified when they learned the nature of the content of pre-employment tests. Their discussion after tours to prospective employers or after visits of employers' representatives focused on the disparity between test content and job description. I, too, think that many job tests are designed to assess general intelligence in a middle-class context. Consequently, young people from minority groups who have grown up in a different cultural environment often fail these tests. Some government officials, industrial executives, and others also believe that such tests often reflect cultural bias. One such official cited a Texas oil firm's experience. Twelve blacks applying for semiskilled jobs all failed a job test which included questions on trigonometry and geometry. When the company was pressured by NAACP and Urban League to revise the tests and gear them to the type of work the men would be doing, ten of the twelve men passed.

Changes in traditional concepts take time. Meanwhile, students have to be prepared for the reality that exists. My negative reactions to tests as measurements of ability did not change the reality. I therefore included pre-employment tests as a part of the course content from the fourth week on.

What were these tests like? Where did I find them? How were they administered? What were the students' weaknesses?

Some companies require a personnel test and a mechanical aptitude test. Failure to pass the former eliminates the applicant even if he passes the mechanical aptitude test. The personnel test covers vocabulary, verbal reasoning, and reading comprehension. The material used, however, sometimes refers to literature and experiences to which young people from ghetto areas have never been exposed. These youths like the mechanical aptitude test, however, and have never complained about it.

Vocabulary tests are presented in several styles: matching words to meanings, selecting synonyms and antonyms, and selecting a word to complete a phrase so that it is analogous to a given complete phrase.

The mechanical aptitude test for students in electrical training includes diagrams of electrical parts of machinery, tools, and other equipment, which applicants are asked to identify, rearrange for proper functioning, etc. Aptitude tests for clerical personnel cover typing accuracy and speed, and knowledge of office machines.

Where did I find pre-employment tests? I prepared my own, patterning them after those I had heard about. In addition, I enlisted the cooperation of the minority group recruitment official of a large utility company and the on-the-job training personnel of the Urban League's local branch.

The minority group official, for example, visited to administer a sample test of ten questions. To simulate realistic conditions, he timed it to conclude in three minutes. The students were not expected to complete the test in the designated time. Only one student completed eight questions, and a few answered none within the time limit.

The trainee supervisor from the Urban League supplied us with sample personnel tests which gave the students practice in coping with an assortment of formats.

In addition to the multiple-choice type of test, I prepared problem-solving situations with which students might be confronted on a job. These were open-ended, to give the students an opportunity to express their thoughts in writing, and were used for both diagnostic and evaluation purposes.

How were they administered? The initial tests had only ten questions, to help give the students a sense of accomplishment and success. Later this number was increased to twenty. In the last six weeks of each program the frequency of timed tests, at the students' request, was increased from two to three times a week on alternate weeks.

The timing was strictly followed. As soon as the bell rang, papers were collected. They were checked while the students were engaged in preparing talks or in reading selected material. Then the papers were returned, and a brief conference was held with each student to acquaint him with his errors. The students were prone to make comparisons of scores; traditional emphasis on grades is difficult to change. I explained that it was more important to understand what was asked for on the test and how to answer than to worry about scores. If they understood and had sufficient practice, their scores would automatically increase.

What were the students' weaknesses? I found many misspellings and much unacceptable usage. Often the students overlooked single words important in the instructions: *opposite, same, underline, check, not.* Their ability to recognize incorrect spelling had to be improved. The students' greatest weakness was their difficulty in thinking in analogies, a form to which they had little exposure; e.g., "*white* is to *black* as *night* is to (a) *evening*, (b) *sunset*, (c) *day*, (d) *blue*, (e) *rain*." It is interesting, however, to see how quickly students respond after they have been given practice.

The minority recruitment official's test also revealed the students' inability to follow instructions because their reading comprehension was below standard. This particular test also indicated the students' lack of understanding of some of the basic principles in mathematics: percentages, decimals, cubic capacities. The wording, which was sometimes tricky, stumped them: for example, "Find which is the perfect square. . . ." I immediately transmitted these findings to the mathematics instructor.

As a result of our frequent practice, students who were sent to prospective employers were now able to pass pre-employment tests. The reports of successful students bolstered the self-confidence of their classmates. The state employment department and interested private agencies sent students to many companies. By the termination of each program, few students failed to pass such tests.[16]

FILLING OUT JOB APPLICATIONS

Actual application blanks were obtained from some large companies and the Urban League's on-the-job training division. The students' first attempts at filling out these blanks proved how necessary it was for them to learn how to interpret questions. They didn't know how to spell such words as *industrial, mechanical, aptitude, accustomed, requirement, painter, plumber, construction, janitor.*

They were reluctant to rewrite their applications after they were corrected. After the meeting with the employers' representatives, however, their reluctance vanished and their motivation hit a new high. Duke, who had rewritten his application at least ten times, finally said, "You know what? I'm getting writer's cramp, but I'm gonna make it. I decided that after I heard those guys. They not going to keep me out. Give me some books to study, will you, Mrs. Dawson?"

We also practiced preparing résumés after I explained what résumés were and why they were helpful. Students worked on these feverishly. When they completed them in suitable form and language, they kept a copy and returned the original to me for transfer to the job development counselor of the state department of employment. We referred to the state employment department's publication *How to Do It: A Guide for Preparing your Résumé.*[17]

DRIVING LICENSES

Most skilled jobs in large utilities companies and other plants require driving licenses. The importance of a driving license arose when the students were ready to be sent out on jobs by the state employment department. Then it was discovered that many men students had never had a license, or, if they had one, it had been suspended or

[16] See Appendixes, pp. 300–306, for sample of pre-employment tests.
[17] You may be able to obtain this from your state employment department.

revoked. (The gang code considered lack of a driver's license no deterrent to driving. Many of their arrests were consequently for traffic violations.)

We focused on driver's licenses from the beginning. This permitted us to discuss each student's driving problem early enough in the program to have it resolved by the time the student was ready for employment. The students began to realize the importance of this requirement to such a degree that they requested appointments with the police community relations officer for his assistance. The text of the motor vehicle code was used for reading and discussion intermittently throughout the program; discussions often arose from students' accounts of reckless driving.

The need for driver's licenses was also stressed by employers' representatives. At such times students often asked the number of violations permitted before one was considered unemployable.

A representative of a utility company told us, "The only way we can determine how you're going to drive is how you've driven. One fellow from a previous program passed all his written tests, but he was washed out: he had six moving violations in the last two years. Do you think there's any excuse for that? I don't. He would have to be breaking the law every time he got into the car. You know we break many laws during the day driving a car, but how many times do we get caught? To be caught six times you almost have to be riding with the police." Laughter.

STATE EMPLOYMENT DEPARTMENT'S VISITS

Early in each program the students were confused about the kind of jobs for which they were being trained, whether or not they were guaranteed jobs at the completion of the program, and other related questions. We were discussing such questions when this conversation took place:

"You're here because I assume you indicated your interest in office jobs."

"Hell, no," said Curly.

"Then why are you here?"

"I want a job. I was told I could get one and that I could also get my high school diploma if I finished this course. But I don't want office work. I'd rather be a janitor and get $2.85 an hour."

"How many of you don't want to be office boys?" Nearly twenty of the twenty-five students raised their hands.

"Yeah, I was guaranteed a job by my employment counselor."

"You're a liar. You got to get your own."

"All right, let's add this to our agenda for the meeting."

"Why do we got to be called office boys? We ain't boys. We's men."

"Yeah, why don't they call us general office clerks? We getting the same course as they. That's discriminating."

"If they get us a job, and we don't like it and quit, will they get us another job?"

"Do we have to take the first job offered, even if we don't like it?"

It was obvious that extreme confusion and dissatisfaction existed. Fortunately we had at the Youth Center a representative of the California Department of Employment who agreed to have a meeting with us to answer the students' questions.

"What good would a meeting do?" said Jim. "We don't believe them anyway. We heard these things before."

Deacon agreed, "What's the use of all this? I ain't never going to get a job in electricity or as a telephone frameman. There are fifty of us in basic electricity. Say even forty pass. You think the telephone company is going to hire forty blacks? Quit kidding, Mrs. Dawson."

The agenda we developed for our meeting was as follows:

I. What can the state employment department do for me?
   A. Job getting (guarantee?)
   B. Job classification
   C. Job security
II. What is my role in this program?
   A. Job choice
   B. Decision to leave job
   C. Salary satisfaction

The state employment department's representative was precise in her answers. "You're mistaken if you think you are guaranteed a job. You are not. If you finish the office boy course satisfactorily, we will send you out on a job interview. However, you will have to sell yourself. You will have to pass the job tests. You will have to conduct yourself with proper etiquette at the interview. The responsibility for getting the job is yours, not the state employment department's.

"Now, as to why you're in the office boy program. You needed training for more skilled jobs. Our surveys showed that there was a need for office boys in industrial plants. This is not a highly skilled job, but if you can do this type of work, you can get experience that will be valuable in helping you get into other, better-paying jobs. You have to begin somewhere. You can't begin at the top when you have no high school diploma and need improvement in reading comprehension. Remember you have to compete with others who have high school diplomas and even employment experience. For most of you, this may be your first regular job with an eight-hour day. If you don't want to be in this program, we may have to drop you. We cannot transfer you to any other, because right now there is no other.

"I'm sorry if you don't like the term 'office boys,' but this is how employers classify such jobs. This is the same way that newspapers refer to 'copy boys.' This doesn't mean you're a boy. If we called you 'junior clerks,' you'd never get a job, because such titles do not classify you for the capacity employers have for males. 'General office clerks' usually refers to women. You need the same subjects, because that is what both general office clerks and office boys require.

"If you leave a job of your own free will without good reason, you're not doing yourself any good. It won't be easy for you on any job at first. You're not accustomed right now to the routine. You won't like it immediately, but if you want to work, you have to learn how to adjust yourself. So, my advice to you is to give yourself time to adjust.

"We may not always send you out on an office boy job. If there is none at the time and something else arises, maybe a job as a gardener's apprentice, we'll send you if you're willing. You can't turn down more than three offers from us. If you do, it doesn't seem that you are really interested in working.

"On a job, your attendance and punctuality are important. You learned this in your course and on your tours. I can only urge you to settle any personal problems before you get a job.

"You can't expect to begin with high salaries. You have to prove your ability and interest first while you are learning. You have to be patient."

Her answers did not completely satisfy the students. The discussion led to a series of meetings with other people from the state department of employment. Students with individual employment problems were urged to discuss them with their vocational counselors in the state department of employment.

These direct confrontations provided another opportunity to demonstrate to the students how important it is to obtain as many facts as possible before jumping to negative assumptions.

INDUSTRIAL PLANT TOURS

Various large industrial plants and utilities cooperated in arranging tours to their facilities. On each tour what the students saw depended on the particular job for which they were being trained. Those being trained for clerical work had opportunities to see clerks in action, those in the telephone framemen group, who were learning basic electricity, saw demonstrations of related work. The rapidly changing computerized equipment made each IBM tour so fascinating that some students were motivated to continue into more advanced electronics.

Tours provided new information. For example, we didn't know that applicants for certain jobs had to meet minimum weight standards because they had to handle heavy equipment. Several students in the framemen group were later disqualified for jobs with utilities companies because they were too slight to manipulate heavy equipment. Others were afraid of heights or of working underground.

MOCK EMPLOYMENT INTERVIEWS

At my request, some large companies sent especially trained personnel to conduct mock employment interviews in our classroom.

Our first experience with such an interviewer took place in the office boys group. Our guest distributed job applications and went over a few questions to familiarize the students with the kinds of information desired. When she asked for volunteers to be interviewed, no one rose. Several minutes elapsed — still no response. I observed the students looking at each other quizzically. It was apparent that fear of failure was still present, and understandably so.

The interviewer laughingly told them she was aware that this was their first experience with this type of job interview, but that nothing embarrassing would happen. Finally Curly volunteered to be the first applicant. Our guest then conducted the interview as she would in reality. She stopped at each question to explain its significance. While the interview was in progress, however, something which might prove embarrassing to our guest was happening: students were leaving in groups for the rest room. This was a manifestation of their fear and insecurity; I did not stop to call attention to it, but waited for our feedback session after the guest had left. The incident pointed out to me how much more preparation we needed for job interviews and filling out applications. Such behavior was not repeated in subsequent groups, because we did spend more time on preparation.

In our feedback session, the students confirmed my assumption on their use of the rest room as a refuge.

"We didn't want her to see how much we didn't know," said William.

There was one question on the job application which infuriated most of the students: "What are your hobbies?"

"That's getting personal, ain't it?" asked Curly. "That's why I hesitated. I don't have no hobbies except dancing and hustling."

The students seemed to be unanimously opposed to answering such a question. They did not understand the possible correlation between hobbies and vocational aptitudes.

"Can you imagine why employers might be interested in how you spend your spare time?"

"Maybe it'd give them a clue as to the kind of person we are."

"Employers like to hire applicants," I said, "who show by their hobbies that they are interested in learning; who read; who draw; who are imaginative instead of just wasting time. They are not trying to pry into your night life. They may not understand that growing up in poverty doesn't always allow you to develop the kind of hobbies to which middle-class people are accustomed. Now that you know the reason for such a question, be prepared to answer truthfully without fear. Let me explain further. I noticed that Jim likes to draw. He calls it doodling, but it reveals artistic ability. Suppose an employer knew this from the job application. Now let's suppose that Jim has tenure on the job and that an opening develops in another department in which drawing and design are involved. Jim may be eligible. Then his hobby has helped him vocationally."

The combination of visits, tours, and other types of cooperation from private companies and government agencies provided the students with opportunities to get firsthand information and to see what conditions they would have to meet on successful completion of the course. After tours, their usual comments were, "Gee, they were so nice to us. Maybe we might even get jobs if we pass the tests. I'm not a high school graduate, but now I'm going to take courses at night to get more advanced electronics training."

Each feedback session after a tour brought out the students' feelings about the practice of discrimination. They compared statistics on how many blacks or other non-whites they had noticed.

"I'll tell you what. If you get a black for a supervisor who's an Uncle Tom, he'll hang you every way but loose," said Allen Williams.

Structure

Course content must have some structural design to be meaningful and meet the needs of youths from poverty areas. There is nothing haphazard about my method of operation. A great deal of thought goes into the structure of each session. Subject matter is not relegated to one session and then dropped. Office etiquette, health, work habits, and attitudes are some of the topics that weave in and out of the Personal Development course.

Structure implies a plan, although the plan may change with the exigencies which arise. Only with a basic plan will you and your students be able to achieve desirable goals.

There must be continuity of subject matter. It is unwise to jump from topic to topic without this thread of continuity. Free association is encouraged, but the students should be taught how to pursue topics in depth. If the students are involved in a controversial discussion when the bell rings, it is your responsibility to note where they left off and to pick up from this point in the following session. When you do this, students become aware that you are listening to them, and their incentive for learning increases.

If you follow this practice faithfully, a basic structural design will evolve which still allows you to provide time for innovation and treatment of unexpected situations. Basic structure ensures a certain amount of regularity, an essential characteristic of educating young people from poverty areas. The students' work habits will improve if they become accustomed to regular daily activities including reading, speaking, writing, and listening. In spite of their initial reluctance, they have to learn how to adjust to a daily routine. But routine can be deadly without injections of spontaneity. Educating youths from poverty areas requires dynamism.

Other structural characteristics I have found essential are timing and flexibility. To arouse and sustain the students' interest, timing is important. It is as essential to effective teachers as it is to successful actors, musicians, and scientists. How much time should be spent on communication skills? How much on field trips? On outside visitors? On special programs? It is difficult to determine such time allotments, since these subjects are interrelated. A plan provides guidance and, especially in the beginning, makes both you and your students more secure. I can only recommend that you try to allot daily time for review, vocabulary development, and discussion. When there are outside visitors, however, or a film, or even an unexpected incident, you may have to shorten or lengthen the planned time segments. Situations, students' moods, and interaction will serve as your guides.

How much time should a teacher devote to field trips? Field trips should begin when you see indications of a reduction of hostility and when a friendly relationship develops. This takes at least six weeks. Don't be discouraged if it takes longer. Each group varies in its collective personality and willingness to adapt to changing situations. It is advisable to begin with one field trip a month. Thereafter, no more than two a month are recommended. The actual tour of a plant should last no more than one and a half hours, because the students' span of attention is limited. This means a half day — either morning or afternoon — when transportation is included. Consequently, the students will have to miss other classes. It will be a test of your persuasive powers to secure the cooperation of the entire faculty for such a new venture. Field trips are so educational if planned intelligently, however, that the students' reactions to the trip can be related to other class material.

Films or slides should not be shown more frequently than once a week, and they can be shown as infrequently as once a month. There are not enough suitable films available with which these students can identify. How films or other devices are used is more important than frequency. If they are used without prior preparation of the students, and if they are unrelated to objectives, they are worthless. If the students are told a film's purpose, the film can be useful in developing listening habits, increasing opportunities for thinking, and enhancing perception.

Another factor to consider in using a film or slide is its effectiveness in helping the students conceptualize. Don't use a film to fill a time slot. Utilize any available free time for students' self-expression.

How much time should be devoted to outside visitors? Outside visitors should not be introduced into the program for the first month. The same reasons apply here: the students' initial distrust of you as an authority figure needs no reinforcement. You are still an outsider, and you will reinforce their distrust by exposing them to other outsiders too soon. Even when you feel the time is ripe, don't confront students with a *fait accompli*. Share your ideas with them to get their reactions and comments before you make final plans. Then invite outsiders once a month, or more if the need arises. Remember these criteria for inviting guests: Can they contribute to the accomplishment of your mutual objectives? Can they communicate with the students? Do they understand what it means to grow up in poverty? Can the students identify with them? Outside visitors can engender much interest, but only when they are selected carefully.

How much time should be devoted to special programs? The same rule also applies here: wait at least a month to get acquainted with your students before planning such programs. Then special programs can take place once a month, or at least once every two months. I introduced "Tomorrow May Be a Porcupine" almost two months after the first program of general office clerks began. Such programs, if well planned with the students, can be effective in developing their abilities to plan, think, cooperate, and apply what they have learned.

Timing also has other applications. Knowing when to terminate a role-playing situation, for example, involves timing. This is a less tangible matter, however, and depends on your experience with this technique as well as your sensitivity to the mood and tenor of your students. Don't overdo any activity. The law of diminishing returns begins to take over after a certain point; the students tune you and the material out, and learning stops.

As soon as you observe restlessness, change the activity; change the writing phase to talking or the talking to writing. In other words, vary the activities unobtrusively and skillfully to increase the students' spans of attention. Students are accustomed to action in the streets, and they become bored in class without it. In the beginning, therefore, each session has to have action of some kind. Operating teletrainers, using tape recorders, acting as moderator, and filling out applications and questionnaires, for example, are all forms of action. Even listening requires action of a cerebral nature. It is natural that the students' need for action will decrease as their span of attention and ability to concentrate increase.

Timing also applies to you, personally. Don't talk too much. Whet the students' intellectual appetites, but never satiate them. Leave them desiring more. When we first had role playing, the students wanted it daily, but I did not allow it, for this very reason.

Another important aspect of timing is your speed in developing new concepts in relationship to the students' pace of learning. Too often subject matter is covered because it is required; whether it has been understood by the students is not always a concern. I believe that facts are not so important as principles. Your students and you must know not only the *hows* but the *whys*. For example, the students have to learn not only how to plan wardrobes appropriate for office wear, but why they should do this. They have to learn not only how to practice office etiquette, but why. You have to adjust the pace of the material to the pace of the students. If the atmosphere is, as Coolsann said, "conducive to our learning," the students will feel free to say, "What does it mean?" or "I didn't get it." If you don't stop to find out, the students will feel left out again.

I don't worry if at the end of the program we have not covered all the material in each chapter. I am much more interested in the student's capacity to use what he knows and its effect on his outlook on life. Quality rather than quantity of learning is our mutual goal. As a result, I have seen students stimulated to continue learning beyond the completion of this course. Opportunities for self-expression and communication boost their self-confidence.

Flexibility in designing structure is very important. Even after you have developed a pattern of presenting and timing material for daily sessions, you have to exercise flexibility. The time slots for vocabulary vary, for example, depending on the students' pace and on introduction of pertinent and analogous material. Strict adherence to a daily schedule will make it hard to achieve mutually desirable goals. In the beginning of each program, you will be able to accomplish little on Mondays and Fridays, and forcing the issue is a waste of time. As a friendly relationship develops, and as the material and your methods of presentation evoke favorable responses from the students, more will be accomplished even on these "bad" days.

For example, on one day you plan a discussion on health. But you note sadness and almost withdrawal on the faces of Wiz, Coolsann, and Edward. Do you go ahead with your plans anyway? If you do, I know from experience that you will engage few of the students. Rather, find out what is bothering these students, who have previously shown interest and leadership.

"Some jerk bumped into my car this morning," said Wiz. "He couldn't see where he's going. I need another engine. The front caved in."

"I was so happy. It was beautiful out. I was driving along. Out of nowhere, this dude comes on my left and—smack! I'm cited. I need the car tonight. I'm stuck," said Edward Emile Edlow.

"It was foggy at seven this morning on the freeway," said Coolsann. "I change lanes, but look first, and then it's foggy and I can't see. So I change back. This stupid dude in front's going so slowly, I slam on my brakes; but it's too late, and I hit him. It weren't my fault. He was going too slow! Now I got no car and no insurance. What am I going to do?"

For this session and the next, we discussed drivers' responsibilities, accident prevention, and laws of physics and their relationship to speed and stopping, and the like. I brought in the motor vehicle code summary, and we read passages that were pertinent. Discussions of the students' conception of basic speed, liability, slowing down, driving in fog, and changing lanes provided us with opportunities for reviewing safe driving precepts. This would never have been possible unless there was structural flexibility. This unexpected incident took precedence over the planned structure.

There were other instances where flexibility was exercised. Late in the frameman program, only seven of the fifteen students arrived for our regular Personal Development session. They had sad and sullen looks, which I had not seen since the beginning of the program. I was disturbed because I had had no notice from the office about scheduled absences. I did know that the class was to be graduated one month from this date and that every opportunity for possible employment was being investigated by the state employment department, the Urban League, and the vocational instructor in basic electricity. At this point we were concentrating on filling out applications and getting practice in taking employment tests. I could tell that there was anger combined with hopelessness this day. I abandoned my idea for the session and focused on the students' problems. I tried to draw them out. Slowly they began to talk.

"Eight fellows were singled out by Mr. Y. to go down to Western Electric this afternoon for employment tests. They don't need money bad as us. We got chilren to support. Anyway, we know as much as them."

"I couldn't believe it. Mr. Y. didn't tell us nothing. The fellows didn't tell us nothing. They're our buddies? The only way I knew was I saw several fellows run out of class this morning in their work clothes and return in suits with white shirts and ties. I'm perceptive and get the picture right away."

Their main complaint was the instructor's lack of directness with them. He had never acted this way before. If he had explained honestly what he planned to do and why, they would have accepted his decision more readily, although they admitted that they still would have been disappointed. The resulting discussion went off in several directions. The facing reality meant being able to cope with competition. This led to the need for accepting one's limitations. The rejected students finally agreed that there were individual differences and that perhaps their chosen classmates had less hostile attitudes and were more punctual in class, but they were still adamant in believing that the selected ones didn't know more.

Each session has to be planned loosely enough so that additional time can be extended to any planned activity or new material suggested by the students' comments or direct questions can be taken up. The examples just cited demonstrate the advantages of this. The students' respect for you will increase, because they are quick to sense your sincere interest when you allow them to discuss their problems. Such flexibility on your part will influence their habits of thinking. Flexibility also adds an element of surprise to class sessions. Films, newspapers, field trips, outside guests, panels, etc. provide the seasoning. As in cooking, however, seasoning must be added with a light hand. Used reasonably, these additions can accelerate learning. Used too much and too often, they can create chaos.

Summary

Educating young people from poverty areas requires new approaches to curriculum content. Textbooks cannot be the only teachers' guides. There are still too few available that have "soul," that can really touch these youths' daily lives. Materials for the younger age groups are being published, but even these are few compared with the overwhelming need. I believe that it is important for teachers to know their subjects; but an effective teacher not only knows his subject but also knows how to interrelate his subject with others. This interrelatedness is often lacking; and when it is lacking, how can the students be expected to think in analogies and associate ideas? Whatever the prescribed content for a particular subject may be, I think it is a teacher's responsibility to keep himself informed on developments in science, literature, cultural anthropology, and current events so that he can interrelate his own subject with them.

My experiences with these young people indicated that they needed much more than was prescribed by the curriculum planners. The prescribed subject matter was a basis for preparing the students for any type of skilled employment. Much more was needed to help them develop as complete persons. For example, more attention to arrest records and their effect on chances for employment has to be paid by government employment services, educational agencies, law enforcement agencies, and the public if youth opportunity programs throughout the United States are to fulfill their purposes. I therefore supplemented the prescribed content with material on the legal rights of citizens, the nature of arrests, and employers' attitudes on hiring applicants with arrest records.

Since education should prepare the students for living and learning throughout their lives, the barriers between school and community must be destroyed. The participation of the community in problems of housing, consumer education, and legal rights should be part of the course.

After working with these youths for several years, you will become conversant with their common problems. These problems will provide course content. Relevant subject matter, combined with innovative approaches, reaches these young people and when they are reached, their self-confidence, feeling of self-worth, and hopefulness increase.

Problems of vocabulary, language structure, and speech arise from discussions of the subject matter; and reviews are integrated into this content. Opportunities for self-expression, to improve the students' communications skills still further, are numerous and varied. Listening is a need for you and them. Various kinds of materials to increase ability to listen should be devised and used.

Preparation for job tests begins early in each program to reduce the students' fear of failure. Tours and class visits by policy-making personnel executives assist in destroying the stereotypes in which these young people and the employers see each other.

Content without objective, or content presented haphazardly, accomplishes nothing. You must have a basic plan, but it must be loose and flexible to allow the students opportunities to present subject matter that pertains to their problems. Both you and the students must be ready for the unexpected.

5 • Broadening Perspective

POVERTY BOXES IN ITS VICTIMS as tightly as a casket. Helping young people to pry open the lid requires a certain type of educator: one with inner strength, dedication, tremendous energy, and creativity. Unfortunately, educators rarely have been oriented to operate in a milieu of poverty. What is needed, therefore, is a broader outlook on life—not only for these youths, but for the educators as well.

This chapter will focus on material considered by vocational educators to be extraneous to job training. Ultimately, however, such material affects the students' concepts of employment and chances for advancement. Their perspective has to be enlarged to extend beyond job training if they are to be educated for living. Exposure to art, music, and literature of other cultures cannot be reserved for the middle and upper classes.

Young people confined in a ghetto environment usually have social contacts with only one cultural group. Association with other groups is brief and generally unsatisfactory. Development of wider relationships requires time for successful maturation. Before this program, the students' associations outside their insulated poverty areas were with white authority figures whom they resented: teachers, welfare workers, the police, and employers. Their exposure to people outside the ghetto has to be extended beyond employers, landlords, food dispensers, clergymen, and law enforcement personnel.

The course content you evolve with them and your shared experiences and ideas will help open their eyes and minds to the existence of another world, to which they will rightfully demand access. Your continuing close relationship will provide you with insight into their problems and their quest for clearer self-concepts.

Opportunities for exposing these youths to new experiences are limited only by ingenuity and available resources. The students' daily patterns of growth and their emerging respect for people with different cultural backgrounds and different points of view are rewarding. Visiting museums, newspaper plants, and television stations and meeting people from other cultural groups are essential to the personal development of these young people, their younger sisters and brothers, and their children.

In this chapter you will note my students' reactions to contemporaries born and brought up in Southern Rhodesia and Martinique and their reactions to university and museum tours. In addition, you will see the effect of these new experiences on their self-concepts.

Guests

GUESTS FROM CULTURALLY SIMILAR BACKGROUNDS

How are their reactions affected by their self-concepts? What are their attitudes toward the African heritage? In order to get answers to these questions from my students, I enlisted the cooperation of a black psychiatric social worker formerly connected with the California State Department of Mental Hygiene. We decided to experiment with the topic "The Black in America Today." The presentation would be based on an actual case study, but the students were not to know that it was autobiographical.

The whole student body was involved in this special program. The speaker radiated warmth and friendly interest as he began. "I'd like to read a story to you. It's really only an incident. I'll stop at certain places to get your reactions. What happens after that depends on you." He paused. The students listened attentively. None left for the rest rooms. There were no sleepers. The guest continued, "The boy in this story is a fourteen-year-old black. His name is unimportant. Listen to him. 'In my first semester in high school, I was talking to my buddy. This was an integrated school. I had known this fellow, a white kid, from the beginning. We were pals. I didn't visit his home, and he never visited mine, but we still considered each other friends. This particular morning, for some small reason, we had had an argument. I can't even remember what it was about. Anyway, we became angrier and angrier, and finally he said, "You dirty black African, why don't you go back where you came from?"' "

I watched the students. Some were shocked and looked to see my reaction. The guest stopped. "Imagine that you were that student telling the story. What would you have done at that point?"

One man student said, "I would have felt sorry for the white fellow for losing his temper. When he calmed down, I would have told him that his real feelings were coming to the surface and that he was prejudiced deep down. I think he had a great deal to learn."

"But is that really the way you would have reacted? Let's be honest. Who else wants to comment?"

"I'd let him have it, but good," said Jim, the former gang leader.

"I would have laid him out, man, so flat he'd have a hard time getting up again," said William.

"Prejudice is deep-seated, and beating someone ain't going to change him. He has to be educated," said Adolph.

"Continue—we wants to know what he did," said Rosetta.

The speaker continued. Instead of reading, he summarized: "He beat the white fellow. I go along with that. I think that would have been my immediate reaction. At that age it would have been difficult for me to control my temper and hurt. The black fellow, feeling better after the beating, proudly ran home to tell his mother the good news. What do you think his mother asked when he finished telling her the story?"

"Did you do a good job?" "How did he react to the beating?" "Did you hit him again for me?" These were some of the students' responses.

"No," said the speaker. "The mother asked none of these questions. You may be surprised, but she said, 'I'm disappointed in you, son. Why get so angry at being called African? Aren't you proud to be black? Don't your ancestors come from Africa? I wouldn't have been so disturbed. Why be afraid of the truth?'"

Then, addressing the students, the guest asked, "How do you feel? Do you resent being called 'African'? Aren't you black?"

"I'm proud of my African ancestry," said Marietta. "In fact I'm studying African dance. I want to learn more about African history. We didn't ask to come to this country. We were brought here for economic reasons."

"I'm not proud to be called African. I'm American," said Jessie. "When someone calls me African, they mean it in a bad way."

"Yeah," said Wilbert. "Black means evil. There are all shades of black among us. The devil is pictured as black, and the angels as white. How can we expect to feel good about this?"

"Look at the TV commercials. Even black cars aren't as good as white cars, because they run out of gas, but white cars always make it."

"That's right, too. I never thought about that," said Mahalia.

"All right. I'd like to know if you think Africans are beautiful."

"I don't think so," said Roberta. "That's why I'm insulted if I'm referred to as African. I think the African woman is ugly with her very thick lips and fuzzy hair."

The next minutes were spent on the subject of standards of beauty. The speaker tried to find out if the American Negro wasn't trying to imitate the Caucasian instead of setting his own standards. In no way did the students want to be associated with the African. They wanted to continue to wear stylish coiffures even if the styles were set by Caucasians. This topic was so controversial that the students continued arguing after the program ended. Their interest was so aroused that a series seemed advisable. In the usual feedback, I discussed this with the speaker, but his limited time did not allow him to continue.

This special presentation showed the need to make the students proud of their heritage by familiarizing them with the contribution of African culture to world culture. Most textbooks will have a blind spot in this area. Black history and African culture became part of the content of Personal Development. Three books were used for reference: Franklin's *From Slavery to Freedom*,[1] Hughes and Meltzer's *A Pictorial History of the Negro in America*,[2] and *The Negro in American History*.[3]

I believe that black history should be taught as part of United States history throughout the regular school system rather than being reserved for black students. It is the responsibility of educators to assist all students, no matter what their race or cultural background, to broaden their concepts on the contributions of minority groups to the development of their country. Since few textbooks give a proper perspective on this aspect, it becomes necessary for teachers to be prepared to fill in the gaps.

I looked for a person who had not only knowledge of black history, but also ability to present it in a manner that would sustain our students' attention. College degrees were not a prerequisite. A black man

[1] John Hope Franklin, *From Slavery to Freedom: A History of American Negroes*, Alfred A. Knopf, Inc., New York, 1963.

[2] Langston Hughes and Milton Meltzer, *A Pictorial History of the Negro in America*, rev. ed., Crown Publishers, Inc., New York, 1963.

[3] *The Negro in American History*, Board of Education, New York, 1964.

in his early thirties was recommended. This man volunteered his services, because we had no budget for such activities. For the past seven years he had been teaching black history without compensation at a community center. His mornings were free because his regular work at a hamburger stand didn't start until one o'clock in the afternoon. This man, Mr. Brown, was married and had three small children. His formal education had ended with high school graduation; but he continued his education by reading newspapers avidly and visiting the library.

We decided to experiment with two sessions on black history, one week apart. Aware of the students' brief span of attention, I urged the speaker to allow time for discussion. After the first session we would note the students' reactions, evaluate the session, and decide how to continue.

The students were receptive because this program was what they had indicated they wanted. As a result, several students volunteered to type the necessary publicity — an unusual occurrence. In introducing the speaker I gave autobiographical data stressing Mr. Brown's involvement in an activity which did not bring him any money, but which helped others.

"He must be a nut, that's all I can say," said Jim. "I don't volunteer. The one I've got to help is little old me. Let the others take care of themselves, see."

Mr. Brown, although friendly and interested in his topic, wasn't dynamic enough to hold the students' interest during the first session. He didn't try to get them involved by throwing out provocative questions, but recited a chronological series of events from slavery to after the Civil War. He tried to cover too much too quickly in monotonous fashion, and he lost the students after the first five minutes. I discussed this with him later and suggested that for the second session he experiment with current events involving blacks, making them alive and more intelligible by historical flashbacks. This he did, and the students interacted. In the duplicating machine operators and framemen groups, student committees were responsible for team presentations on black history which were taped and then criticized.

GUESTS FROM OTHER CULTURAL BACKGROUNDS

A few weeks later, at the University of California Adult Education Center in Berkeley, I met a group of students representing thirteen new

African republics who were studying adult education methods and materials in the United States. Mr. Sataure from Southern Rhodesia was very much interested in our program and readily agreed to visit us. The students were delighted because they had many questions to ask about modern Africa and this would be their first direct contact with an African citizen.

Mr. Sataure's visit generated unusual excitement. The students looked especially attractive in order to impress the visitor. The young women wore freshly starched blouses and skirts; the young men wore short-sleeved open-necked sport shirts. Hairdos had been so altered to conform to office appropriateness that they were no longer recognizable as those of the same students we met the first day of the program.

The students assembled on time. They didn't know how the visitor would be dressed. Some envisaged a headdress, long robe, and sandals. They recognized the visitor only when I greeted him. There were murmurs and surprised looks: Mr. Sataure was dressed like any other man they knew.

After a brief introduction he began his presentation in a friendly manner distinguished by humor and a sonorous voice. Exhibiting remarkable poise, he opened by writing his name on the blackboard: E R N S T   S A T A U R E. He pronounced it several times. He said that this was the name of his guardian, who had bestowed his surname on his father. In a system comparable to that practiced during the period of slavery in the United States, his father had worked for this wealthy ranch owner. Both the ranch owner and Mr. Sataure's father wanted the son, our speaker, to have a university education. Mr. Sataure told how interested he had been in reading and learning from the time he was a child. The ranch owner paid for his education at Oxford University. Since our students had never heard of this university, Mr. Sataure briefly explained Oxford's international reputation. His manner of speaking was not pedantic, but the students found difficulty in understanding his speech because it seemed to combine an African tribal flavor with British overtones. This afforded an unexpected opportunity to develop listening ability.

Mr. Sataure put two words on the blackboard side by side:

FIGHT   FLIGHT

"I'm going to talk about these two words, and then I'll stop for questions. In my country it's difficult for any ordinary citizen to get an education."

"Where is your country?" asked Rosetta.

Mr. Sataure drew a map and pointed out the location of Southern Rhodesia. "Education is not free there as it is in the United States. My father taught me the value of learning. He began to read to me when I was a child."

He then talked about discrimination against blacks in Southern Rhodesia, which made getting an education so difficult. He could have chosen flight as escape. He knew, however, that without an education he couldn't help his people, and so he worked days and with the help of his father studied at night. "That's the alternative for you. You don't realize how fortunate you are. Not only do you get free education, but in this program you get paid to come to school. In spite of this, I understand there are some of you who don't come to school often. Well, you fool only yourselves. You won't be able to get jobs by fleeing. You have to have an education. A high school diploma is not enough. Automation has reached our country, too, and our people have to be prepared. Of course, many still live on the farms and near mines. Our standards of living can't be compared with yours, but we are improving. Many of our people don't read and write. This presents serious problems. When I return to Southern Rhodesia, I shall head an adult education program for my government. I can only urge you to study and work to improve yourselves. That's all. Fight to stay in school rather than escape into flight. If you don't study, you're really in flight. I hope I made my point. Any questions?"

"Will any young people our ages be interested in exchanging letters with us?" asked Roberta.

"Yes, I think that would be a splendid idea. If you send me a list of your members, with addresses, I'll have some of our people write to you."

"You don't speak like us. In fact, I can't understand you. Why?" asked Belle.

"I can't always understand Americans, either. In different parts of each country people speak with the particular accent of that locality. I lived in England for several years and acquired a British inflection."

"Are you married?" asked Jessie, who always asked personal questions.

"Yes. I have a wonderful wife and five children." Oohs and aahs echoed throughout the room.

"Do the young people do the watusi or swim or even the monkey dance in your country?" asked Jim.

"I really don't know about such dances. I don't spend time dancing. I'd imagine you could discuss that in your exchange letters."

"How do young people dress?"

"Do you imply that they wear headdresses and few clothes? These you see in movies. In modern Africa, clothes look like yours. Notice my suit. You must visit us and see for yourselves."

In our feedback session the following day, Roberta, now student council president, organized a correspondence committee. She also asked me for photographs from the students' original production, "Woman in Black." Letters and photos were mailed to Southern Rhodesia—marking another step in the students' personal development.

A few weeks later ten visitors from Martinique made an unexpected entrance, accompanied by an interpreter from the United States State Department and a representative of the local International Hospitality Center. These men were recent high school graduates on an educational tour of the United States planned by our State Department. San Francisco was their first stop. The visitors were shyly friendly at first. They spoke only French. Knowing this, I spoke to them in French, explaining the purpose of our program. During the dialogue, my students' reactions indicated complete amazement. What were we talking about? In what language? It was not my intention to keep the students in suspense or make them feel left out, so I translated our conversation.

"Mrs. Dawson, ask them what they're going to do when they get back to their country," said Mahalia.

"Where do they come from?" asked Rosetta.

"What do they do for fun?" asked Jim.

"How come they don't speak English?" asked Bailey.

Soon our visitors moved closer to the students and we were engaged in a crossfire of French and English. Such rapport was established that the State Department's representative had difficulty in persuading his group to leave for their next scheduled stop.

When our visitors departed at lunchtime, my students surrounded me and an unofficial feedback session ensued.

"Gee, where'd you learn French? It sure sounds good."

"Yeah, how come we don't learn French? I'd like it better than typing," said William.

"Why don't we have a few words in French every day? Maybe I might go to Martin—"

"Martinique," said Rosetta.

In each subsequent Personal Development course I have included visits by students from other countries. Universities and colleges have provided exchange students from Liberia and Ghana, too.

At our next Personal Development session, the students asked me to talk to them in French and then translate.

"All right. Listen and see if you can understand from my tone. Everybody ready? *Je suis la professeur. Je m'appelle Mme. Dawson. J'aime beaucoup la langue française. J'ai travaillé en France il y a plusieurs années. Alors, c'est tout maintenant.*"

"Let me try first," said Bailey excitedly. "You're Mrs. Dawson and you're in France and the Lord is everything."

"You a dope," said Rosetta. "You ate an apple with your girl friend, Jeannie, and that's all."

"You're listening and using your imagination," I said.

"What did you really say?" she asked.

I translated.

"Do you speak any other languages?" she went on.

"Yes, a little modern Greek, Russian, German, and Spanish." I said "What is your name?" in each of these languages as a sample, and the students were flabbergasted. Again they asked me to include French in our daily sessions.

"That would be fine, but let's learn English first. To express our thoughts in acceptable English is still our number-one goal. It is important to know that many cultures contributed to the English language. We are grateful to others for their contributions: language, customs, and ways of looking at things. Even food is a part of culture. Have you ever tasted French cooking?"

"What is it?" asked Bailey.

"It sure ain't chitlins," said Wilbert.

"Well, if it ain't soul food, I don't want it." ("Soul food" is fattening, but also nourishing: corn pone, corn bread, baked sweet potatoes, apple turnovers, mustard greens with bacon, baked ham, and chitlins.)

"Continue. Tell us about French cooking."

"All right. Tomorrow I'll bring in some menus, and we'll talk about a few dishes." (The students' contacts with restaurants were limited to refreshment stands. Eating seemed to be an afterthought rather than a delight. Many times I heard several say, "Gee, I forgot to eat. Then I looked at the clock, and it was late at night. I remembered I was so busy standing on the street or shooting craps I didn't have time to think about eating.")

Understanding menus was essential to living. Introduction to exotic foods also added to personal development and expanded the students' horizons. At the next session I distributed menus from a moderately expensive French restaurant in San Francisco. The students hadn't the slightest conception of what hors d'oeuvres are. At their clubs' social functions, the women prepared small sandwiches and served olives, celery, radishes, and pickles. These I said could be considered hors d'oeuvres. They were appetizers.

"Oh, yeah," said Bailey, "With alcohol they whet your appetite." Laughter.

I gave several examples of hors d'oeuvres in a French restaurant and their counterparts in an Italian, Greek, and Balkan restaurant. The students were very much interested. Wilbert said, "Wow, I'm getting hungry. I think I'll get me some more potato chips. Hey, Bailey, got anything to chew on?"

Another dish on this menu was coq au vin. I put this on the blackboard. We pronounced it, and I explained what it meant. When Rosetta and Mahalia asked for the recipe, I gave it to them. Roast prime ribs of beef au jus was another dish. This was enough French cuisine for an introduction. Once a week for three weeks thereafter we allowed fifteen minutes for descriptions of unfamiliar foods.

In the general office clerk and office boy groups, we enacted a restaurant scene. I brought in eating utensils for two, place mats, etc. We demonstrated proper positioning of utensils. Jessie and Wilbert were the first pair. The rest of the group named the restaurant "Chez Ricardo" to show their knowledge of French and Spanish. When Bailey, playing the waiter, approached for the order, Jessie took over, interrupting Wilbert as he began to order for both. This led to a discussion of etiquette.

Dick, who was one of the few working after school at a legitimate job, wondered if he would be embarrassed if he took his wife out to a fairly expensive restaurant in San Francisco. I understood what he meant, but I didn't think there was much discrimination practiced in San Francisco. My students thought differently.

Jim said that if he were refused service, he would get his gang and they would jump the dude. Bailey said he wouldn't feel comfortable in a high-class restaurant.

I suggested a group visit to various restaurants to sample food from different countries. The vote was unanimous in favor of such an arrangement. In each group we managed to visit at least two restaurants during the program — French and Italian restaurants which served a seven-course dinner for under $2.50 a person. These youths were now becoming part of the outside world.

After the successful student production of "Woman in Black," William, representing the office boy group, was inspired to do something creative, too. He arranged for a student vocal quartet for a special program on a Friday. His idea coincided with the planned visit of a professional calypso singer from Kingston, Jamaica, who was about to open in San Francisco. The next Personal Development session of the office boys was devoted to planning publicity for this event.

Daily thereafter, including the morning of the special program, lunch hours and coffee breaks were enlivened by the harmony of the quartet rehearsing. They were accompanied by a fellow student, a self-taught pianist whose fingers stumbled uncontrollably over the keys of a piano badly in need of tuning. Frank, Adolph, Curly, and William made up the quartet. Frank, Adolph's alter ego and his partner in karate and judo, was selected by his classmates to be the master of ceremonies. He approached me immediately after he received this honor to ask me to listen to his introduction. In our rehearsal Frank, who was overly self-centered, had to learn that the M. C. doesn't monopolize the center of attention, but is the liaison between audience and entertainers. His remarks, therefore, had to be short, and humorous rather than forced. He learned quickly, and his improvised introduction showed thought and humor. We planned to borrow a tape recorder for the occasion.

Dick, who had exhibited drawing talent, volunteered to design a backdrop. Other students helped under his supervision. The backdrop was extremely colorful and represented Dick's impressionistic conception of a romantic cove in Kingston, Jamaica, where he had never been.

Friday came, and again there was great anticipation and excitement. Frank, for his role, was resplendent in a gold cloth vest with black jet buttons, dark trousers, and no sunglasses. His hair was greased and his sideburns were grown long for the occasion. He looked more like a flamenco dancer than a folk singer's M. C. His remarks were laconic, funny, and well received. He set the scene, and the rest of the student body waited anxiously for the performance to begin. The quartet was excellent. They sang in harmony without musical accompaniment, an improvement over their original plan. While they were singing, two of their fellow students left and returned quickly with African drums.

The calypso singer had a dramatic manner which engaged the audience's attention immediately. Before he sang each song, he explained its content; he sang it solo first and then a second time with student participation. He asked the drummers to join in, too. The church rafters vibrated with the music. A wonderful time was had by all, and it had been another opportunity for expanding the students' horizons.

Speech was a problem, as was obvious from the first day. I thought that if the students could hear good speech from someone outside the classroom with whom they could identify, there would be an unconscious carryover and added incentive to improve their own speech. I was looking for someone with personality, experience, and enthusiasm.

One evening I chanced to turn on our educational television channel and saw my choice. The program was produced by a handsome, personable, intelligent young black who spoke beautifully. He discussed aspects of racial discrimination in depth with interviewees.

The product of a middle-class family, he had only recently come in contact with black youths in poverty areas for the first time. He was appalled to find that racial discrimination existed in San Francisco. San Francisco's educational channel hired him to produce a weekly program that would highlight various aspects of discrimination.

I told the students about my discovery and asked them if they would be interested to talk with him if I could make the arrangements. I told them that I had never met the man, but that I would call the station, explain the purpose of our program, and try to enlist his cooperation. The students and this producer liked the idea. I asked him to talk briefly about himself and how he got into television, stressing the educational requirements for other types of television jobs.

Our guest followed the planned format, stopping for questions. At this first meeting few questions were asked about television as a career. This disturbed the speaker. When the two of us discussed the possible reasons, we thought that the students still felt inadequate as high school dropouts and despaired of ever being able to qualify for any television job. This fear was seen previously in the reaction of office boys group to mock employment interviews conducted by companies' representatives. The students were especially concerned about how many blacks were employed in television. In each feedback session the students expressed their fascination with the guest's precise speech, which furnished a model for them to emulate.

The producer continued his interest in succeeding programs. He acted as host for visits of the students to the television studio. The students enjoyed these visits. They were excited to be taken behind the scenes where they could watch rehearsals of live productions and see engineers, floor managers, and artists in action.

Meeting the Public

VISIT TO A TELEVISION PROGRAM

When we were two-thirds through the basic electricity program, I thought the students had had sufficient practice in discussing a variety of topics and were now ready to meet the public. The public's conception of these young people is still negative, and understandably so. News reports on the crime rate in slum areas usually identify black youths or youths from other minority groups as offenders. The youths themselves have rarely, if ever, been given equal time to be heard. I was anxious for the public to see these young men and women on television and hear what it means to grow up in poverty. Such direct contact might also bring about better understanding of the numerous problems involved in the education of these youths.

The television producer enthusiastically endorsed my idea. For the first program I selected Ali-Tees, Coolsann, Deacon, Wiz, Edward Emile Edlow, and Allen Williams.

This type of program required no rehearsal, since its spontaneity gave it its special flavor. In our Personal Development session we talked over possible topics for a first program and certain ones were unanimously chosen: employment, racial discrimination, the police, and arrest records. Before this preparatory session ended, the television participants insisted that I join them on the program. I explained that I wanted this to be their program, with no assistance from me. I did promise, however, to be present at the studio for the videotaping — the program was pre-recorded.

We arranged to meet at five o'clock sharp at the studio. I was fearful about the time element because the students had not yet developed punctuality to any great degree. Not only were five students on time, but three of them even arrived early. Only Coolsann, who worked after school, arrived fifteen minutes late.

Although the producer had said they could dress casually, Deacon, Ali-Tees, and Wiz wore suits and white shirts with ties. The others wore sport shirts. "We want to show the public we ain't slobs and know how to dress even if we're poor," said Wiz, whose hair had been cut and slicked down for this momentous occasion.

In the warmup before the actual videotaping I sat in with them while they talked over with the producer how they would begin. His manner made them feel comfortable in their strange surroundings. The signal for videotaping flashed. I left to sit in the dark as a nervous spectator. I was amazed at their poise and the deference they showed to each other.

Their opening discussion centered on their arrest records, resulting from juvenile offenses which they attributed not only to poverty, but to their own ignorance. This led to the effect of arrest records on chances for employment. I will pick up only points you have not yet heard.

The producer commented, "You told me that five of you have police records. What does this do so far as preventing you from getting a job?"

Wiz answered first. He spoke quietly and with great self-assurance. "Well, first of all I believe that the two, they go hand in hand, and with arrest records it's impossible to qualify for civil service or something of that nature, if you have felony convictions and things like that. What I'd like to clarify is, if you get arrested and you don't clear up the records, that record will follow you all through life, because it's there."

The producer added, "And you're stamped as a criminal."

"Well, you stamp yourself, literally. You don't try to conform once you find out you can't get a job. You just go along with the group. 'Well, now, he's not going to give me a job anyway—forget it.' Next thing you're back, fighting it again, marking off that time."

The others continued, relating incidents about their encounters with the police with which you are now familiar.

The host asked, "Do you think it's possible that perhaps you're being overdefensive?"

"You see," said Deacon, "if it didn't happen frequently, we wouldn't be overdefensive. It's not our fault . . . because we don't go around looking. When we see a policeman, we don't sneer or something like that. . . ."

"All right," said the producer, "What, in your estimation, can you do . . . to build a relationship between yourselves and the police? . . ."

"I don't know if it's possible to build a relationship with the police," said Deacon. "Let me give you an incident which is repeated too often in the way police handle us. We react, that's plain and simple. We'd be inanimate if we didn't. Last summer I saw this happen, for instance. It was during the track season. This was a track team, a school track team, and one of the boys—I don't know whether he was on the track team or not—anyway, all were on the bus. One of the boys took the man's changer. Now he didn't know which one did, so he started running around, grabbing all the little boys, twelve to fourteen. The juvenile detail came, and they took all of them and stuffed them in the wagon. Yeah, stuffed. 'Get in there!'—and they pushed them like they were cattle. Policemen think they're gods, almost, the way they act, looking down on you."

The host replied, "Then actually what you're saying is that you don't trust the police."

"That's right," said Allen Williams. "Just go down to the Fillmore district (in the black belt) and sit there. You'll see how the cops treat people. . . . We would never call upon the police if there's trouble. We saw what happens. I've seen people come in with their heads bashed when I was in jail. I saw one guy—his eye was swelled all the way out over his eyelid. Couldn't even see. They hit him with a billy club. . . . Maybe that's why we seem to be on the defensive."

"Until the police change their attitudes," said Deacon, "I don't see how we can be expected to trust them or respect them."

The producer brought up community organizations interested in preventing delinquency and asked our students' opinions on them.

Allen Williams said, "They can't penetrate too deep, because these kids don't want to open up to students with degrees. . . . They been in a big hassle since they were six years old."

"Then it's fear."

"Yeah," said Edward Emile Edlow, "fear and humiliation."

"What about your younger brothers and sisters? Are they defensive, too?"

"Even more so," said Coolsann. "How can they help it when they see this stuff and come home with, 'I seen a cop this morning beat a man on the head.'"

"I try to help the younger kids not be so defensive," said Ali-Tees. "I give them encouragement and tell them, 'Keep on fighting. . . . Get yourself an education. . . . Don't quit school.' I give them money. I don't want them to steal."

They continued to talk about injustices practiced in the courts. "A lot a kids make the mistake of pleading guilty so they can go and get it over with. A lot of times they'll get probation, but this leaves a scar on their employment record. . . . In the morning you go to arraignment, then you get a court date five or six weeks down the calendar, you have to sit in the county jail. . . . I feel," said Edward Emile Edlow, "that a lot a people just plead guilty to keep from going through all this."

"And a poor man, he'll be in jail from now on, because he don't have a lawyer, only a public defender . . . who speaks with you five minutes . . . and tells you to plead guilty. . . ." said Allen Williams.

It was at this point, when the discussion was lively, that the half-hour program had to be concluded with many comments still to be made. The students were disappointed that this seemingly abrupt ending had to be, but they were satisfied when the producer told them how well they had done, how lively the program was, and that he wanted them for a second program to continue where they left off. He promised to keep us apprised of audience reaction, favorable or other.

I threw my arms around the students and expressed my pride in their performance.

"Was I articulate?" asked Wiz. The others wanted to know, too, and felt relieved when they heard praise.

"I could of used different words," said Edward Emile Edlow.

"Different words?" questioned the others. "Man, you talked so much we had to slip in sideways to get heard. On the next program you got to give us a chance, too."

"See, Mrs. Dawson, we sure learned something. Remember when we couldn't talk to each other? We were too busy yelling and couldn't stay on any subject," said Wiz.

"Tell your friends and neighbors to watch you tonight. I'll watch, and tomorrow we can evaluate your performance." We left in a happy frame of mind. This occasion marked another step in the personal development of these young men.

The next morning the Personal Development session was abuzz with the students' comments. Those who had not participated had only negative responses at first.

Duke led this group. "You think you're smart because you were on TV. Ali-Tees, you hesitated, and when you did speak I couldn't hear you."

"Wiz, you looked sharp and talked all right, but you put on a little like you really educated. You were seditty. Next time be yourself."

Edward Emile Edlow had to defend himself against his critics. "I didn't interrupt. I had enough experience in moderating and discussing in this class. I just tried to keep the discussion going. After all, millions of people was seeing us, and they didn't just want to see our faces. They wanted to hear what we had to say. I only spoke when there was an awkward pause in the conversation. You guys got to be on the ball. Don't complain about me because I'm alert."

After these comments we got down to evaluating speech and diction. Several students had taken notes while they watched the program, and off we went on correcting pronunciation and usage.

Several days later the television producer advised me that the station had had numerous calls and letters indicating the public's favorable reception. What impressed the people most was these youths' ability to express themselves, their honesty, and their poise. They clamored to see them again. I relayed this to the students.

"You're not putting us on, are you, Mrs. Dawson? People really like us? Geez, that's different. Maybe we punched a few holes in their bag," said Wiz.

"You mean we destroying their stereotypes," said Coolsann, proud of his ability to use new vocabulary. "Maybe they begin to see us as people."

Members of the board of education responsible for our MDTA program never made any comments, and there were no letters of commendation from any of the agencies' staff members. In spite of this, the new experiences were increasing the students' feelings of self-worth and hopefulness.

VISITS TO COLLEGES AND UNIVERSITIES

After the students' successful television appearances, their desire to meet contemporaries in a college setting burgeoned.

"Mrs. Dawson, we think we're ready to go to college," said Allen Williams. "In fact, I'm making application to city college for the fall term. I ain't waiting for the end of this program."

"Yeah," said Wiz, "I been studying all this vocabulary every night before I go out, and I got it. No smart college kid can rip me off now. I think I can outsmart them."

"Let's not get swelled heads or become arrogant. You have improved, but there's still a long road ahead. I'm sure you'll make it if you continue to learn. How would you like it if I were able to arrange for a weekend visit at San Jose State College in a social setting? I know an English professor who is very much interested in our program and in extending opportunities to you for your personal development. I'll call her and see what can be planned if you like the idea."

"That'd be swell, but will there be any trouble for us on a weekend? That bothers me," said Sebastian, a quiet student from Texas who was slowly beginning to assert himself in the presence of his peers, whose social groups he had not joined yet. His drawl evoked ridicule from his classmates, but he never became ruffled, and after seven months in the basic electricity program he had even won their respect by proving his ability to take it. I knew what Sebastian meant by trouble. He wondered whether he and his colleagues would be welcomed cordially when their hosts saw they were blacks. I assured them that our hosts considered it a privilege to meet them. I also made it clear that under no circumstances would I ever subject them to any humiliating experience. In fact, if anything unpleasant ever occurred while we were together at any place, any time, we would take proper action together, not singly. It was saddening to note their continuing fear of rejection. The students were assured that there would be no such problems on this visit.

Arrangements were made one month in advance to allow us time for psychological preparation. The president of the San Jose State College student group called to tell us how excited his members were about our coming. In fact, his committee would even travel to San Francisco to pick us up if necessary.

Representatives of the San Jose State College student body were to meet us at the San Jose bus depot and escort us to a private home for a buffet dinner prepared by the hostess, a professional writer. She had seen our students on television and was very anxious to meet them in person.

After dinner the students were to be driven to another private home where there would be dancing to records. Opportunities for conversation in informal settings, with no attention to ethnic or racial backgrounds, would be numerous. To complete our students' visit, thirty miles from their San Francisco homes, San Jose State College students had arranged to serve breakfast to those whom they housed overnight. How receptive my students would be to this arrangement remained a question until the day of the trip. After discussing the advantages of staying overnight, five accepted. In each case the students' parents were notified.

On the day of the trip the administrative staff predicted a fiasco. "You'll see, no one will show up. They'll disappoint you."

"You're assuming a great deal of responsibility to go that far — and overnight, too. I wish you luck."

Eleven students had signed up in advance. When I arrived at the bus depot in San Francisco at 4:15 P.M., six students met me, seemingly apprehensive.

"You're two minutes late," said Edward Emile Edlow, with a twinkle in his eye. He had a record of tardiness but was slowly changing.

As we waited for the five remaining students, a woman who had just arrived looked over at us and then in a most friendly manner said, "Weren't you the young men I saw on television?" When they shook their heads in amazement, she continued, "You were simply wonderful. You were for real. I'd like to see you again."

In a few minutes, the remaining five appeared. We had been told to dress casually, and when Sebastian arrived in a dark suit, white shirt, and tie, the others made him so uncomfortable that he secretly left for the men's room to make changes. He missed our bus, and we waited for him in San Jose. Our hosts were on time and greeted us warmly. Only Coolsann objected to their welcome, which he described as "condescending."

We were driven to dinner first, and met our hostess and at least twenty other people. We joined them on the outdoor patio for the "soul food" our hostess had especially prepared: baked ham, baked yams, baked beans, corn bread, greens, and apple pie. Her delightfully soft voice and friendly manner immediately impressed the students. Her appearance belied her years.

The dancing began later at another home. The timing coincided with the end of a repeat broadcast of the students' program. My students were most concerned about the reactions of those present. When the program was over, my students were surrounded and complimented for their fluency and spontaneity on the program. I, too, was pleased with their reception. Viewing the program a second time was even more satisfying to me because I was more relaxed and could discern the ease and directness with which the students answered questions. They listened to each other, demonstrating how far they had progressed. I was pleased, too, with their graciousness in accepting compliments as they wandered from group to group. I heard them enter into discussions with noticeable self-confidence. They were expressing themselves in improved English unaffectedly.

In the home where dancing to records took place, we met in a basement decorated like an island in the South Seas. I tried the watusi and other steps my students were patiently teaching me. I observed and listened, but never gave my students the feeling that I was hovering around them in any supervisory or "mother-hen" way. When I left shortly after midnight, the party was sailing full speed ahead.

I taped the feedback session the following Monday. The students' comments on this trip were interesting because they showed development of perception and a growing awareness of relationships to other people. The "old lady" delighted them. "She swings," said the group.

"I think some of the white girls I talked to were scared of us," said Coolsann. "When I sat down in between dances, an attractive blonde came over and sat down next to me, right under the head of the witch doctor staring at us from the grass-covered wall. 'Hello,' I said to this blonde, casual-like. 'Enjoying yourself?'

'Yes, but I feel a little uncomfortable. Don't you?'

'Should I? Well, I don't. I'm sorry you feel that way'."

"At the party where we first had dinner," said Allen Williams, "some of the people I was sitting with were talking about sports or science, but as soon as I sat down, they immediately changed the subject. 'How do you feel about civil rights? What do you think about this and that, to do with blacks?' I told them I didn't come to discuss blacks' problems. I came as any other citizen to meet people and to enjoy myself. I could talk about sports and science, too, and told them to try me out. 'I know you mean well, and I hope you understand I'm not being hostile, either.' Gee, Mrs. Dawson, ain't I becoming articulate?"

"You certainly are."

The students who were overnight guests told the rest of the class about their experiences and how comfortable they had felt. Since that time two of my students have developed lasting friendships with two of their hosts. To show their appreciation for the weekend, Deacon suggested letters. These they completed a week later.

The students were so fired with enthusiasm at their reception by college students that they wanted to visit the University of California's Berkeley campus and Stanford University and note contrasts between a public and a privately endowed school. I timed our University of California visit to coincide with the week ending in the annual California-Stanford football game.

Arrangements were made for chartered buses to transport the entire Manpower Development Training student body in this youth program. We were to leave at 9 A.M. from the school in San Francisco. Lunch would be available at nominal cost in the university cafeterias. Those wishing to bring their own could still eat in the cafeterias. During lunch and immediately after, our students could avail themselves of the recreational facilities in the associated student union buildings.

The trip to the University of California followed our discussion on Theodora Kroeber's book *Ishi*, which interested the students so much that they looked forward to visiting Kroeber Hall, a new anthropological museum, the first stop on our itinerary. When the day arrived, the skies opened up, and those without rain coats were allowed to remain indoors when we reached the Berkeley campus. The inclement weather, however, had no dampening effect on the merriment within the student union building where we met our ten guides. Their friendly welcome enlivened my students' spirits. Walking in sunshine never appealed to them, but their willingness to walk in a deluge was surprising. As we walked along, my students immediately felt like part of the campus. They mingled as if they were students there. We visited art galleries, the main library, classes in session, and the Campanile, and heard anecdotes on which my students tried to take notes for our feedback session.

After a refreshingly healthful lunch, we returned to the main floor of the student union building, which was rocking to the music of a jazz combo. Almost everyone present became a participant in a spontaneously creative mélange of interpretive dancing. The young women in our group were asked to dance by the university men and our young men asked the university girls. This entertainment lasted one hour.

The heavy rains never subsided as we returned to school in San Francisco, drenched but happily content. In our feedback session the following morning, my students had only praise for their reception by the university students.

"We felt they liked us," was the refrain.

"I want to go to that university," said Allen Williams. "I think I can make it there."

What impressed the majority of my students was the freedom enjoyed by university students in matters of dress, class attendance, etc.

"We could never walk around without shoes or stockings and our hair uncombed, with big dogs by our side, and be able to bring dogs into class with us," said Wiz.

"I looked into one room and saw 800 students. Our guide told us the number. I didn't have time to count. I asked her if this was an assembly. She said it was a regular class in philosophy. Students didn't have to attend if they didn't want to, as long as they got good grades. How come they're always on us at this school on attendance? Don't seem fair," said Duke.

This led to discussion of the differences between their program and ours, between their educational background and ours, and between their objectives and ours.

"We saw few like us there," said Ali-Tees. "Were they hiding?" At that time only 2 percent of the student population was black.

The Stanford University visit contrasted strongly with the visit to the University of California. The annual game, with its accompanying excitement, was over. The highlight on this tour was our visit to the site of the nuclear accelerator. This was a disappointment, however, because we were able to view it on film only. We did get some idea of its immensity by a drive along its route before returning to San Francisco. The complete itinerary consisted of a visit to the church, internationally known for its stained-glass windows, a walk around the campus, lunch, and use of recreational facilities. The friendly spirit was missing. Even the sunshine had no visible effect on our spirits.

In the feedback session the following day, Sebastian said, "As we walked to the cafeteria, students stopped and looked us over, like we were strange animals escaped from the zoo."

"What were they expecting?" asked Anton, "War whoops and a snake dance, maybe? They seemed naive to us."

"Another thing," said Von, "at my lunch table, we sat with several white Stanford students who kept asking us one by one in a frightened way, 'Are you going to be students here?' Another interrupted with, 'If you are, it'll be like the movie *Blackboard Jungle.*' I was surprised at my maturity. I didn't jump him. When we said we were only on a visit, they relaxed."

"You going to find even fewer blacks here than on the University of California, Berkeley campus," said Duke.

"You got to be rich to go to Stanford, so what do you expect?" said Edward Emile Edlow. "Their parents taking care of them. They don't have to scratch for nothing to eat."

The only discipline problem on any of the trips arose on the Stanford visit when a new student, unaccustomed to our method of operation, brought a "shortneck" (half-pint) of vodka and frequented the rest rooms to take drinks, exiting each time with increasingly staggering steps. One of our faculty members was watching closely. At the cafeteria counter, this student almost precipitated disaster. Having to wait for his hamburger annoyed him. Vociferously he attributed this delay to racial discrimination. As soon as I heard what was happening, I went over. His charges were invalid. I spoke to him quietly and waited until he got his hamburger. Then I escorted him to a table where Duke and Edward Emile Edlow, immediately perceiving his condition, handled him knowingly.

On our return to San Francisco that afternoon, the faculty member in this students' bus immediately reported his behavior to the principal. This disturbed the other students, who wanted to work out some form of penalty through their newly established student organization. They resented being bypassed. This new student was suspended by the principal for two days, the two days' pay being deducted from his weekly stipend.

When he returned, we had several private discussions. He was at the stage of hostility and belligerency the other students had been in at the beginning of the program. In his short time with us, however, I had observed his acuity in understanding verbal concepts and told him so. His behavior began to show slight changes for the better by the time the program ended.

Trips to colleges and universities opened up new worlds to these young people who never imagined that they, too, might be able to enter. Incentive for continued learning reached an all-time high as a result. Self-confidence and feelings of hopefulness were now increasing rapidly.

VISIT TO A MUSEUM

Toward the end of the program in the basic electricity and duplicating machine operators group, the students expressed interest in visiting museums. We chose to visit the Palace of Legion of Honor museum. Its architecture and location were unforgettable.

I made arrangements for the museum's curator of education to be our guide. A petite, dynamic woman, she immediately established rapport by her vivacity, sparkling humor, and warmth. Her British accent added to the students' fascination. Before they were able to identify her accent, Sebastian whispered in my ear, "She's German, huh?"

Changes in behavior patterns were becoming evident. Most of the students met me at ten o'clock sharp. Duke, who had been reluctant to come, limped over to me.

"I hurt my knee getting into this peanut of a car (Von's Volkswagen), and I got to go home." He was teasing, and I recognized teasing by this time.

Our guide greeted us in the lobby of the museum, introduced herself, and asked the students to call her by her first name. "I can't do this," said Sebastian. "That's not right. I got to treat her with respect."

In the rotunda, she showed us a bronze statue of a nude young woman. "How do you like it? Look her over and let me know. I'll give you time." The students walked around the figure, observing it from every angle as if they were art connoisseurs. Most liked it, but the consensus was that she was too thin. Monster thought she was shy and possibly ashamed and therefore trying to hide. The curator was delighted with their reactions and discussed styles and artists' changing tastes in feminine figures. She joked about models in today's women's magazines. This evoked laughter.

We then entered a large room with many oil paintings by artists of the Renaissance period. We stopped before one depicting two nudes, a male and a female, with Cupid on the left, dart in hand. A strip of diaphanous material rippled across the couple's genitalia. The guide again asked the students for their reactions.

"She'd catch a cold in the San Francisco fog," said Wiz.

"They look like gods," said Ali-Tees. "Maybe from mythology, eh?" he said, as he looked at me questioningly.

When the guide confirmed his guess by saying that the couple depicted were Mars and Venus, the students looked at Ali-Tees with pride. The veil in the painting had been used to make the nude figures acceptable. The guide went on to tell about the artist and his technique.

"Will you please reiterate? I didn't get you," said Coolsann, in the outer circle. His voice sputtered in his effort to make an impression.

While we were listening to the guide, Von wandered off to another painting. Soon we heard him yell, "What we got here? Looks like a murder in a bathtub."

The rest of the students looked over at him, annoyed. "What's that word to describe what Von's doing?" Pause. "Yeah, I got it," said Wiz, "irrevelant."

"It's irrelevant," corrected Allen Williams.

In the next gallery, we saw a painting of a French king. "What a feminine dude," said Deacon. "That feather sure is long on his hat. Look at the jewels. He don't look like a man." The guide explained that men in those days wore bright colors while women preferred more subdued shades.

A Rembrandt portrait of an old man pleased them most. They showed their sensitivity. "You can just see what the man is thinking."

Deacon was so interested that he wanted to know who owned the paintings. The guide said, "They really belong to us all. We are tax-payers, and our taxes help maintain this museum."

As we were leaving this room, Deacon said, "Please wait. I want to take home my Rembrandt."

On our way out we looked at hand-woven tapestries covering the walls, depicting the Crusades. They had been done in the twelfth and thirteenth centuries. Several students asked if they were valuable. One said, "I'm coming around on a night and take them down. If I hustled them, I could get a load."

In the French room, which was decorated with gilt, Duke said, "If this is real gold, I'll bring a saw and take it with me."

"How did these things get here?" asked Sebastian.

"Somebody left them, you dope," said Duke. He liked the fountain in the middle of the rotunda. "Anyone for swimming?" he said as he threw in a penny, which he immediately retrieved, getting wet to the elbows — anything to attract attention.

The tour ended with the guide's pointing to a painting of a king's mistress and saying she was often referred to as "B. S. Annie." When one of the students asked what that meant, she said, "I'll let you figure that out for yourself. Now, are there any questions on any part of your trip?"

The students expressed their appreciation of her stories before asking questions. Several wanted to know why there were no African paintings or sculpture. She explained that this museum specialized in paintings and sculpture of the Renaissance and that other museums with collections of modern art might have these pieces. Other questions had to do with artists' techniques, training, and patrons. The guide was pleased with the students' concern. She asked them to return for an exhibit on Toulouse-Lautrec, whose life she briefly sketched. Their response was immediately favorable.

In our feedback session the next day, Deacon expressed the reaction of the whole group: "That was the most relaxing time I ever

had. The guide was so interesting. She had a story behind each painting. We could have stayed forever. When are we going again?"

Several months later we did go to the Toulouse-Lautrec exhibit,
which they equally enjoyed. They were especially pleased with the
guide's reaction to them: "I think you're wonderful. You have more
spark in you than any of the high school students who come through
here regularly. It's a pleasure to be your guide."

VISIT TO THE INTERNATIONAL SOCIETY OF GENERAL SEMANTICS

After these visits the students grew more eager to meet people
outside their immediate environment.

"Mrs. Dawson, when are we going to go to public meetings? Can't
we go to one of the organizations to which you belong, the society on
communication?" asked Wiz.

"You once said you were so proud of us you wished the public
could hear us and change their stereotypes of culturally disadvantaged
youths living in ghettoes," commented Allen Williams.

"Yeah, you said we had brains. Now we can see how we get along
with others. We got to continue our own advertising," said Edward
Emile Edlow. Laughter.

The society on communication to which Allen referred was the
International Society for General Semantics, headed by Doctor S. I.
Hayakawa, Professor of Language Arts at San Francisco State College.
I explained very simply what general semantics is about and how it
differs from semantics, with which it is often confused. Semantics is
concerned with symbols and their derivations, whereas general semantics is concerned with the reaction of human beings to symbols.

"Let's take the symbol *police*. In the study of semantics, we would
learn that it derives from the Latin *politia*, 'a condition of state, government, administration'; from the Greek *politeia*, which has the same
meaning; from the Greek *polis*, 'state'; and from the French *policer*,
'to govern.' It is understandable, therefore, how the symbol *police*
comes to denote law enforcement and protection of citizens and the
state. Just mention the word *police* to you, however, and what are
your reactions?"

I arranged for my students to meet the members of this society
and present a program similar to the one they had presented on television: their attitudes toward labels, school, employment, and arrest
records. The panelists chosen by the class were the same students who

had appeared on television, with the exception of one. They were Deacon, Edward Emile Edlow, Allen Williams, Wiz, and Coolsann, and Anton, substituting for Ali-Tees, who was working at night.[4]

This general semantics meeting took place on a Friday evening at eight o'clock. The panelists were not paid, but they were dinner guests at a French restaurant. It was interesting to observe each student watching me to see which utensil to use. Those seated on either side of me whispered questions on what to order. Only two ordered French cuisine; the others felt more comfortable with pot roast and apple pie.

The meeting was jammed — standing room only. After a brief introduction, I opened by addressing a question to the panel. Thereafter Deacon assumed the role of moderator.

"We hear people refer to you as 'culturally deprived,' 'culturally disadvantaged,' 'high school dropouts,' 'juvenile delinquents,' and 'hoodlums.' How do these labels affect you?"

"First of all," said Coolsann, "most people throwing out these labels, I really don't feel they know what it's all about. . . . People say, 'He comes from a socially deprived area.' Well, he was forced into this. So what can you do? You apply for a job and you write Hunters Point. What does this man say? 'He's from the black belt.' If they can find someone else, they hire the person. You can't get the job. Society has stereotyped ideas about us."

"Labels do make people think in restricted ways," said Edward Emile Edlow.

"I don't feel it's right to call me a hoodlum, so I ignore it," said Anton.

"Oh, yes," said Allen Williams, "an employer will say, 'We talked about you . . . your type, that is. We don't want your type here.' "

[4] Anton, a self-labeled nonconformist, who had dropped out of high school in his senior year, had been with our group for two months. He was the first white member of this class. The principal had been working with the state department of employment to expand the area of recruitment to cover the city rather than one area.

Although only eighteen years old, Anton was an alcoholic when he entered the program. Intelligent, sensitive, and articulate, he had an arrogant manner at first which alienated him from his classmates. In their eyes he was an intruder, and they avoided him. He sat alone for the first three weeks. When the students saw how understanding he was and how he never usurped discussions, even with his advantage of "heavy" reading, (Huxley's *Brave New World*), their aloofness vanished and he was in. He was later elected a representative to the student council.

Laughter from others on the panel. " 'We feel you might be a disadvantage to our company.' See, these are the things we run across from day to day."

Wiz said, "And another thing I'd like to say is, when you're going to school and trying to learn, the teachers are trying to get over with you, but it's just that hostility in you because you don't have what the average person has. OK, like the doctor's son, the lawyer's son, he's sitting there clean and he's learning. Now I'm sitting in my corner raggedy, you know, and trying to think of where I'm going to get my next nickel so I can make it. I think that my whole teen-age life was very unhappy. . . . Now that I've gotten back to school and I'm learning . . . life is much more beautiful." [5]

"Labels trigger some people's minds to the point where they know all about you before you open your mouth," said Deacon.

"Yeah, well, I mean, basically, like in the public school, you get up in the morning," said Coolsann, "you go into the classroom. The teacher say, 'This assignment . . .' — he doesn't stop . . . to figure out how you feel. You might be sitting . . . with holes in your shoes. You cold, because your clothes aren't sufficient. You're hungry, but you tell people these things and they would laugh. It's hard to get a person to understand some of the things that the so-called minority group go through because they have never been exposed to this."

Their comments on the next topic were unexpected. Anton was talking about the reasons for his dropping out of high school in his senior year.

"I didn't drop out of school because I had nothing better to do. The teachers were at fault, too. When I first came into Mrs. Dawson's class . . . I didn't believe she could be that way — hip, I mean. She used some of our language. What's the matter, can't she speak good English? . . . But I learned she was translating new vocabulary into our language. We were learning English as if it were a foreign language. I sat there. She's not for real, I thought. Later I learned she is for real."

"Yeah, when you meet a teacher who speaks your language," said Edward Emile Edlow, "you say to yourself, 'What's she up to?' This is unusual, you know. I just sat back and studied her real hard." Laughter. "Because I wasn't sure. I had been through so many before with that color. I didn't trust her. You see I changed. She got next to me."

---

[5] Wiz entered this program after having spent a year in jail for stealing cars. He was still on probation, but he had had no further trouble.

Coolsann's comments on the problem of prejudice and its close connection with thinking in stereotypes showed how he understood other aspects of the concept.

". . . I feel that everyone is stereotyped on certain things. . . . Take a simple thing like a cigarette. All I smoke is one brand. I'm prejudiced. Toward diverse groups, now, I ain't so prejudiced. I try to get along. . . . There's good, bad, and what else in everyone."

"When talking to somebody with a racial barrier hanging over your head," said Edward Emile Edlow, "it shows up in communication."

"I think there'd be less prejudice if more people understood what it's like to be black and grow up in poverty. You're included in that group, too. For example, teachers don't understand. You might be sitting in class with holes in your shoes, cold, because your clothes aren't sufficient. You're hungry, too. But you tell people these things, and they laugh. They never been exposed to this. Like if someone was to tell you, 'I had to sleep in a room with six people on the floor.' I mean you would find this rather hard to believe. This really does exist. I'm the oldest in my family. My parents and younger sisters and brothers look up to me. I try to figure out, 'How can I get some money?' You try and get a job. You can't. So you become discouraged. Your friends mock you for trying to work. You keep trying. Then your spirit breaks, and you turn to crime. Then you have a prison record. Then you try to get a job when you're out, but now it's impossible. You may have a serious desire to conform to what society expects, but you got no choice. I feel that a lot of minority groups are forced into situations."

Anton said, "Labels don't help destroy prejudice either. You put a label on a cat, and that's it. You really don't bother to talk to him to find out how he feels about anything. . . . Labels trigger people's minds —where they know all about you before you open your mouth. How the press feels about race comes out, too. Like, for instance, in a swanky part of the city there's a 'wild party.' In the poverty area where there are few blacks, they call it a 'gang fight.' In the black ghetto, they call it a 'slashing.'

"All these ideas tend to draw pain," said Edward Emile Edlow, "when somebody approaches you and tells you this. . . . I don't blame anybody. . . . I'm not like the cat that fooled with the yarn and got all wrapped up and fell down the stairs. . . . I'm looking before I step." Laughter.

"I don't blame anybody. . . . I look at him, and then I see how he really is. I check him out like I did Mrs. Dawson. I don't let myself be fooled by pretty speeches and broad smiles. Still, I give him a chance first and try to see him with an open mind. I ain't naive. I'm sophisticated."

Wiz had a partial solution to the problem of prejudice. "There should be more black history known by everyone. Only in this program did I learn what blacks invented. If I could've seen this in high school, it might've made things a lot better for me."

"Let's get back to the topic of school," said Allen Williams. "They always played up my brother to me. I said, 'Man, how am I doing? I don't always want to hear about my brother.' They didn't give me any goals to go after. I couldn't get motivated. I lost interest in school and dropped out."

"When you leave elementary school and go to junior high school — well, if you were a bad boy — say your father or mother broke up while you were nine or ten," said Edward Emile Edlow, "not like a kid who has a mother and father's affection — he'll kind of grow up right with the sense that someone cares. In my case my mother and father broke up, and I had a complex. . . . My mother married again, and I definitely didn't accept this dude. That's what he was." Laughter from the audience. "I rejected him because he was nothing like my father. To me my father was a god. With this complex, I didn't want to conform. . . . I wouldn't participate in school. You know. I didn't want to read. I didn't know how to when I was fourteen, so I got in trouble. The teacher didn't understand what was bugging me. When he called on me to read, I was ashamed. I'd sit and mope. Finally I got kicked out."

Anton brought the discussion to a close by this interjection: "You know, in our Personal Development class we specialize in interaction. We've talked enough. Now, how about a little interaction? We're ready for questions."

The first respondent didn't ask a question; he made a speech. It was interesting to note how the panelists were listening and how they picked up the essence of his remarks and threw them back at him.

"I have a great sympathy for your feelings," he said. "But look at the other side. . . . You say you couldn't care less about labels; but you do, or you wouldn't complain. . . . When I was a young man, I didn't have it good either. . . . I have a job that involves hiring people. . . . You have to put labels on people and stereotype them. . . . You discover that a certain background will almost inevitably bring you a certain type of trouble, an inability to perform the work, or unreliability, or maybe a criminal type of individual. . . . I can't entirely be on your side. . . ."

Every panelist was excited, but Allen Williams spoke first.

". . . When you said you were a young man . . . I don't know what year, but back in those days you were free, but we weren't. Do you understand that?"

"I wasn't talking about color or creed. . . . I was talking about people. . . ."

"That has to come in. . . . Let's not pretend. We've got to be frank with each other. This is communicating, right?" said Allen Williams.

Coolsann jumped in. "I'll give you an example. From the age of seven to the age of nineteen, I was labeled 'incorrigible.' I might still be labeled 'incorrigible,' but at nineteen I saw the light. I said to myself, 'Well, I'm always incarcerated. I'm always in trouble, breaking my momma's heart, I'm going to straighten out.' I go down to get a job. I couldn't get a job. I walk around for eleven months looking for a job. I'm the oldest one in the family. Everyone's looking up to me. When I come home—'How did it go?' My mother didn't seem to understand. For twelve years I resorted to crime to get what I want. All of a sudden I decided to do the right thing. This is very disgusting. I can't get employment. So I have to turn back to crime. I didn't. I have enough will power to keep on trying. After eleven months I got my first legitimate job at $1.25 an hour. I didn't like the job, but I took it and tried to advance myself. I stayed there fourteen months. I asked for a raise. The Man was always patting me on the back. 'You're a good boy, Coolsann. You do the work of three men.' What about a raise? 'I'm doing all I can, you know.' I worked for $70 a week for a ten-hour day. So he told me to go somewhere else. This goes to show you."

The man from the audience continued, "Maybe I didn't make myself clear. . . ."

In unison the panel cried, "We think you did."

"I've been trying to hire someone from the colored group to do work. . . ."

The panelists asked what type of work, and he said work on heating equipment.

Allen Williams came back again, "You mean you haven't had any success? You mean you tried to hire blacks, and they couldn't sell heating equipment? Are you really serious? Come on. You know what? Let's get back to stereotypes. You should be ashamed of yourself. You know, that really bugs me. People say that all the time."

"Get his real name," said Edward Emile Edlow, taking out his pad as if he were a newspaper reporter or the police. Laughter.

Edward continued, "With the idea that everybody has that the average black is a thief, there's a lot of things going against us. It makes a lot of people afraid of us that don't know us or hardly ever tried to talk to a black. . . .

"I had a taste of this in my experience selling magazines from door to door with a white partner. Everybody he talked to talked to him, but when they saw me they slammed the door in my face. . . . They don't give you an opportunity to put across what you're trying to get over to them."

"You said about labels. . . . I'm not letting you get away with anything. This is supposed to be a society interested in communicating — well, let's communicate. To do this I learned you just don't talk, you listen. So, please listen. I listened to you. . . ."

"I wasn't thinking of minority groups," said this same man. "I was thinking of alcoholics." There was laughter from the panelists.

Wiz said, "Alcoholics? We're not alcoholics. We don't know anything about that. . . ."

"Let's try to communicate to this man," said Edward Emile Edlow to his fellow panelists. "Let's play it cool and not lose our heads. I want to say something to this man. Sir, it seemed this way to you because that's the way you looked at it. To me I was probing to find out why you think this way. I wasn't attacking you. I'm trying to understand you, but you have to try to make yourself clear, too."

Everyone was excited. Several more members of the audience asked questions or sought advice from the panelists on how to deal with de-facto segregation in the schools. When the meeting was officially adjourned, the panelists were surrounded and engaged in discussions while we had refreshments. Before we left, each student asked me how he did and beamed at my laudatory comments.

The following Monday at our feedback session, I played the tape for the rest of the class to hear and evaluate. Attention was intense.

"You know what?" said Duke, who had not been at the meeting. "I'm not prejudiced, but you fellows sounded more articulate and direct than those in the audience. These semantic people made long speeches and took hours to get to the point. You're really learning. You were pacific and down to the nitty gritty, not way out in space." Applause from the class.

We concluded this session with the reading of a note I had received from the president of the Society stating that this had been the most interesting program ever presented. Each panelist received a copy of the society's newsletter, which had this to say: "Our November meeting featured a unique panel of students who told of the ways they've changed in this semantically oriented Personal Development class and also of the way the world looks to a young man in a black ghetto. A fascinating presentation of issues seldom discussed openly. . . . A welcome note."

Summary

Exposing young people from poverty areas and ghettoes to new cultural experiences adds another dimension to the concept of educating. Educating for living must transcend the narrow boundaries imposed by prescribed texts and restriction to the classroom. The development of these youths stymied by poverty and racial prejudice is hampered by failure to include the cultural resources available in urban areas.

In urban areas the opportunities for broadening your students' perspective, and your own, are numerous. Universities and colleges have many student exchange programs. Unfortunately, they may not be familiar with your particular program and needs; it is therefore up to you to be an unofficial public informant and to initiate the various contacts. In so doing, try not to be deterred by any pessimistic comments by administrators and colleagues. Fear of the unknown is not confined to youths from poverty areas. It is present among people at many levels of human endavor.

This expansion of the students' horizons is also possible in rural or suburban areas. It may be possible for universities, colleges, and museums in urban areas to provide you with mobile programs if you plan far enough in advance.

You have observed the eagerness and delight with which my students met each new cultural experience. Changes in feelings such as this do not happen by chance, but occur when these young people are accepted as intelligently functioning, important individuals. What they learned in Personal Development prepared them to meet the public and present themselves as they are, not as the public imagines them. Television appearances, visits to universities and colleges, visits to museums, visits from exchange students, and participation in intellectual programs — programs often considered suitable only for people with greater educational advantages — these all help to destroy existing stereotypes. Often, these youths' ability to cut through a dense forest of redundancy and ambiguity put so-called "intellectuals" to shame.

Opportunities like those recorded in this chapter allow these youths to test their newly discovered perspicacity and demonstrate their growth in perception, self-confidence, and ability to accept criticism. At this point in their personal development, they are beginning to slough off their feelings of rejection and emerge with a realization of how much they can contribute to the world around them.

6 • Emerging Changes in Attitudes and Behavior

WHAT A MEMORABLE day it is when Duke enters and says, without the accompaniment of the usual four-letter words, "Know what? I got a question mark in my head, just as you said. For the first time I didn't think I knew it all. I let Von disagree with me."

He seemed pleased with his new behavior and yet surprised at it. I was pleased, too, because Duke was one of the few students in the basic electricity group whose attitudes and behavior midway through the program still reflected their hostility, hopelessness, fear of failure, self-hatred, and intense anti-white feelings. He continually interrupted and snarled at his fellow students and occasionally me. He insisted on memorizing, and he derided those who tried to learn.

He had leadership qualities. If only they could be channeled into constructive activities! I continually urged Duke to open his mind. Repeatedly I selected him to chair discussions. On two occasions I left him in charge while I attended a meeting of the student council, of which I was adviser. He was to tape the session, which would be played back the following day for discussion and evaluation.

When I opened the door as the session was ending, I heard Duke say to his fellow students, "Hey, fellows, down. We here to learn. If you don't, get out. Don't be selfish and stop us. We dig this class, see?"

His brow wrinkled, his eyes flashed, and he greeted me with, "I had it. I couldn't get nowhere with them. There was always someone interrupting or blocking when we tried to get a discussion going. All right, don't say it. I get the pitch, but I'm learning. If some want to be stupid, that's their problem." This seemed to mark the turning point for Duke. Changes in his feelings about himself and others, although slow in coming, thereafter became more perceptible.

In the general office clerk program, behavioral changes began to emerge after the sixth week. More students were punctual; fewer were absent; sunglasses, hats, and head scarves were no longer worn in class; students no longer chewed gum noisily or passed notes; those who formerly slept in class or stayed in the rest rooms were now involved in what we were saying and doing. In fact, as my students would say, "Things were swinging."

Roberta and Cindy, perpetual interrupters and know-it-alls at the start, stopped interrupting and began to listen when they were given opportunities to demonstrate their leadership qualities by co-chairing the student council and moderating discussions. It was another great day when Roberta felt secure enough to part with her head scarf and coat in the classroom. She had a beautiful face, which was now completely visible. Her figure was still too ample, and she requested counseling on proper diet.

Outward changes in appearance, although pleasing, are not as revealing as increased feelings of self-worth and hopefulness. Such changes never come about overnight, but result from continued daily exposure to challenging situations in an atmosphere of mutual acceptance. The students' violently defensive reactions, developed as survival measures in the streets, are difficult to overcome. Substitution of non-violent responses for violent responses is understandably slow in coming.

It is important to remember that in the process of learning and changing there will be setbacks to infantile and socially unacceptable behavior from time to time. Neither you nor your students should be discouraged by such regressions if both of you understand the nature of change. The struggle between changing and remaining the same is a natural human phenomenon.

I was pleased by the slightest favorable change, but never lulled into a state of relaxed complacency. I didn't know when the storm would break, but I knew it would break sometime. It happened at a different time in each group. In the general office clerk group an incident illustrating behavioral retrogression occurred at a most unexpected moment in a most unexpected way with the most unexpected participants.

Our first general assembly meeting with the head of the state employment department had just concluded. The students had had their say: they had asked questions and made comments about their chances for employment. The meeting was adjourned. The speaker and I were appraising the program during the coffee break. The usual pandemonium reigned: the piano was attacked by one-finger players, transistor radios blared forth, and the monkey dance was in full swing.

This upheaval followed a period of unaccustomed concentration; the pattern of increasing spans of attention was still in its embryonic stage, and now the students were letting off steam.

Then it happened. I heard a thump on the floor and yells. My guest and I turned around in utter amazement to see Dick with his arms tightly wrapped around Belle, whom he was banging on the floor like a yo-yo. I thought her skull was being fractured. Each time Dick raised Belle's body, her feet wiggled and her hands fought the air. I ran over to stop the slaughter, only to be barred by Chops and William, who said, "You might get hurt. Let us take care of it. Don't worry." They pulled the couple apart, and while one dragged Dick out, the other took Belle to the door; then they saw that each was taken home at a different time.

Our guest was initiated. She began to understand the problems involved in educating youths from poverty areas — of which subject matter in the traditional sense was the least.

The president of the student council, Roberta, heard of the incident and immediately called her executive committee together. They went to the principal's office and decided to summon both Dick and Belle to a meeting the following day.

Dick and Belle had never before shown any antisocial behavior toward anyone, and certainly not to each other. That same afternoon rumors began to spread that Dick was angry with Belle because she had spurned his advances. Dick's wife, eighteen years old, had just returned from the hospital after breast surgery for a malignancy. According to the gossipmongers, Dick had decided that Belle should take his wife's place during her convalescence. These rumors had little foundation, and I tried to squelch them. I asked the students not to make assumptions until we could talk to both Dick and Belle.

I remembered that at the beginning of the general office clerk program, Dick had occasionally tickled Belle, who sat in front of him. When she paid no attention, he tried to wrestle with her. She was strong and hit him; then he stopped. But both had laughed; on the few occasions that this had happened, there was only friendly interaction.

The following morning Dick was waiting for me as I arrived for counseling. "Can I see you privately immediately? It's urgent."

I canceled my other appointments. He continued, "I don't want to come up on charges. Really, nothing serious happened."

"No?" I said. "I was shocked, Dick. I thought Belle's skull was fractured, the way you pounded her head on the floor."

"It wasn't her head. I held my arm around her head so I wouldn't hurt her. It was my hand and elbow that took the beating. See the bruises." (There were bruises on his elbow.) "I've heard bad things being said about me and my relations with Belle. They ain't true, and I don't want my wife to hear them. She's had enough trouble. I had a hard time explaining the scratches Belle made on my face. These things they're saying ain't true. Anyway, I wouldn't choose Belle for my girl. She's too full of religion."

"Suppose you tell me what happened and why."

"I admit that yesterday I began to tease her too hard. I just felt like it, I guess. I'm nervous, and I'm tired of staying home every night with my two small children and a sick wife. I've always been out every day after school trying to get a job because I need the money. I've teased Belle before, and she never acted like this. When the speaker finished explaining about employment, Belle dug her pencil into the back of my neck, and that's all I needed. I got so mad I grabbed her and started to fight. She's strong, but I'm stronger, and I held her arms down to prevent her from scratching me. She did anyway. I'm sorry it happened, and I would like to shake hands with Belle in your office now and apologize and tell her I'm still her friend. Can I do that?"

"Maybe. First I'll have to see Belle and ask her if she's willing. You wait here, please, Dick, while I talk to Belle. I'll be back in a few minutes."

I left and got permission to talk to Belle. She confirmed Dick's story about the teasing. Dick had done this before, and she had taken it. "This time Dick pinched my behind, and this got me mad. I began to fight. When I got home, I was still mad. After I put my baby to bed, I had time to think. I was sorry I lost my temper. I remembered when we talked about maturity. I guess I'm still immature. I thought about it all evening and decided I would shake hands with Dick if he wanted to."

I told her that Dick was also disturbed and wanted to apologize. She came to the office. I stayed in the background while Dick and Belle smiled and talked. Then they shook hands and apologized.

I spoke to Roberta and to the principal, giving him a written report and recommending that the incident be closed. There was never a recurrence.

The ability to accept criticism from others as well as to be self-critical slowly emerged as we proceeded in each program. The time involved, of course, varied with the individual and the group. Initially, violence was the usual response to criticism. This reaction manifested itself dramatically in the basic electricity program. Fortunately, the incident happened during a coffee break when only a few students were in the room. I entered the room early and to my surprise found Deacon and Allen Williams glaring at each other. This wouldn't have been unnatural, but each had a huge desk chair raised in front of him as a shield. Monster and Duke stood by, cool observers. As I looked down, I saw a knife in Deacon's right hand. He saw my surprise and apprehension.

"Don't worry. I'm only playing, but I'm mad," said Deacon.

"I can't hear you," I said. Addressing both combatants, I said, "Why don't you put your knife away and put the chairs down and discuss the problem like civilized people?"

"We're sorry. We didn't want to get you into trouble."

"Yeah," said Deacon, "but Allen Williams called me a name, and I wasn't going to let him get away with it. I pulled the knife in fun. He's in no position to criticize me. I don't like it."

Had this incident occurred during the session, it could have started a chain reaction resulting in damage and injury.

That session, and many sessions thereafter, we dwelled on being able to accept criticism as well as being able to criticize others. This was related to conditions on a job; it applied to reactions to an employer's criticism of work habits or procedures. The person who reacts uncontrollably in an infantile way harms himself. The precepts from our class discussions had to be internalized before they could rightfully be considered educational.

There was much evidence later in the program that such internalization was taking place. In one session we were discussing attitudes and behavior and how important it was to make certain changes in them. We were citing concrete evidence of change observed in class. Deacon said he could see changes in Allen Williams. Allen disagreed and said he was the same as when he entered.

Deacon said, "You're not. You're changing."

The dialogue became more heated. Deacon continued, "You probably don't know whether you learned anything, because you haven't reached far enough back in your mind to find out. You have changed, if you'll only look."

"I know I'm readier than you think to be able to criticize myself, Deacon, but you know what? We were in the service together, but you didn't learn shit."

We all sat upright. How would Deacon react this time? "You know what?" he said. "Let me tell you something about you. . . . You're kind of mentally off, or something like that. Anything that comes up, you have to object. You've got to have your say, and half the time you don't know what you're saying. You're full of initiative—energy and everything—but you're pushing it the wrong way."

Allen was startled at Deacon's reaction. While he struggled for words, Edward Emile Edlow addressed Deacon, "You know when Allen talked to you like that, you know what you supposed to say? 'That's your idea. I don't feel the way you do. You think what you want about me. I know myself. I'm getting an open mind. I'm able to accept criticism. I feel sorry for you.' That's all you had to say. If you're a man you don't have to argue with nobody. Whatever you think I am, OK. You have a right to your opinion, but don't abuse me. That's all. Then it be all over with."

On many occasions later in the program, Deacon demonstrated his ability to accept criticism in a mature, dignified way, never demeaning himself by violent reactions. The rivalry between him and Allen continued in an academic context, but never again did it flare up into antisocial tactics.

There was something else I observed from this incident: the courage of Allen to criticize his peers in the presence of the gang and in violation of the gang code. With each succeeding program I noticed not only changes in individual behavior, but in group behavior as well. In the office boy program, the group followed the leader. If he slept in class, they followed. If he provoked the teacher, the others did too. Those who didn't want to go along with the gang absented themselves to avoid reprisals. Allen was among the first to assert his independence and unwillingness to conform to what he now considered antisocial behavior. As the students' self-confidence increased and they came to feel that someone was truly interested in them, they developed courage to disagree openly with their peers without fear of punishment.

We were talking about group behavior and the need for gang adherence one day, with Ali-Tees moderating.

Edward Emile Edlow had the floor. "See, if you get cast out, you say to yourself, 'Who else is on my side?' No one else. Therefore you stick with the code regardless of anything. If the group disapproves, you're out. And with man being the gregarious creature that he is, he has a tendency to get hooked up."

I said I understood the problem, but I was concerned about each individual's being allowed to develop. His development was blocked if he had to conform to his gang's behavior patterns.

Randy said, "Even individuals, if they see the group is doing wrong, they're going to see that as individuals and drop out."

"Yeah," said Duke, "if someone has a normal amount of common sense, they would drop out of a group that's doing wrong."

"You know, you're not exactly right," said Edward Emile Edlow. "You know that people you used to hang around with hung around in gangs in the street, and they still doing that. That ain't using common sense."

"If they got something out of it, they would still do it," said Coolsann. "Take a certain bag. . . . I'm going to tell you about one I grew up in . . . where everybody now, they own Cadillacs and stuff—that's just how progressive the cats were, you know, and everybody is on their job. I mean, they doing this thing and that thing, and yet I don't know nobody that goes to work and punch a clock for eight hours a day. I was in that bag once."

"How did you get out of it?" asked Ali-Tees.

"I'll tell you what. First of all, I got tired of being arrested. . . ."

"I got out of the bag, too," said Allen Williams, "and I was the poorest on the block. Who wore sweat shirts and tennis shoes every day? I did. I was hooked up in a bag, sure. But gosh, common sense'd tell you. . . ." Laughter.

"See," said Edward Emile Edlow, "some people, it takes them quite a while and institutionalization before they get more mature."

"What about the fellows you worked with and those you met in prison?" asked Wiz. "Do you still associate with them?"

"I still see some of them. One just got out, bought himself a brand new Impala, and I'm afraid he's busy again, but I'm not with him."

"Yeah," said Wiz. "It's not easy to change behavior when you're growed up. We've been given a raw deal by whites and feel we want to get what's our due, so we take it when we can. That's how I felt before I joined this program. Now I'm changing. Maybe I'm more mature, too."

Ali-Tees, the moderator, was a city college student, and he was anxious to sell his friends on their need to go on to college. "What you guys ought to do is get deep on a few things. Because this is an interesting world, and if you take time and slow down, there's a lot a things that interest you out there."

He had some effect, because later Edward Emile Edlow and Allen Williams went to the city college to register.[1]

Other changes were noticeable. One morning toward the end of the basic electricity program, Wiz asked to be excused. "Duke has an employment interview. It's too cold to wait for a bus, and he's nervous. Could I be excused to drive him there?"

"I would say yes, but I don't have the authority. Furthermore, I don't want you to lose any weekly allowance for such an absence. I would suggest you ask the office."

I happened to be in the office when Wiz made his request. At first he was refused, but he persisted: "Gee, that's not being very cooperative. I thought you wanted Duke to get a job. Give him a break. I'll return. I'm reliable now. I promise."

Permission was granted, and Wiz returned as he had promised. This incident occurred after we had been working together more than seven months. Repeatedly in our daily discussions and in our experiences we were helping each other and demonstrating the need to persuade with words rather than with violence.

The process of behavioral and attitudinal change is often carried out deviously by the students, to avoid antagonizing nonstudent buddies. Many times I saw cars pull up to the school, filled with friends waiting for our students. The security these young people find within their close-knit peer group makes up for their rejection by outsiders. It is not surprising, therefore, to find that the students are reluctant and afraid to disturb this security and that they allow their nonstudent friends to interfere with their intellectual and social progress.

However, as our students became involved in schoolwork and aware of others' concern for them, the frequency of nonstudent visits lessened and the students began to have a favorable influence on their nonstudent friends. In fact these friends were welcomed as guests to special programs, and several later became willing recruits of the school.

---

[1] College was too difficult for Edward Emile Edlow, but Allen Williams was still attending at the time of this writing. He planned to go to a state college and earn his bachelor's degree when he completed junior college.

Throughout each program I have observed a tug of war between students born and raised in Southern rural areas and those raised in Northern urban areas. Because their value systems contrast so sharply, those from the South — designated by the northerners as "country boys" — are constantly the target of ridicule. In Southern rural areas, gangs and gang influence are not as prevalent, and young people have more close-knit family units. They go to church on Sundays; they seem more eager to learn; their dress conforms more closely to standard office attire; and few have police records.

Therefore it takes strength for the "country boys" to withstand the daily provocations and jibes — "dirty white nigger," "stupid Uncle Tom." The "city boys" now have underdogs. They try to establish themselves as the superiors in this relationship, thinking the southerners are vulnerable and will succumb to their taunts. The Southerners who are unattached and live alone are more vulnerable than the married ones.

If reverting to unacceptable forms of behavior is the entree to the city group, then that is the solution for the Southern boys. The Thumper, nineteen, had just arrived from a rural area of Texas when he entered the basic electricity program. It was interesting to see the changes in him after two months: he no longer sat with the country boys; he now sat near the city boys and usually close to a window, where he could pull cords, knock on radiator caps, and annoy the teacher; his hair and sideburns were longer; and his schoolwork showed signs of deterioration.

When he came in with eyes half-closed, I knew he was really in — now he was smoking marijuana. I called him for counseling. My assumptions were confirmed.

"I had to, you know. I met some girls up here, and they gave me an education."

As the months went by, however, and the city men increased their self-confidence and became engrossed in what we were doing, they began to reprimand the Thumper for his infantile behavior. Now they were reconverting him.

There are many adjustments to be made between rural values and customs and urban values and customs. When these problems are compounded by sectional differences, Southern youths are confronted with gigantic obstacles.

My counseling sessions provided me with keener insight into behavior problems as well as increased understanding of their genesis. Several students seemed to me in need of long-term psychiatric care, which was not then available. William was one of them. He showed the scars of years of poverty, racial discrimination, and rejection: his erratic behavior and moods revealed this. He was referred for psychological counseling at the Center. At first he was reluctant to go, assuming that this implied he was "crazy"; but he was willing to enter an experimental group therapy session conducted by a psychiatric social worker.

Because his intellectual ability surpassed the others', he was transferred to a more advanced Manpower Development Training program, still in the Youth Opportunity School but located in a regular vocational adult high school outside the ghetto. This transfer necessitated an academic break with his peers and somehow convinced him that he no longer needed psychological counseling.

Several days after he was transferred, I heard that he had been threatened with expulsion the first day because he had insulted a faculty member. About a week later I was just about to conclude my counseling hours and break for lunch, when the loosely hinged wooden door was forcibly swung open and William barged in ferociously. He didn't look straight at me. He was wearing his small-brimmed hat and sunglasses again, an indication of retrogression, and his voice was strident, threatening, and angry—not at me, but at the perpetrators of his expulsion.

Dispensing with the usual amenities, he said, "Those dirty bastards! Did you hear what they did to me?

Under the circumstances I didn't interrupt to remind him to take off his hat or to call attention to his rudeness.

"I'm going to shoot them, that's what I'm going to do," he said, as he put his hand in his pocket menacingly. I didn't know whether he had a gun or not, but it was very likely he did. I had no intention of asking him for proof. I was more concerned about trying to quiet him and get him back to the reasoning stage. I felt complimented that he had voluntarily come to me with his problem.

I let him spew out his anger. "You think I'm crazy, I bet—don't you? Maybe I am, but no one's going to step on me. I'll kill them first. What I got to lose? I'm not going to get a job anyway. Now they took my last opportunity away—by expelling me. I'm back on the street. I can only get into trouble and do time."

When he paused for breath, I said quietly, "William, tell me your story. So far I've heard only rumors."

He didn't sit down, and I didn't ask him to. But he stopped pacing the floor and stood still. "You really want to hear, huh? Well, I got to school the first day. I saw a lot of dudes, and I knew maybe one. I felt as smart as any of them, and I'd show them. I did swell in math and knew I was good in English. The English teacher spoke all right, but he wasn't paying enough attention to me. So I tested him. 'What's an abstract noun?' He didn't answer, but he answered the other dudes' questions first. I got mad. 'Hey, Mr. Homo, how come you don't answer my question? I asked you first.' He got so mad he ran out of the room to the office and demanded that I be expelled. I don't have to tell you the office's decision."

"Well, William, put yourself in the teacher's place. How would you like it if you were called a name? You knew what you were doing. You knew you were trying to provoke the teacher and attract his attention. I thought you had gotten beyond that by now."

"You're right. I did know what I was doing, but I wanted to show him and the others that fellows from Hunters Point are smart, too."

"All right, let's follow this further. Don't you think you deserve some disciplinary action?"

"Yeah, but not expulsion. It takes away my motivation and initiative."

"But didn't you have some responsibility for such a decision? If you did shoot or attempt to shoot the principal or the teacher, maybe it would have satisfied your immediate anger—but what about the consequences?"

"What would I care about that? I'd still have the satisfaction of getting this out of my system. Who cares if I go to prison? No one. It's the white man's world. I hate them all. They're devils."

"William, I think by now you know you're not telling the truth. If no one cared, would anyone want to help you? If I didn't care, would I have taken verbal abuse?"

"Maybe you're right. I know you're no phony—but what about the others?"

"The psychiatric social worker is certainly trying to help you. He cares."

"Yeah, maybe."

"You're young and very intelligent. What about returning to psychological counseling—today? I'll call up the psychiatric social worker and try to get an emergency appointment. OK?"

After a few moments of thought, William sat down and sighed. "Do I have to go today? Can't I wait until tomorrow?"

"I would recommend you do it right now." I telephoned and got an immediate appointment.

"OK, I'm going to keep it. Thanks. You'll hear from me."

William's expulsion was reduced to suspension. Psychological counseling has helped him. He is working in the community with young people who have similar problems. On one of his early days off from school he stopped by to visit me. His outward appearance reflected his inner changes: his hair was cut short, he had dispensed with his small-brimmed hat and sunglasses, and he dressed elegantly. What was even more significant was his quiet and friendly manner.

On later visits he expressed pride in his scholastic achievement: he was the top student in mathematics and basic electricity. Finally he succeeded in fulfilling the requirements for his high school diploma while simultaneously completing the program in basic electricity and obtaining the MDTA certificate—his first academic success. I asked him if he would enter college if he could get a scholarship.

He said thoughtfully, "I'm not ready yet. I guess I'm afraid, but I've got a lot of adjusting to do and so much to learn about myself. It'll take a while. I got to go slowly. People don't understand."

William proved to be reachable, but not every youth in these programs is. Not reachable was the Lamb, a younger brother of Wiz. The Lamb, eighteen at the time I met him, was tall and gracefully lithe, with large brown eyes and handsome features. Too often his eyes were clouded with sadness, the corners of his mouth drooped, and his general air indicated despondency and despair to any sensitive observer. He had been among those who taunted the teachers, using any delaying tactic to thwart progress in learning. He was a follower, and William was his leader—in the beginning.

There is usually a correlation between poor academic progress and behavioral aberrations. This was borne out in the Lamb's case: he was at only a fourth-grade reading level. His method of compensating for this reading inadequacy was to try to cause disruptions. Despite tutoring in remedial reading, he was too restless to sit in class for more than two minutes. He couldn't listen.

When his leader, William, became interested in class activities, the Lamb at first showed behavioral changes: he came to class with his notebook, and his span of attention increased. Such changes were short-lived, however. Not long thereafter the Lamb was absent without notice for four days. He returned in a sullen and belligerent mood, threatening to beat up the principal. He was tired of going to school. He was bored. I talked to him in private counseling sessions. His remarks were incoherent, and he had a glassy stare. He seemed so emotionally disturbed that long-term psychiatric care was indicated, but it was not available.

If the Lamb had been able to take advantage of psychiatric care, the sad series of events that followed might have been prevented. The Lamb was dropped from the program for nonattendance; he lost a series of manual labor jobs provided by the State Department of Employment; and he was "kicked out" of his home.

The Lamb's father was searching for his stolen pickup truck and found it in the neighborhood. When he looked into the cab, he saw his son, the Lamb, with a silk stocking covering his head and face, slumped in the driver's seat as if sleeping. His father opened the door of the cab, and as he did so, the limp, cold body of his son fell out. The Lamb had been shot in the lower right side of his back. The police report indicated instantaneous death.

It was later learned that since being dropped from school, the Lamb had gone back to his former companions, who were engaged in nightly criminal forays. On this particular occasion he had taken his father's truck as a getaway car and with two accomplices had stolen $200 from a neighborhood grocery store. They were not caught.

The police figured that the Lamb's accomplices, fearing he would confess and implicate them, killed him. Two days later they were apprehended, and they are now serving time for robbery and murder.

Among these young people, moodiness is a common deterrent to learning. Frequently, especially in the early stages of each program, you will observe students sitting there completely abstracted. When you talk to them, they snap back, "Don't bother me. I'm not in the mood to work today. I'm thinking of my problems."

Marietta was subject to such moods. She was tall, slender, and always neatly groomed. Her large dark eyes, heavily made up, gave her a brooding look. Her hair, worn in a high style, had two curls plastered down, one practically covering the right eye and the other reaching to her left nostril. She was overly attentive to her coiffure, making innumerable trips to the rest room to keep it in place.

Her moods were unpredictable. On days when she felt good, she worked conscientiously and participated vigorously. On such occasions she revealed her keen ability at repartee. Her retorts to her classmates were witty and humorous. She was seldom absent or late. She had potentialities for developing into an effective clerical employee, if only she could be less inclined to yield to moods.

Emerging changes in her behavior were noticeable as the general office clerk program proceeded: her tolerance of frustration increased, her visits to the rest room decreased, and her periods of sulkiness became more infrequent.

There was other evidence of changes in attitudes and behavior. Mahalia, previously quiet and nonparticipating, was also beginning to change. Her voice, once inaudible, almost went to the other extreme. She was dressing more stylishly, whereas previously her clothes had looked frumpy and matronly. She was trying hard against great odds: she had two out-of-wedlock children and often had severe asthmatic attacks. When we discussed her need for professional help, she willingly assented, but a long waiting list at the county hospital precluded individual therapy sessions.

One day toward the end of the general office clerk program, when the men had been sent out on job interviews, we had girl talk on dating and men. Both Marietta and Mahalia were vituperative toward men.

"No one fools around with me," said Marietta, one of the few with no out-of-wedlock children. "I carry a knife in my bag at all times. I never had to use it yet, but I wouldn't be feared to. If the guy pesters me, like one did last week, I tell him; and the way I say it, he knows I mean business."

"Marietta, I can't say we've been very successful in Personal Development." Laughter.

"That's true," said Mahalia. "I go with Marietta. We double-date and know many of the same fellows. I carry a gun in my bag . . . loaded, too. I've been fooled a couple of times, but no more. I don't trust guys, but I still like them. . . ."

These revealing comments have to be understood in the context of these young womens' world and not compared with middle-class standards of dating. The defense of young women in their circumstances against unwanted male advances, although seemingly primitive, is effective. It is the responsibility of those working closely with them to listen, observe, and try to understand the cultural patterns they have evolved to maintain their self-respect and dignity.

It is always encouraging to observe favorable changes in attitude and behavior after weeks of daily struggle. It is frustrating when these changes are blocked by administrative procedures, as an embolus blocks the free circulation of blood through a living organism. Such a man-made embolism occurs when the students' weekly allowance from the Manpower Development Training Act funds are delayed. In the beginning of each program there is a two-week delay, at least, in receiving the weekly stipends. This is understandable, because administrative procedures have to be activated. Still this delay is unfortunate at any time in the program, and in the beginning it comes at a time when the students have to adjust to school routine after undisciplined days and nights in the street—a difficult time for them.

When the students begin to receive their checks, it is then possible to work. For example, it is now two months into the basic electricity program. Things are running smoothly. Hostility has abated. Effective rapport has been established. A few students are beginning to budget. Many, for the first time, are involved in learning, so much so that they are suggesting assignments and completing them. They are taking an interest in their appearance and becoming aware of their capabilities. Suddenly, without warning, the weekly allowances are again delayed— two, three, and four weeks. This is a terrible blow.

"Just when I was beginning to pay my debts," said Deacon. "Now what do I do?"

"Yeah," said Coolsann. "I was figuring on getting out of my nightly racket. Now I'm stuck. What's the good of all this learning if I got to worry about eating and feeding my two kids? I can't afford to go to school without pay. I got too many responsibilities."

Delay in receiving checks often meant returning to hustling at night, with all the risks involved: possible arrest, and absence from school and subsequent expulsion.

The few students who arrived during these periods of check delays were so sleepy and hungry that they were in no condition for learning. The process of favorable change was broken.

In order to prevent the students from reverting completely, they had to be fed. I brought in cheese and crackers, which they ate ravenously in spite of their dislike for cheese in any form. Then we were able to discuss action: we decided to investigate reasons for delays. Two students, official representatives of the recently organized student council, and I met with the principal, who advised us to see the head of the state employment office because this problem was outside his jurisdiction. We received even less satisfaction from the state employment office, whose representatives had had no success in learning reasons for check delays from their superiors in the state capital.

What should we do? "You know what?" I said. "Why not write to our state assemblymen?"

"They don't do anything, so what's the use?" replied Deacon.

"I'm not discouraged. You'll change your attitude when you see results, but these won't be brought about by sitting still. You have to use every legitimate channel, and this you haven't done. I'll make you an offer. I'll write letters to the assemblymen, too, but I won't mail them until you write yours. I've already talked to the principal and the heads of the state employment department, and we have their approval.

We wrote the letters. The procrastinators were again goaded on by the others, and individual letters were ready by the end of the week. When the students' will to correct their letters waned, I reminded them of our agreement. They asked me to read my letter.

"Did you write that all by yourself?" asked Randy. "It's terrific."

After we had mailed the letters, the refrain still persisted: "You'll see, nothin's going to happen. No one cares if we get evictions or are hungry. We just statistics."

Two weeks later there was great excitement; we had received replies from the two state assemblymen. For the students it was their first response from a government official, and they were proud.

"I was addressed like a person. I was called 'Mr.,' not 'boy.' "

There were still the doubters and suspicious ones.

"You fools," said Duke, "the politicians playing with you. Nothin'll happen. We not important to get excited over."

A week later we had another letter, concluding the assemblymen's investigation. Accompanying the letter was a copy of a letter from the head of the state employment department. It consisted of a list of projects and students' names with dates when checks were received.

"He's trying to evade the issue, that's what," exclaimed Stewart. "With those statistics, he's trying to make it look as if checks were on time and as if we be lying. He's saving face, that's what."

Shortly thereafter the checks began to arrive regularly once again, and there have been no recurrences of check delays.

The success of this episode turned the tide in favor of constructive action by the students in community affairs. In one of the ensuing class discussions, Ali-Tees said, "How about our own political group? We can now begin to speak for ourselves. Many of us are over twenty-one, and the rest will be soon. We got rights. Let's use them. If we don't want Uncle Toms in government office, let's organize. We should get a name first."

Several names were suggested: Youths for Reform, Youths for Rehabilitation, and Young People's Committee for Advancement.

"The first two are no good. Want the world to think we criminals? We aren't, so why give that impression?" Von was speaking out.

Young People's Committee for Advancement was selected. Now we had to inform the public of the new organization and its purposes. The students decided on a newsletter. For several Personal Development sessions thereafter ten minutes were allotted for organizing committees to prepare the newsletter, which was to be an out-of-school activity.

So far the students' community interest was only talk. It was not translated into action until the appearance of a guest, a retired black naval petty officer. This man, in his early forties at the time of his retirement, had entered the Navy at the age of seventeen with only a tenth-grade Louisiana education. Currently he was completing requirements for a bachelor's degree. The students were questioning: What had happened to him to change his attitude? How did he do it?

He grew up in poverty and had been angry at the world. Before he entered the Navy, he was always ready for a fight. If there weren't any, he'd start one. He provoked teachers and dropped out of school in the tenth grade. Violence was always his answer to frustrations. Even in the Navy he got into fights, and this delayed his promotions.

"I finally got sense. I decided to get to know as much as my white commanding officers. I began to read—books, articles, etc.—and finished my high school requirements. When I retired from the Navy, I enrolled at junior college, finished that, and then went on to regular college. I get my degree next week. I'm still not satisfied, and I'm already set to go on for my master's degree in social science. What's all this for? Just for me? I want to be a big shot? No. I want to help my people. Fighting and staying at the bottom of the ladder won't help.

His speech overflowed with imagery and interjections of profanity. The students were listening to every word. He had captured their attention with his humorous style. He was speaking their language. He was talking at the nitty-gritty level.

"I haven't finished yet. I got a purpose in coming here. I need your help. We got to help our people get an education. I feel we got to work with the children. How many have had fairy tales read to them? Did you? Will you help?"

"How?" asked Edward Emile Edlow.

"By volunteering at night to tutor little children in this free school I've set up in a church in this city. I've had it going for two months, five nights a week. It's not limited to children, either. Even college students want to learn how to take examinations. They need tutoring. Funny thing, the majority of tutors who volunteer their services are white. Know what? They're the most steady, not our people, and they're teachers, lawyers, businessmen who work hard all day on their jobs. And yet the rest of the neighborhood that don't even know what we're doing are hostile to these whites—just because they hostile to any whites, as I was, too, before I got sense. Why should it be this way? So I need your help. You know what it means to be in a bag. It'll make you feel good to be doing something constructive for your own people. Let's get names and the times you can come."

Duke said, "That's against my principles, to help for nothing."

"That ain't for nothing, you dope," said Wiz. "It's for us. We doing a lot of talking about getting out of the bag, so how about a little action?"

Several of the students volunteered. The next morning Edward Emile Edlow, Lionel, and Wiz reported on their first tutorial experience.

"Gosh, what a night! I could never get the kids to sit down long enough to teach them to read. They were parading or going to the tiolet." The students laughed knowingly, shaking their fingers at each other.

Lionel was pleased with his ability to teach mathematics and interest a few children. It bolstered his ego. Each day following their volunteer work they returned to class with an evangelistic urge to transmit their enthusiasm to the others.

When the antipoverty program under the Johnson administration was being organized, Anton came in one morning during the last weeks of the basic electricity program with exciting news.

"Know what? With all the discussions we been having on assuming responsibility for our actions and changes in our conditions, I've been campaigning for council member of my area's antipoverty board. I wanted to surprise you and tell you only if my campaign was successful. It was. Last night I was elected. I'm the only teen-ager on the board. What's more, I'm not getting paid, and I'm still doing it. Ain't that a change? I knew it'd please you."

Anton has not only persisted in his efforts to improve conditions in his area, but he has managed to inspire other students in the group to take similar action in their communities.

Two-thirds of the way through the first general office clerk and office boy programs, we were really learning how to work together. By this time, the students were interested in showing their parents, their friends, the Center staff, and the school administrators how much they had learned. They decided to hold an open house. Committees, selected by the students, immediately went into action, planning and preparing the program, invitations, decorations, refreshments, signs, exhibits, and reception. There was tension and excitement in the air for the next two weeks.

Committee chairmen met each afternoon after school to report on their progress. Committees that needed prodding got it. The two office boy members of the signs committee were missing at each of these meetings. For two days no one had seen them. I became worried and investigated. They were closeted in the counseling room; I found them sitting on the floor, surrounded by newly made signs, glitter, paints, and ink. They were so absorbed in printing that they never heard me open the door. I closed it and quietly left.

The students decided to create a skit as the entertainment feature of the evening.

"Why don't we role-play it?" said Jessie.

"That'd be great," said Mahalia. "Why not two scenes, a 'Before Training' and an 'After Training,' to show where we had to start when we came?"

"At the bottom," said Bailey, laughing. "We better hope the audience don't get confused and think the 'Before' is what we learned." More laughter. Mahalia volunteered to make up a few lines to introduce the scenes, to prevent misinterpretation by the audience.

"Let's work the 'Before' scene out now. The 'After' one will be easy. In that one we'll show how to act right in an office, how to dress, how to cooperate with others, how to conduct yourself in an employment interview, how to follow instructions, and how to act on a job," said Susie.

This Personal Development session was devoted to structuring the "Before" scene, selecting the cast, and deciding on props. Marietta was the leading lady; Bailey was the boss; Susie, Belle, Sarah, and Dick were the general office clerks and typists; Jessie and Rosetta were job applicants; and Mahalia was the stage director.

There was still too much delay in preparing the imaginary stage. "You're wasting your own time," barked Bailey authoritatively. "Act like real actors. Come on."

"Well, I'm the leading lady," said Marietta. "I has to look good, you know." She took out her comb and for the hundredth time poked it through her bangs and curlicues. Her large eyes caught your attention. They were round, expressive, and encased in layers of eyeliner and mascara.

The "Before Training" scene was now being improvised. Bailey, playing the boss, was lying on top of the desk with his head down, poring over pictures of a beauty contest in *Ebony* magazine. His lascivious grin was visible each time he raised his head.

Suddenly there was singing in a loud voice—Marietta's. With a cigarette holder swinging in her right hand and mincing as if she were wearing an evening gown, she practically fell into the imaginary office— obviously having come directly from an all-night party. The students were as amazed as I at her improvisation.

"Man, was I popping last night!"

Dragging herself over to the boss, who by now was seated with his legs up on the desk, she threw her arms around him, overpowering him with kisses and hugs. The class roared.

Belle, playing one of the clerical employees, arrived at 9:30 A.M., an hour late, with her hair in curlers. As she entered and saw Marietta on Bailey's lap, she yelled, "Why don't you fire her? That ain't right. She's drunk. I smell it from here."

Marietta jumped off Bailey's lap, drew herself up to her full height, and said, "Look who's talking. You wearing curlers and sandals. At least I was here on time." Then she burst into unintelligible singing, as if drunk.

"You'd better go home, Miss A. Sober up and return tomorrow," said Bailey, the boss.

Marietta exited. Belle went to her typewriter and sat down. Three other employees arrived, a few seconds apart, each in disarray: one had on capri pants and a low-cut blouse; another, a house dress; and the third, a coat, a head scarf, and sun-glasses, which she continued to wear inside the office. All were chewing bubble gum furiously.

The phone rang and rang, but no one answered it. One typist was asleep at her desk, while the others ignored the rings. Finally a clerk from another office, Susie, rushed in excitedly, "Belle, how come you don't answer?"

"This is my napping time, that's why. Call back in ten minutes." Laughter.

Then Jessie and Rosetta barged in without giving the receptionist a chance to ask their purpose. Bypassing her, they went directly to the employment interviewer; and Jessie said, "We're here for jobs, my friend and me." Her chewing interfered with her speech. "In fact we'd like your job." Laughter.

"You can't have it."

"Is that so? Well, we don't like your attitude, and we're reporting you to the FEPC (Fair Employment Practices Commission)." More laughter.

This was a natural ending for the "Before Training" scene. Now we assembled for comments and criticism.

"With your rears to the audience," I said, "your voices are hitting the walls. Your lines, so impromptu and funny, will be lost."

"Marietta has to cut her part. She's dragging it out too much," said Mahalia, the stage director.

"She has to make it clearer, too, and not so jumbled."

"This is our first time. Now we've worked out the idea. Let's do it over."

They did the "Before Training" scene over and over until they were satisfied. Such voluntary perseverance was something new.

Creating the "After Training" scene took much less time. The way they arrived at the office punctually, spoke precisely and politely, answered the phone promptly, came to interviews singly, and conducted themselves—without coaching—showed more effectively than written tests what they had learned.

The evening of the open house was unforgettable. Over three hundred neighbors swarmed in an hour early. The cries of infants pierced the air, adding to the din. No one had foreseen that there would be so many people. The only publicity had been by word of mouth from the students.

Everyone was dressed in his Sunday best. The young women looked like fashion models. The older women's freshly starched blouses and dresses sparkled. Roberta, the president of the student council, made a dramatic entrance in her black basic dress, dark brown wig, and high-heeled shoes, with a long, bedraggled fur stole slung over one shoulder. Pulling her boyfriend, the same one who had previously kicked her in the stomach, she dashed over to introduce him to me.

The young men, too, looked like fashion illustrations. Their hair was crew-cut or slicked down; some wore shirts with ties, while others were more gaily dressed with colorful vests and expensive sport jackets.

No sunglasses or small-brimmed hats were to be seen. Belle's and Sarah's infants were dressed alike in clothes made by Belle. The colors, pink and white, were chosen to carry out the color scheme decided on by the decorations committee.

Elaborate wire cages, decorated in pink and white, were suspended from the ceiling. Pink crepe paper hung in scallops all along the bare walls, only partially concealing them, and colored balloons were gay, vulnerable pendants. Signs, many decorated with glitter, were visible from any angle. The bulletin board, edged in pink and white, was artistically designed to exhibit the students' typing, mimeographing, and outside activities. It was enlivened by photographs taken on tours and colored snapshots of Frank and Adolph demonstrating their weight-lifting prowess.

At 7:45 P.M., the reception committee, dressed in pink and white, arrived. They wore badges and immediately circulated among the guests as hostesses. Four, stationed at the entrance, distributed programs just off the press. They were so nervous that they kept dropping the programs. The hosts acted as guides to the typing room where both men and women students were typing madly to show their speed.

As I walked around talking to visitors before the program began, I was introduced by my students to their parents, sisters and brothers, cousins, aunts and uncles, and friends, who beamed with pride at what they saw. I was overwhelmed by their warmth, affection, and kind remarks. Marietta's mother, a large woman with a beautiful face and large dark eyes, was among the most articulate. She said in a soft voice, "Thank you for being so kind to Marietta. You must have such patience. She's a problem because she's so moody. She's not a stupid child, though. But if she doesn't get her way, she gets mad. She was good in school, but she got bored quickly. Now she reads and uses big words. I don't understand what she says. She doesn't call me stupid, but explains them. I'd like to go to school, but I'm too tired after a hard day's work. Maybe later, when the children are married, I can do it. I still have five small children besides Marietta at home. I'm so glad to meet you."

The educational administrators arrived so early that they became impatient and kept urging the performance to start earlier than planned. The refreshment committee sacrificed their participation in the entertainment by remaining in the basement throughout the program frantically preparing hors d'oeuvres and sending out for more food. Frank and Adolph were setting up the amplifiers and tape recorder, which they were going to operate. Mahalia was rounding up the cast. It was now 8:15, and the educational official designated to make the opening remarks was becoming more and more impatient. We couldn't begin: Bailey, who was to play the boss, was nowhere to be found. This was catastrophic. I dashed over to two of the office boys, Jim and Curly, explained our predicament, and was delighted by their response. "Sure, we'll take chances on playing the role. I'll be the boss in the 'Before' scene, and Curly the boss in the 'After' scene."

The performance went on without a hitch. Afterwards, the refreshments were served on huge trays decorated in pink and white. The cast was overwhelmed with praise from their friends and neighbors. The open house was a great success, and the students talked about it for days.

What had happened to Bailey, the original boss? I was in my counseling office several days later when the door opened slowly and a swollen head appeared. The face was unrecognizable: the eyes were so black and blue that they were shut, and the mouth was twisted to one side. The laugh was Bailey's.

"I'm so glad to see you," I said.

"You are, even after I let you down? You must think I'm terrible. Here's the story. That day of the open house, about six o'clock, I picked up my girl and was going to bring her with me. I was all dressed up, too, with a shirt and tie, like a boss. We went for a ride first and had a argument. She made me mad. I grabbed some beer and had a few. Then I drove madly in my brother's car. It has only front tires—the back has rims, but no tires. I guess I was going too fast down the hill. I lost control and went through a man's garage . . . with the door closed. The dude's suing my father for $4,000 damage, but my dad'll help him rebuild. I'm sorry. I guess I slid backwards, huh?"

Bailey continued to slide: his attendance became more sporadic, and he had to be dropped from the program.

The open house was an exercise in teamwork, self-control, planning, concentration, creativity, and communication skills. It afforded the students another opportunity to demonstrate their ingenuity, intelligence, poise, and increasing self-confidence. It marked a turning point in self-realization. These young people were beginning to prove to themselves and others that they, too, could achieve. Everyone was pleased with the students' personal development, but few administrative heads had ever been close enough to view the daily struggles to reach this point. They saw only the finished product.

What about these changes in values, attitudes, and behavior that we saw emerging while each program was in progress? Was this pattern developed strongly enough to persist in the face of obstacles when the program ended and the daily reinforcement of our personal contact was missing? How many of our students were able to find jobs in the capacities for which they were trained? What was the effect of being turned down? If these young people found jobs, were they able to stand the routine? Would there be a carry-over of punctuality and good work habits? What happened to their relations with their friends who were still hustling nights? Did my students return to this way of life when they lost jobs? What about police records? Were there any more arrests at the end of the program? What about the students' attitude toward family life—how did that reveal itself? What about their new approach to thinking and tolerating differing opinions? Would they be involved in improving living conditions in their communities?

Each program saw at least one out of ten students dropped—some for personal reasons, others on account of poor attendance, emotional instability, or need for remedial academic services. Those who remained successfully completed the requirements for the program, receiving the much-coveted certificate from the Manpower Development Training Office attesting to their employability. Those without high school diplomas remained six months longer to complete their high school course of study. They received both their high school diploma and their certificates simultaneously.

The final month of each program was focused on job referrals. The state employment service counselors at the Center, the vocational instructors with contacts in industry, private agencies like the Urban League, and the students' independent search through want ads and clues from other interested sources provided the job referrals. Many students who took the employment tests before the program ended and failed to pass returned only slightly disappointed. Instead of their former despair and hopelessness, their new-found faith in themselves gave them courage to take more employment tests with other companies until they succeeded in passing. The first group, as is to be expected, did not have the advantages of subsequent groups: employers' readiness to give these young people a chance increased with evidence of satisfactory job performance.

About 70 percent of the first general office clerk and office boy groups obtained jobs, although not all in capacities for which they were trained. The larger the company, the greater the possibility of employment for minority groups, especially blacks. It was therefore natural for our students to be placed in banks, utilities, insurance companies, department stores, and other large operations. A few students who took civil service tests received temporary assignments while they continued their search for more permanent employment.

The office boys had the greatest difficulty in finding employment the first year. The job development section of the state employment service had not been able to find enough office jobs for the graduates. This made clear the need for intensive examination of every possible avenue of employment for MDTA recruits.

At the time of this writing, one-half the general office clerks are still employed at their original jobs in telephone companies and banks, some having been promoted twice in the past two years. About a quarter have changed jobs at least twice because they were unhappy with working conditions or with the attitude of the employer or fellow employees. Those who are not working have personal problems like pregnancy, poor health, and care of children. The few office boys who succeeded in obtaining warehouse jobs have kept them.

The duplicating machine operators had difficulty in finding work in this capacity. However, they were one of the most persistent groups. Most of them took every possible civil service test for which they were eligible and pursued openings for clerks and typists in hospitals, army posts, and private industry. The interval between the end of the program and their first jobs was necessarily long. They were often discouraged but never sidetracked. Currently one-half of the thirty men are employed. However, only two have jobs as duplicating machine operators.

The graduates of the basic electricity program—all men—have been the most successful in finding employment, in spite of their police records. Only a few had difficulty in passing employment tests the first time. In fact, some received high scores in both the middle-class-oriented intelligence test and the mechanical aptitude test. A few basic electricity graduates are working as framemen for the telephone company and several are groundmen with the public utilities company. A select few were hired by IBM. Some have passed civil service tests and are now employed by the Hunters Point naval shipyard. One has been among the first blacks to be hired as brakemen for the railroad. Two whose police records prevented them from being bonded obtained employment through the Urban League's on-the-job training services.

Most of the students have been able to hold jobs even when the going was rough. In so doing they have shown their ability to forgo current pleasure for future gain. They have told me how difficult it has been for them to leave their friends at midnight in order to have time to be well groomed and establish a pattern of punctuality on the job. They reserve partying and staying up all night for the weekend. Mondays and Fridays are now treated as ordinary working days. In their leisure time these young people still visit their friends in the street, but they also spend time reading. Several are continuing their education into city college and urging their former fellow students to do likewise. What is most gratifying is that many have discontinued hustling and pimping to maintain legitimate jobs.

With the advent of the War on Poverty, some of the men have become community organization aides in the Community Action Program. They are responsible for working with young people to change their negative attitudes and behavior.

It is obvious that my former students have changed their views of society. They have become more active in community affairs, and many are now vociferous leaders in the movement for changes in conditions in poverty areas. Even more satisfying is the fact that only one student has had a major conflict with the law, and traffic violations have diminished.

My students have been instrumental in changing the food and work habits of their friends and younger sisters and brothers. Parents have been so pleased with these changes that many have enrolled in evening classes for adults.

Because of his arrest record, Duke was the last to be hired. However, a change in his attitude was apparent. When the community relations representative of the police department and other whites took such an interest in him that his probationary period was reduced, he said. "Well, I can't say now that all whites are devils, but I'll still work it out on an individual basis. When I find other whites changing, I'll change more."

Duke took his first job with an equipment manufacturing company, although the initial salary was lower than that of any of his friends and far below his previous nightly hustling income. He had to get up at six in the morning and go 16 miles by bus, but not once did he arrive late. Although he was the only non-white, he got along with the other employees because "I minded my own business while still cooperating." He didn't like the job because there was little chance for advancement. Through his own efforts he found a job as brakeman with the Southern Pacific railroad and now has earned tenure. He is enthusiastic about his job for the first time and gets along with his fellow employees.

Coolsann was without a legitimate day job for more than a month, but he continued pimping at night to support his two out-of-wedlock children. Finally, with the help of the Urban League, he got a job with an elevator construction company. He called to tell me he would have to ascend 150 feet, surrounded by only the metal framework of a sky-scraper under construction.

"Gee, I'm afraid of heights. If I'm sent up, I'll have to quit."

By the end of the week, Coolsann called to report that it had happened: he had lost his job because he was asked to ascend to the top of the building under construction.

"I told The Man I suffered from acrophobia. How do you like that? I guess the boss didn't understand and fired me."

Shortly thereafter Coolsann was in trouble. I was disturbed because for the entire year I had been working with him, he had had no brush with the law. Coolsann bought two tires for $20 from a bar acquaintance. The tires, however, were still on this acquaintance's car, which was parked on a side street of a San Francisco suburb. At 4:30 in the morning, while Coolsann was removing the tires, he was picked up by the suburban police for tampering with a stolen car. The police community relations officer of San Francisco who acted as liaison with the suburban police admitted that although Coolsann's account of the transaction seemed improbable, it was possible. The charges were later dismissed for lack of evidence: there were no fingerprints inside the car and no ignition keys.

Since that unfortunate encounter, Coolsann has located another job with a steel company. He is now living with the mother of his second out-of-wedlock child. He plans to marry her and discontinue his pimping when he gets tenure on the job.

Allen Williams calls regularly, too. He has been working part-time and attending a small private college in San Francisco where he is now in his sophomore year.

"Know what? I've been getting all B's in my courses, including English. I'm thinking creatively, too, now that I have more experience. You introduced me to poetry, and I really like it. This Dylan guy from Wales fascinates me. So does Edna St. Vincent Millay."

Ali-Tees has had a full-time job with a steel company. He has accumulated enough money from overtime pay to return to college full time.

"I decided when I was in the program that I wanted to be a social worker and help my people, and that's what I'll do."

Edward Emile Edlow, who had been among the first to volunteer to teach remedial reading to children, has been employed as a community action aide by the antipoverty council in his new multiracial neighborhood. Although he has moved out of Hunters Point, he has maintained his former friendships. He became so interested in working with teen-agers that he finally decided to help organize a club that would initate creative programs. He hoped that the streets would lose their attraction for the teen-agers. His hobbies now include creative dance and jazz. His brothers and he now constitute a vocal quartet, available for club dates.

Anton, the only white student in Edward Emile Edlow's group, has increased his status in antipoverty council activities, while still maintaining an interest in the club he and Edward helped organize. From a group of twenty, the ranks have increased to over three hundred. Membership is multiracial, with no restrictions of race, color, or gang. The club is being sponsored by government funds and private funds from churches.

William and Jim, the gang leader in the first general office clerk group, visited our basic electricity class the last week of the program. Both young men, employed by the Economic Opportunity Council, were distributing questionnaires to get youths' reactions to and suggestions for the program plans in the community. They were dressed conservatively, spoke in well modulated voices, and exhibited great poise and maturity. What a contrast with our first day!

Bailey has had several jobs since he left the general office clerk program shortly after his automobile accident. He passed the Federal civil service test and is now employed by the Hunters Point naval shipyard. When I saw him at a student dance recently, he proudly displayed his first month's salary expenditure: a set of upper dentures.

"Remember what you said? Well, I finally did it. How do they look? I got them yesterday." He looked wonderful, and I told him so.

Roberta, the first student council president, had married the boyfriend who had kicked her in the stomach. He had enlisted in the Armed forces and was in Vietnam. While Roberta's mother took care of the baby, she worked as a receptionist in a hospital.

"Notice my hair," she said when we met recently. "I don't wear scarves or coats indoors any more. Before my husband left, he bought me a wig. He hated head scarves, too."

Belle, who never could type and didn't want a clerical job, is employed as a restaurant aide in a cafeteria of the telephone company and is very happy. Her friend Sarah is home with her second child and, at her husband's request, will remain at home until the children are old enough to go to school.

The picture was not entirely rosy. Cindy worked as a file clerk in a social agency for over a year. She never missed a day and was never late. However, she had to leave to have a second out-of-wedlock child.

Marietta, who had never been able to keep a job because she was too temperamental, was now home with her first out-of-wedlock child. The father of her child, a former student in the office boy group, loved her and wanted to marry her, but she still was meditating.

In the fall of 1966 an unfortunate incident arose in Hunters Point, on the block where the first Youth Opportunity school had been established. This incident triggered the San Francisco outbreaks. The incident involved a young member of the black community and the police. The sixteen-year-old youth, suspected of riding in a stolen car, was pursued by a policeman and shot to death when he refused to stop.

The Hunters Point community immediately reacted, demanding that the policeman be charged with murder. Some people resorted to violence, and there was fighting in the streets for two nights. National guard troops and additional policemen were brought in, and a martial curfew was vigorously enforced. In my opinion, these outbreaks were less the effect of the death of one youth upon the Hunters Point community than they were the result of years of civil neglect, poor housing, inadequate recreational facilities, and rising unemployment.

However, in comparison with what happened in other cities, these outbreaks were mild. Although the War on Poverty had only lightly touched this area, it had provided the people with a new feeling of hope and shown them the benefits of constructive action.

The results of such a feeling were shown by my former students. For example, Duke and Edward Emile Edlow demonstrated leadership qualities. They took to the streets before any policemen or national guardsmen arrived and tried to persuade their younger brothers and friends to come into the neighborhood community center and discuss problems rather than resort to violence. Afterwards, their newly established committee, Youth for Action, suggested a program to prevent future outbursts. It was the consensus that the committee and the community could have controlled the situation without the intrusion of the national guard. These young people considered the imposition of law enforcement agencies an insult. By now they believed that they had enough self-respect to enforce law and order on their own.

These youths were, however, adamant in their demands for action, from government or established agencies. They wanted no more talk. They also wanted resumption of job training programs — which had been discontinued — and increased attention to job development.

They reiterated these sentiments on television when they were interviewed by the San Francisco press and later by the host of a weekly public affairs television program. Of the ten in the group being interviewed by the press, six were my former students. Among them I was happy to see Duke. I marveled at the continued application of what they had learned from our practice in class discussions. Wilbert, who was now in his sophomore year at junior college, seemed to have been designated by the group as moderator in what became a freewheeling discussion. He performed his role with dignity and poise. He allowed each one who wanted to talk to do so. He was alert, however, to check repetitions and to insist that everyone participate.

Each member explained clearly and logically the causes of the outbreak and offered constructive suggestions for resolving the problems. The members of the press were attentive and interested. In conclusion, Wilbert summed up the remarks by reading from a prepared "agenda of action" a list of each grievance, with the proposed treatment for it. The group demanded that action be taken on the proposals within two days.

Only six young men participated in the second program, but they were vocal and did not allow the regular host to change the direction of the discussion to follow his preconceived pattern. When the host became distraught at his inability to direct the discussion, he said to William, the leader on this occasion, "We have to hear from the Chamber of Commerce representatives. Stop interrupting." William replied, "You've been interrupting us all our lives!"

Both programs demonstrated improvements not only in the students' communication skills, but also in their ability to listen, concentrate, and pursue a topic in depth. The programs also showed that these young people were willing to go through proper channels instead of resorting to violence. Television had given the public the opportunity to meet youths categorized by negative labels, to hear how intelligently they analyzed their problems, and possibly to change their stereotyped thinking about these young people.

It was interesting for me, too, to observe that it was the young men and not the young women who took the initiative and assumed leadership on a community problem. This marked a significant change which, if it continued, could destroy the matriarchal concept associated by sociologists with black culture in poverty areas.

There was something else very evident, too. People from the ghetto were beginning to speak for themselves and to produce their own grass-roots leaders. This trend, if continued, could greatly affect the political picture.

The conduct of these young people during the two years since the first program of general office clerks and office boys ended is substantial proof of the impact of educating for living with its mutual exposure and continuing interpersonal relationships. The students and I call each other regularly. I have met the students' parents and friends, and they have met my friends; and I have tried to buoy their spirits at times when it was needed.

Surely we miss the excitement of our daily encounters and are sad that this program had to end. What we learned from each other and about each other has made us more fully developed human beings. For this we are grateful.

Summary

Sparks of change in attitudes and behavior among young people from poverty areas and ghettos are rewarding for you and for them. It would be naive and unrealistic, however, for you to assume your complete effectiveness from the single appearance of one change—and that only in words. The change has to be translated into action, and the action has to be consistent, to indicate the development of a new pattern, before either you or your students can pat yourselves on the back. Only time and continuing follow-up can tell the true story.

Retrogressions to infantile behavior, so noticeable in the early stages of each program, have to be understood as inherent in the process of learning and change. To chastise or reprimand at such times is to assume a punitive role inconsistent with the concept of learning as a mutual process.

Students can be self-reflective and self-critical if they have been exposed to a climate of mutual acceptance in which condescending attitudes are excluded and mistakes are accepted. If these youths have been responsible for breaking the cycle of favorable change, they will voluntarily return to it, resuming where they left off, with the necessary encouragement from you. Teachers must realize how difficult it is for them to change when nightly they must return to the foul conditions of poverty that beget antisocial attitudes and behavior.

It is understandable, therefore, that change and learning must be a process. Time is involved, and instant changes should be suspect. What you may assume are instant changes may be only a camouflage to win approval.

The struggle to survive in a ghetto-like environment leaves such scars on some young people's mental makeup as to make them incapable of being reached. Such youths need psychiatric care at an early age. Of course, removing the causes of poverty and rejection is the ideal solution; but some psychiatric care, even if too little and too late, is better than none at all.

When you observe how rationally most reachable youths operate and how creatively they learn to confront frustration and criticism — and contrast this with their former violent reactions — you realize the extent of their growth in self-confidence.

In working with these young people to effect changes that will make them employable in the middle-class world, you have to be ever mindful of a danger: that they may be trained to be robots, wired to react mechanically to daily problems. To do this — intentionally or unintentionally — is destructive to them and consequently to society. Contrary to stereotyped thinking, these youths have a contribution to make to the human condition. It is up to you to help them develop their individuality. You have to reinforce their positive traits, among which are their creativity and their keen sensitivity to hypocrisy. Your pattern of behavior has to be as consistent as theirs. They are watching you to see if your actions match your words. You have to be able to accept criticism as much as they.

Over a period of time, then, if a close relationship develops between you and your students, numerous changes in attitudes and behavior will be evident: increased spans of attention, more attention to detail, greater ability to follow instructions, improved work habits, more sense of responsibility, increased self-discipline, and reduction in self-hatred, anti-white feelings, and feelings of hopelessness. Imbued with newly found faith in themselves, impoverished youths strive to be recognized as the warm, intelligent people they are.

The test of what they have learned, however, is whether these changes you observe can endure and whether the students' lives are affected after the program ends. What is the carry-over — to jobs? to family life? to the community? This you will never know firsthand unless your relationship continues. Continuation of the relationship is essential: it gives these young people the reinforcement they need to cope with the daily frustrations and inequities with which they will still be confronted. After you have been working so closely, you will not want to sever your relationship.

Words are inadequate to express the feelings of pride, comfort, and joy that fill you when your students voluntarily keep you informed of their progress. Their new outlook and conduct of life is assuring. No longer will these young people allow themselves to be ostracized from the mainstream of society. Educating for living has given them purpose, dignity, courage, and hope.

7 • Conclusions

EDUCATING YOUNG PEOPLE FROM POVERTY AREAS and ghettos cannot be approached in the same way as educating those from middle-class backgrounds. Young people who grow up in poverty with problems compounded by racial discrimination have been compelled to develop customs, language, attitudes, and values entirely foreign to middle-class culture. I consider ghetto culture a different culture rather than a subculture. Middle-class values and ways of looking at life are common to middle-class blacks, middle-class Puerto Ricans, middle-class Chinese, middle-class Japanese, and any other middle class group. The middle-class black will have just as much difficulty in reaching these youths as the middle-class white unless he understands the crippling effects of poverty. The problem, therefore, is not so much racial as it is economic and cultural. Racial conflicts are there, however, and we should not forget it.

Ability to relate to these young people depends not at all on the number of academic degrees accumulated. These youths couldn't care less; in fact, degrees may even be obstacles. Success in communicating depends on how interested you are in learning about people in poverty and on how aware you are of their problems: what it means to grow up with every nerve tuned to a daily struggle for survival; how this affects family life; how our historical attitude toward minority groups, especially toward blacks, has emasculated the male; why life on the street is so attractive and gangs are so much a part of life; and how conditions of poverty have generated hostility and defiance toward authority, whether it be school, church, or law enforcement agency.

When you understand that gangs provide the feeling of belonging so essential to human growth, which exclusion from the mainstream of society has prevented, you can interpret antisocial forms of behavior more scientifically. When you understand that leadership in a gang is earned by fearlessness in operating for the welfare of the group—and that the greater the disregard of accepted institutions, the higher the status—you are learning about poverty. When you understand that status in the gang is the man's proof of masculinity and that violence is a manifestation of intolerable frustration, you are attuned to reality. When you understand gang influence, you understand classroom behavior.

Poverty must be the concern of everyone in the society. Educational administrators, teacher training institutions, employers, the church, law enforcement agencies, parents, government officials, and the general citizenry have to be awakened. Failure to heed the growing signs of discontent which are exploding into violence in big cities throughout the nation will result only in a holocaust. Our energies must be geared to prevention and not to repression. We do not need more studies to find the causes. Anti-poverty councils have given us opportunities to hear how eloquently the poor can diagnose and explain the causes of their frustrations despite their difficulty in expressing themselves in middle-class English.

Changes in attitudes and approach at every level are needed. Those in the vanguard of effecting changes must not be affected by fear of reprisals, such as loss of jobs, or by the taunts of those in opposition; we must have the courage of our convictions. Experience has proved the need for change in concepts of educating; and it is natural that change should involve tension and conflict.

Teachers afraid of losing their jobs, and educational administrators afraid of offending the public and legislators, must rather educate the public in the reasons for change. But no lone, small group can resist the pressures of opposing forces; what is called for is a new breed of teachers and educational administrators with leadership and strength who have open minds, who listen and observe, who are unafraid to try the untried, and who have one purpose in mind: to reach those in poverty and help them break the shackles that destroy their humanness and deprive the rest of society of the contributions these unique individuals can make.

Why was I successful in reaching these young people and in estab-lishing a meaningful relationship? The key—from the first day—was my attitude and approach. I approached each student as one human being to another, with honesty, compassion, interest, humor, imagination, and patience, and not as an authority to be obeyed. I saw each student as an individual with hopes, feelings, and needs, not as just something to be manipulated and molded into an employable product.

I didn't allow myself to feel disturbed or threatened by any outburst or unexpected behavior, but tried to interpret such acts as the students' way of communicating something. Therefore their initial acts of hostility and defiance — their restlessness and sleeping in class, among other things — were ways of telling me how they felt about me, about each other, about themselves, and about the world outside their environment. I didn't react by criticizing or giving orders, but accepted them as they were. Even on that first day I saw what they needed in order to feel like people, and what they needed if they were to improve their condition — in other words, what they needed to develop their inner resources. Preparing them for jobs became secondary to buoying up their spirits, crippled by continued rejection, and removing their protective cloak of seeming apathy and lack of motivation.

I listened and observed daily, and I found that the biggest obstacles to learning were hopelessness and fear of failure. Throughout their lives these young people knew few if any outside their gang who cared what happened to them: teachers considered them incorrigible and stupid; they were dropped from school; they had arrest records, and the police harassed them; their housing conditions were so terrible they had little room for sleeping; their mothers were tired after working and had no time to spend with them; and hustling was risky but necessary — what difference if you were arrested? The future was so bleak that you didn't worry about it. You lived for the day, and you really lived — action, action, action. Who wants the boredom of sitting in a dull classroom? You were labeled to begin with, and you had to live down to your labels: "lazy," "hoodlum," "delinquent," "dropout."

It was sad for me to hear Marietta say after the first month, "Why are you so good to us? You're the only one. You really like us, huh? But we won't be anything. We failures."

This is what I worked so hard to dispel — this feeling of hopelessness. It was gratifying to see that by the end of each Personal Development course, these same young people showed signs of increased self-confidence and fearlessness about facing the unexpected. Even those more difficult to reach, like Duke, were now eager to tackle problems because they knew they had the ability to handle them.

How are hopelessness and fear of failure and rejection manifested in classroom behavior? Sleeping in class is one form. To diagnose this as laziness and lack of motivation is to judge superficially. Sleeping in class may be saying many things: I'm afraid to face you; I'm bored; I don't mean anything to you; I was up all night and I'm tired; I didn't have any dinner or breakfast because there was nothing in the house and I didn't have money to buy anything. Other forms of behavior have to be examined in the same light. You have to be willing to face each apparent discipline problem with this kind of understanding.

Critics may say, "You're too soft. You have to show these delinquents you mean business. When do you teach them obedience and who's boss?" What is your answer?

Such comments reveal a conception of educating and communicating that confuses educating with exacting compliance and communicating with preaching. Educating is bringing out the student's talents and helping him develop fully as an individual with pride in his accomplishments and ability to think creatively and critically.

This broader concept of learning and educating is not common among educators and administrators. Educating as traditionally conceived shies away from a close relationship to the community and the student, thereby perpetuating the dichotomy that prevents learning for living.

Educating cannot be restricted to the classroom, but must carry over to each student's world outside the classroom. To pursue the development of a broader concept of educating you must not confine content to classroom and textbooks, but must interweave subject matter continually with your students' lives outside the classroom. In the beginning of each program, students associate school learning with textbooks—to which they are allergic. They do not realize that listening to others' opinions and being exposed to others' cultures is also learning. They have been so conditioned by their environment that they want no contact with the world outside their gang or social group. But as such subjects as housing, health, welfare, and employers' attitudes toward arrest records are included in the content, their negative attitudes toward learning change and they are inspired to participate in class and in their community. This principle of relating learning to life applies to any subject and at any age level.

If you judge your students' behavior by middle-class standards and leave each session hopeless about their ability to conform, you're off on the wrong foot. Changes in behavior do not result from lectures on what's right or wrong. Changes come about when we are aware, when we understand reasons, when we understand how we fit into the new picture. Change involves struggle and suffering. Therefore I caution anyone working with these young people to understand that educating is a process and requires time. Nothing will happen because you will it or force it. Favorable change will come only if each day you enter the classroom with no grudge or hurt for any verbal attack you received the previous day. But that doesn't mean you should not talk about it with your students. You have to let them know how you feel and why, but you should not place the onus of change on them. Learning, to be effective, has to be mutual. Your students learn to respect you only if you prove your lack of prejudice and interest in their welfare. You show your interest by including in the course content things that concern the students. Sometimes you work out solutions together; and from this they learn what it means to plan and prevent crises, what it means to think creatively, and what it means to criticize constructively and to be able to accept criticism. Do not criticize their actions, language, or appearance when you first meet them; wait until your relations have progressed to the point where you can both discuss these things.

From the very beginning you can set the scene for friendly give-and-take by arranging the chairs in a semicircle and removing the barrier of the desk. You sit down with the students rather than stand. Condescension and patronizing characterize the traditional approach in the classroom, so you try to make yours unlike the usual classroom. You allow yourself the freedom to be yourself and your students the freedom to be themselves. You respect each student as an unique individual even if he doesn't react to situations the way you do. You are learning from him as well as about him. You have enough strength not to give up even when things are worst. Soon your students will respect and trust you. Only then will their minds be open to learning. What about the discipline problems? When this happens, they disappear. You are not vengeful in spite of the way they act. You have set an example of patience and understanding.

This approach to educating is strenuous, because you have to be involved with every fiber of your intellectual, emotional, physical, and spiritual being. Every minute requires alertness. You have to be quick to pick up clues and use them, to spot moods and find out why they occur. The daily interaction, the mutual involvement, the affection transmitted by you, the element of suspense always present—these give each session the life the students need to replace the action they miss on the street. No longer are they bored. Finally learning becomes exciting and school interesting. Stereotypes of teachers are questioned. You find, for example, that when new vocabulary is presented in a meaningful context, the students learn it quickly. You find that when each success is praised, they get the needed reinforcement and their self-confidence and hopefulness are increased. The sad expressions you observed so frequently in the beginning are now replaced by expressions of intentness and greater inner peace.

In your use of innovative approaches you will do much that is overlooked or frowned upon by traditional-minded people of many ranks and professions. Instead of imposing a set of rules and regulations, you encourage feedback sessions on a regular basis. You want your students' reactions; only when their feelings are expressed can you have discussion and interaction. No matter whether the subject is police brutality or dissatisfaction with school policy, the students must be allowed to express themselves. Dissent is not only permitted; it is encouraged. You will be amazed at these young people's ability to cut through hypocrisy and pick out the kernel of truth. If you show them that you recognize their strategy of survival as proof of their mental acuity, you are accepted. You are "in." But you do not then condone violence as a reaction to frustration because you understand it. You are presented with a challenge; and I have seen this challenge met constructively. How my former students reacted to an explosive situation in the fall of 1966 is ample proof of their ability to react nonviolently to crises.

When you have earned the acceptance of these young people and they trust you, you are a friend and not an authority. You see their side. Now you have a chance to provide opportunities for channeling the strategy used in the numbers racket to solving problems on a job or in daily living. Even pimping should not shock you—this is a way of earning money for essentials. The ability shown in figuring out ways and means of earning a dollar illegitimately can now be transferred to the study of mathematics, to the study of language, to improvement of speech, and to reading.

In other words, to stimulate motivation and remove the sham attitude of apathy, you have to relate subject matter to the students' own life experiences, not to those of the middle class. Soon their brief spans of attention become longer, visits to the rest rooms are less frequent, and language is less punctuated by profanity. Changes are being brought about not from without, by telling, but from within, because the necessity for change has been understood and internalized. The students have been treated with dignity, not coerced. Their language and habits have not been criticized, but have been understood and discussed on a person-to-person basis.

Language is both verbal and nonverbal. These youths are extremely sensitive to nonverbal communication; any slight nuance of expression — a lifted eyebrow, a curled lip — may be interpreted as revealing your disgust and dislike of them. And you observe something like squirting water as their form of nonverbal communication. On the verbal level, you and they learn to listen to each other. You learn their language and work at teaching English as a foreign language to prepare them for jobs and entering the outside world. You do not interrupt, but carefully take notes of expressions which you will incorporate into your teaching of language. You do not criticize them for speaking ungrammatical English. You permit them to retain their language to maintain the security they need. Soon they will also learn the second language, the language of the middle class. Many are exceedingly intelligent and catch on quickly, even in conceptualizing, which is one of the academic problems you will face in the beginning.

Once your students understand your language and you understand theirs, they are motivated to learn. You have to be aware of any vocabulary you use inadvertently which they may not understand. When you become aware of your own language, you can translate into language they will understand. Then you generate their interest. You have seen how my students learned and loved vocabulary, incorporating into their own speech such new words as *conducive, chaos, psychological, belligerent, improvise.*

Most teachers are strictly authoritarian. They do not tolerate talking back, speaking out loud when not spoken to, leaving the room too frequently, sleeping in class, or expressing opinions contrary to those of the teacher. The textbook is their guide, and they adhere to it rigidly. The workbook is the test of the students' understanding of problems. Interaction and involvement are not considered. Obedience is the important key. Communication is a one-way process. Any variance from the middle-class standard is criticized and punished. Students are constantly ousted from the classroom, sent to the principal's office, suspended, and often dropped.

Authoritarian teachers are not able to reach poverty-stricken young people. Their unwillingness to let go of authority shows their insecurity; inability to relate follows naturally in such a situation. Two-way communication is impossible, and meaningful relationships never develop. Authoritarian practices imply a boss-subordinate relationship. In a classroom in which you are trying to dispel stereotypes of authority figures and reduce hopelessness, such practices doom you to failure. Authoritarian teachers never approach students as participants—only as recipients. Educating to them means accumulating facts. This is a narrow concept of educating, and it must be changed if students are to be prepared to face life intelligently and think creatively rather than conform blindly.

How do these authoritarian teachers evaluate their students' progress? Tests and tests alone are their criteria. If a student is absent for a test, his grade drops a level. I am opposed to tests as indices of ability and progress. I believe that learning is so personal that no one but the individual learner knows what is important to him. I consider written and oral reviews important for the student and the teacher if they are given a different connotation: evaluating the students' understanding of principles and diagnosing weaknesses. The student has to understand that he is competing with himself. Mistakes should be accepted as a part of learning. If repeated mistakes are made, however, your ability to communicate may be at fault. I object strenuously to a teacher's calling out grades and embarrassing the students of more limited ability. I use individual conferences. Using conferences implies small classes. In educating youths from poverty areas, MDTA classes have been effectively small, averaging between seventeen and twenty-four students.

If less emphasis were placed on tests and grades throughout school, students would be more concerned with learning. A grade on a test is no indication of a student's creativity, nor of his ability to get along with others. His day-to-day activity in class is more important. His degree of involvement is a better indication of learning, and a better measurement of your effectiveness, than any test. Tests that require regurgitation of information instead of critical thinking accomplish nothing in depth.

There are tests and tests. I do not like to use the word *test* in class because of its adverse effect on these insecure youths. I like to think of tests as opportunities to express thoughts in writing and orally. Therefore, I prefer problem-solving tests. You will note in the appendices that those I provided fall mostly into this category.

Am I being inconsistent when I include job tests in the course content? I do not think so. Ideally I would like to see jobs obtained on the basis of an interview and a performance test rather than the general intelligence test, which is oriented to the middle class.

Hiring policy in a few industrial plants has been changed so that applicants from minority groups can be evaluated on their ability to perform functions that will be part of their job rather than be eliminated by their inability to deal with standard employment tests geared to middle-class education. The satisfactory performance of such employees — those who were followed up — attests to the need of other companies to reexamine the content of employment tests. However, since I must face reality and want these youths to get jobs in the fields for which they are being trained, I am in favor of simulated employment tests.

How do you prepare students to pass employment tests? You do not focus on this in the early stages of the program. Preparation for employment tests is integrated into the curriculum after the students' confidence in themselves is built up. You may perpetuate their feelings of failure by confronting them with such tests too soon. You orient them by giving regularly scheduled written reviews, including problem-solving employment situations; these seem so natural that the students are not disturbed. As the students succeed, you increase the difficulty of these reviews. Gradually the students feel less threatened. Then you introduce timed tests. The practice the students get in working under pressure and the exposure to various formats increase their self-confidence; and increase in self-confidence is a criterion continually considered in evaluating any content item.

A few organizations and farsighted employers have united to try to change attitudes of other employers toward job tests as the sole evaluative device for prospective employees. Some employers who have hired executive personnel because they did well on psychological tests have become disenchanted with such methods of selection; they have learned that there is not always a correlation between high test scores and good performance on the job. They prefer to base their selection of high-level employees on intensive interviews and on performance in previous employment situations.

The kind of test to be given should be determined by the examiner's purpose. Multiple-choice tests do not allow for original or critical thinking: answers have to be chosen from a given set. Open-ended questions give the students opportunities to reason creatively, even if an answer disagrees with the examiner's. Am I being inconsistent, then? No; I am saying this: put less emphasis on tests; give diagnostic significance to them; and use them as only one of many ways of measuring students' progress and especially as potential means of pointing up your own weaknesses in communication.

Should students be grouped according to ability in reading? I can only use my experience to substantiate my thinking. The students in the first program of general office clerks and office boys had never had standardized achievement tests before their entry into the program. From the written and oral reviews, it soon became apparent that the teacher's difficulty in communicating and dispelling hostility was increased by the omission of such pre-entry tests. The nonreaders, or those whose reading levels were below fourth grade, could not understand explanations from teachers or peers. Consequently they acted in an infantile way, disrupting the class and blocking progress. Nonreaders and those who are below a seventh-grade reading level do not belong in training programs which are geared to the more highly skilled jobs. But such youths cannot be left out; they should receive remedial instruction to bring their reading levels up. This is a delicate situation; your approach must be sensitive, so that the lower-level student doesn't feel you are trying to alienate him from his friends or categorizing him as stupid.

I do not place too much value on the standardized achievement test. I have found that students catch on to the format and soon find ways of locating the key. They feel compelled to cheat because they fear failure — emphasis on tests as sources of grades is that destructive!

When students with reading levels ranging from seventh grade to over twelfth grade were in the same group, the upper-level students helped the lower-level ones and increased their incentive for self-improvement. The constructive effects of such cooperation were reciprocal.

What about grades? Although you may dislike them, they are still part and parcel of the educational paraphernalia. I am encouraged by experimental college programs where grades are omitted, and I would like to see this at all grade levels. However, since grades are still required, I prefer just *Satisfactory* and *Unsatisfactory* to letter grades. I am trying my best to institute this. Letter grades cause unhappiness and upset. On the day grades were given out, students who received C's and lower grades from other teachers — grades based on tests and not on such things as changes in spans of attention, etc. — were so discouraged that their learning progress was set back almost weeks.

To assist you in grading, and to give the students a feeling of sharing, you should have the students grade themselves and give you reasons for their conclusions. It will be interesting to see how honest they are in spite of their eagerness for A's. You must, of course, give the students the necessary instruction on the criteria for appraising progress: daily participation, attitude, behavior, initiative, poise, speech, etc.

"I sure changed," said Edward Emile Edlow. "When I first came in, I came for the weekly allowance because I was sure I'd be bored. I couldn't read well either. Now look at me. I can speak. I'm articulate. I like to learn, thanks to this class. I've changed for the better, but I still have far to go. I deserve a B."

How do you measure success in changing attitudes and behavior? Do you use a sliding scale in a series of psychological tests? No. Any favorable change in attitude and behavior — no matter how slight — from what you saw at first is a measurement of success. For example, if a young man who wore his hair piled high with bleached ends comes in with a crew cut, that's a measurement of success. If a gang leader who continually yelled profanities shows interest in learning and respect for himself and others, that's a measurement of success. When those who spent much time in the rest rooms as means of escape become involved and reduce the frequency of such trips, that's a measurement of success. When students who thought in "either-or" terms now consider a broad range of answers possible, that's a measurement of success. You have also seen many other changes, all of which I consider measurements of success. Each activity, each film, each guest, each new experience has to be appraised as a contribution to the furtherance of your objectives. And your objectives must be an integral part of the course content.

Does the disappearance of the authoritarian approach to education imply anarchy in the classroom and a completely permissive atmosphere in which the student reigns supreme? Of course not. No one rules in this new, broader concept of educating because there is a continual sharing. Teacher and student listen to each other in an atmosphere of freedom of expression. Through creative interaction they learn about each other's worlds and are exposed to each other's values and ways of confronting daily problems of living. The stigma attached to authority in these youths' minds — a result of former unsatisfying educational experiences — is gradually removed, and with it their seeming lack of motivation. The reciprocity implied in this concept of educating engenders mutual respect and effects communication. Instead of anarchy or dictatorship, there is truly a practicing democracy in the classroom. When this happens, stereotypes go by the board.

Not every teacher is equipped to be effective with these youths. What about this new breed of teacher? How do you describe him? Sex, color, age, religion, place of origin — these are of no consequence. The most important prerequisites are sincere interest in working with these young people and faith in their ability to achieve. There must also be warmth and tenderness, humor, imagination, a broad perspective on life, many interests, curiosity about things and people, intuitiveness, and an open mind filled with question marks instead of periods. These must be combined with faith in oneself, respect for others, strength to withstand verbal attacks and other forms of expressed hostility, physical stamina, and integrity.

Even for teachers with these attributes, effectiveness is limited by the administrator's concepts of educating. If the administrator clings to the authoritarian approach, a teacher can become as frustrated as his students. The kind of attitude and approach we have been talking about cannot be relegated to the classroom, and the burden of responsibility cannot be placed on the teacher alone. Administrators have to become more aware of the problems of the ghetto and poverty and feel the need for changing the educational system; and this is true of administrators all along the chain of command, right to the central offices where teachers are selected and where educational policy and curricula are formulated. When administrators understand the character of poverty, they know that credentials cannot be the sole criteria for selecting the specially qualified teacher.

The problem then arises: where can we find this kind of teacher? In the ranks, in teacher training institutions, and in the community. Teachers with these qualifications are to be found at all levels in the educational system, but because this broader concept of educating is not popular such teachers have not been duly recognized. They constitute a minority, and they would welcome a new look at their creative talents as well as the opportunity to utilize them.

Administrators have to break out of the authoritarian bind and establish regular lines of communication with teachers. Both groups will increase their understanding of the problems involved in educating youths from poverty areas if dialogues are encouraged between teachers with relevant experiences and orientation and teachers without them. The lively discussions that would ensue would change the complexion of in-service sessions, which could become a delight instead of a chore.

Teachers who have been effective in working with youths from poverty areas could, by sharing their experiences, destroy the myths attached to culturally different groups, and fears of assignment to poverty areas would be allayed.

The criteria for assignments of teachers to poverty areas have to be reevaluated. A teacher's own feelings, his willingness, and the attributes I have discussed should be the criteria. An arbitrarily assigned teacher may be an unhappy teacher, an affront to the dignity of these sensitive youths. As broader concepts of educating replace the traditional ones, and as the format of in-service sessions changes, more and more teachers of the new breed will become available.

Teacher training institutions—or, as I prefer to call them, teacher education institutions—also have to reexamine their concepts of educating and their curricula in light of this era's needs. Student teachers usually practice in laboratory schools where they are confronted with children from middle-class homes; and therefore these student teachers are being deprived of learning about the problems of poverty. Some of the more farsighted institutions are experimenting with work-study plans in poverty areas; teachers so educated will be assets to any community.

The criteria for teachers' credentials also need reexamination. In poverty areas, teachers with broad interests and experiences in other fields—if they have what these students call "soul" and can get down to the "nitty-gritty" level—can be more effective than teachers who have had only teaching experience in the more formal sense.

More effective lines of communication are still needed to bring about better understanding among teachers, administrators, other professions, and the community. Among the teachers now engaged in teaching impoverished youths, there must be regular channels established for sharing common problems and evaluating practices. The frequency of meetings can be determined by the students' needs, but the fundamental ingredient must be continuity. It may be advisable when discussing some students' problems to have them present to give their own interpretation. At others, psychologists can be invited to participate—not to lecture.

At intervals, too, there should be interagency sessions, with representatives from social services, health departments, hospitals, housing administrations, and law enforcement agencies, to examine problems more broadly. If this were done regularly, the various professions would learn about, and dispel their stereotypes of, each other.

Changes indicated by such mutual-exchange sessions should be translated into action. For example, the comments of teachers who have worked effectively in poverty areas should be considered in formulating educational policy and planning curricula at the top level. Instead of having administrators represent teachers on planning committees, teacher practitioners from the poverty areas should be the participants, not the observers.

For a more comprehensive approach to educating, the educational hierarchy and teachers must work more closely with parents and the community. The residents of each poverty area or ghetto should be consulted and included in the planning and execution of programs. Their opinions on who their leaders are should be considered. Leaders publicized and sponsored by established agencies are seldom the real leaders. Any program—whether it be job training, health, recreation, welfare, or law enforcement—has to be evolved with those living in poverty or in the ghetto, not presented to them as a *fait accompli*, if it is to be effective. The poor are no longer inarticulate or submissive. They are more sophisticated in many areas of living than any middle-class group. As a result they will rebel against attempts to prevent them from being heard and effecting changes in their condition.

The salary and fringe benefits of teachers working in poverty areas need reexamination. I am in favor of a bonus payment as an incentive. The teacher would not be eligible for such a bonus, however, until he served a probationary period in which he would have time to prove his ability to relate to these youths, with feedback from them as a criterion in determining his effectiveness. Teachers paid by the hour only in this strenuous area of teaching are being discriminated against. They have to be credentialed as do teachers in any other educational division. Therefore they should be entitled to tenure and to all the benefits of tenure.

Under current practice, teachers in the job training program are as insecure as the young people they are teaching. Between training programs there may be a lapse of weeks or months when they are unemployed. The lack of continuity of programs is a major defect in the administration of the Manpower Development Training Act. It is a waste of taxpayers' money not to continue to utilize the valuable experience of teachers who have proved their ability to work with these young people. As a result of current practices, the committed and creative teacher often has to find work elsewhere. This is just as much a waste of human resources as society's neglect of impoverished youths.

The necessary changes I have been discussing would be more easily effected if more dynamic public information programs were in operation. Public education is not a single lecture at school-bond time. It must be continuous and carried on simultaneously with educational innovation so that problems of education can be understood in the proper perspective.

When these young people complete their job training program successfully, are they able to find work in their fields? Often they cannot, because they have arrest records. Attitudes of employers also have to be changed. Confrontations with the law have to be understood as concomitants of the struggle to survive under grim conditions, and must be evaluated in that light. Government agencies should lead the way by reassessing requirements for civil service jobs. It is ironic that private industry is now showing leadership in this area.

More emphasis must be placed on the job development phase of the government's job training program. Investigations of the job market have to be more scientifically and more strenuously conducted. The duplicating machine operator's program was an example of poor job development. Over forty students, women in the majority, were trained, but only three were able to find employment as duplicating machine operators. You can imagine the students' and community's frustrations and suspicions. Some private agencies can show the way in job development: Urban League and PACT—Planning Action for Changing Times—for example.

There is another important point to consider. In my experience, it has been easier for women to be placed than men. Government employment service management answers that this is not their fault; there are more openings in the labor market for clerical skills. This is true in part; but what about the men—especially the black man, whom society has already emasculated? If black family life is to be reconstituted, the men must have jobs. They have to be educated and not given meaningless jobs like raking leaves in parks and other clean-up jobs.

Only a small fraction of the population of young people in poverty areas and ghettos has been touched by MDTA programs. Recruiting has been at fault. Youths who have been made to feel rejected do not rush to enter such programs in answer to posted signs. Agencies responsible for recruiting have learned this, and now young people are being recruited where they are actually to be found—in pool halls, on street corners, and in other hangouts.

Ideas on the disbursement of funds for job training also have to change. The administration of MDTA has a tendency to allot funds for job training only to those cities in which violence has occurred or in which violence is imminent; this is foolish and dangerous. For example, San Francisco, because it was considered "quiet," was bypassed by MDTA, receiving no funds to continue job training programs in the fall of 1966. Instead, San Francisco's MDTA programs were to be phased out: programs in progress were to be completed, but no new programs were to be instituted. Then this lack of vision and thumb-in-the-dike approach boomeranged. San Francisco became a trouble spot, like Oakland, Stockton, Watts, and other cities throughout the country. Ghetto problems are all part of one fabric. They are not isolated instances. The causes of ghettos have to be attacked nationally.

Are these young people to be the pawns of political machinators? Should these programs be stopped when an area is "quiet"? What happens to youths, then, if they are denied opportunities that their brothers and sisters had? Are they to be compelled to live in a cesspool of human degradation? The Manpower Development Training Act has only limited life. What happens after it expires? Job training and education of young people in poverty areas and ghettos must continue. The education and training programs must become parts of the adult education structure, not stepchildren dependent on politics.

Jobs alone will not change conditions of poverty. Job training has to be seen in perspective, as only one of many ways to improve the condition of the poor. Ideally, changes in attitude and in the approach to educating should be happening simultaneously with changes in housing, health, law enforcement, and job opportunities, and—most importantly—with changes in public attitudes toward minority groups, especially blacks. However, the fact that in reality this is not the case should provide no excuse for waiting. Waiting and doing nothing until the emergency arises presages only national disaster. These youths' voices will be heard.

The narrow concept of educating young people from ghettos and poverty areas is obsolete. The more comprehensive approach to educating, with its acceptance of change and innovation as part of growth, must be propagated. Why shouldn't the educational hierarchy assume leadership in bringing about the needed changes instead of waiting until they are pressured to do so from below—from the people living in the ghetto or in poverty? To ignore their responsibility is shortsighted and callous. This is a many-leveled, changing society; and educational management must demonstrate its willingness and ability to foresee future needs and must have the courage to change accordingly. Failure to do so is to live in a false security, in an antiquated, unimaginative state of isolation and stagnation. The time for complacency is over. Changes must be instituted *now*.

Appendixes

Teaching Techniques for Teachers of Youth from Poverty Areas

The following techniques are a digest of the factors I found most helpful in educating young people from poverty areas and ghettos. The Criteria for Evaluating Content and Yourself should be used not only at the conclusion of a specific segment of content, but at the end of each class session. They will serve to keep you on the right track. Don't lose sight of the fact that the ability to be self-critical is just as necessary for you as it is for your students. Face your own weaknesses with self-tolerance, and don't lose courage if your students seem to progress at slow pace.

The Practices to Avoid are self-explanatory. Failure to avoid them can result only in perpetuation of the students' hostility. You are constantly under your students' surveillance. Try to match your practices to your principles without equivocation.

Procedures for Conducting Tours are again applications of the recommended techniques for reaching youths who have to develop a more acceptable pattern of attitudes and behavior in order to become employable.

Criteria for Evaluating Content and Yourself

NOTE: If the following questions can be answered in the positive, the content is meeting the students' needs.

1. Are you relating subject matter to personal experience?
2. Is the content helping the students to become more aware of the world around them and of their relationship to it?

Pg. 4

⎯dicate that the students are gaining in ⎯l self-worth?

⎯⎯⎯⎯ arousing the students' motivation, so that they become personally involved and interested in continuing learning outside the classroom?

5. Does the content include new and review material?
6. Are the students being given all possible opportunities for self-expression?

Pg. 5

⎯heir wavelength? ⎯t to talk too much?

⎯⎯ content helping the students to develop more realistic concepts of their responsibilities as prospective employees?

10. Are the students becoming less fearful of failure on a job?

Practices to Avoid

1. Don't criticize a student in the presence of his peers.
2. Don't preach. (In fact, talk as little as possible.)
3. Don't be condescending or patronizing.
4. Don't judge by middle-class standards.
5. Don't think of things in black-and-white terms if you want the student to be able to see more than one side to a question.
6. Don't be authoritarian.
7. Don't subject the students to changes without advance notice; they are insecure enough already.
8. Don't expect consistency in progress toward more acceptable standard social behavior. There will be many retrogressions precipitated by environmental influences.
9. Don't be afraid to admit your own mistakes.
10. Don't expect to reach every one of your students.

Procedure for Conducting Tours

1. *Share ideas with the students.* Share your ideas on tours with your students. If they don't want to visit a plant, don't make the visit. Ask for their suggestions.

2. *Make the necessary arrangements well in advance.* Make arrangements with the relevant personnel manager, tour director, etc. at least a month in advance, once the decision has been reached by the students democratically. When you are making the arrangements, explain the purpose of your program, and therefore of the tours, and the composition of the group. Ask for guides so that the group can be broken up into smaller sections. Where this is not feasible, or where the entire student body cannot be accommodated, take different classes on different days. Ask that the students be allowed to regroup in a conference room after the tour to be addressed by whoever is in the appropriate position. For instance, the personnel director of a company where there are possibilities for employment could speak to them. He can inform them on company requirements for employment, pre-employment tests, the company's attitude toward hiring applicants with arrest records, punctuality, appearance, employees' attitudes, working conditions, and fringe benefits. At least a half-hour for questions and comments from the students should be allowed. A tour should usually last from an hour and a half to two hours.

3. *Make tours after rapport has been established.* If they are to have effect, tours should be begun after the students are familiar with some of the basic concepts of teaching-learning and you are able to communicate with them. Tours should follow many discussions on work habits, attitudes, and dress. The readiness factor varies with each group, but on the average at least six weeks are needed to cover the prerequisites.

4. *Give the students, other teachers in the program, and the administration tour information in advance.* After the plans are made, share them with students. Keep your lines of communication open. Information—including date, time, location, address, and transportation available—should be on a bulletin board.

5. *Make daily announcements of the tour in class.* Every day prior to the tour, announce the place, time, and date of the tour. In spite of this, there are always a few on the day of the tour who forget or say they didn't make the necessary preparations.

6. *Have the students meet you at the site of the tour. Don't take them in a group like children.* Always make arrangements for the students to meet you at the site of the tour. You want them to assume the responsibility of being on time and of traveling on their own. This way, they are being treated like adults. Education should make a person independent. And it should instill the ability to meet new situations with confidence.

7. *Give out transportation tickets the same day—not ahead of time.* Wait until the morning of the day of the tour to give out any transportation tickets. (In my experience, when tickets are given out in advance, the students may lose them, give them away, or sell them.)

8. *Before the tour, explain its purpose to the students and prepare them for feedback sessions in class.* The day before the tour, review with the students what they are to look for, what notes they should take, and what feedback is to follow.

Role Playing

This is a sample of what these young people can do when they are encouraged to create. Their description of the plot is recorded as it was first devised, without editing. Remember that any misuse of language in role playing, as in any situation, can serve later as a basis for the teaching of English. Role playing also provides for the application of the students' ability to organize and their understanding of their relationship to others in a group. When role playing is elaborated as it was in this instance, it can also give the students an opportunity to use skills they have acquired—typing and mimeographing, for example.

STORY—WOMAN IN BLACK

> Written by Jessie, Mahalia,
> Jim, and Edward Emile Edlow

A man has been murdered and Mahalia has been accused for murdering James Mason. But she was supposed to have been at John and his wife's house playing cards on the night of March 16, 1964 between the hours of 8:30 and 11:30 P.M. The witnesses whom are John and Bailey are on trial now. John is Mahalia's witness and he says she was at his house playing cards with him and his wife. Bailey is against Mahalia and he said he saw her kill this MR. JAMES MASON. Mahalia was suppose to have killed him for his money and run off with John, the physician. But as it really happened, Bailey killed the man because he had money, and he tried to blame it on Mahalia for murdering this man.

Friday, April 14, 1967

WOMAN IN BLACK

An Original Sketch by students in Personal Development

Directed by Jim

Hair styles by Susie
Makeup by Mahalia
Costumes by Marietta
Stage design by Wilbert

Cast (in order of appearance)

Master of Ceremonies	Jim
Jurors	
Nurse (the foreman)	Belle
Author	Mahalia
Dress buyer	Sarah
Engineer	Dick
Attorney for Defense	Jim
Defendant	Roberta
Attorney for Prosecution	Emile Edlow
Witnesses	
Fashion editor	Rosetta
Doctor	John
Friend	Cindy
Bailiff	Bailey
Judge	Jessie
Court stenographer	Susie

Place: Courtroom
Time: Today

Sample Materials for Educating Young People from Poverty Areas

The following materials were found effective in stimulating thinking and discussion: Health Questionnaire, Vocabulary Development Test, Listening Techniques, Self-evaluations, Criteria for Evaluating Effectiveness of Employees, Characteristics of a Mature Person, Preparing for an Employment Interview, Pre-employment Tests, and various audiovisual materials. These help the students to become more aware of their need to improve their communications skills, and they provide the students with opportunities to practice these new skills.

Health Questionnaire

This questionnaire can be used early in each program. When the students find that you are truly interested in their health, a more friendly atmosphere will develop between them and you. Their replies will also provide you with content for future sessions. Health habits constitute an important area of educational content.

Self-Inventory Chart on Health Habits

FOOD

1. Do I have the daily requirements of essential food elements?
   Yes _____ No _____
2. Do I know what these are? Yes _____ No _____
3. Do I eat three meals daily? Yes _____ No _____
4. Do I eat breakfast? Yes _____ No _____
5. Do I eat at regular hours? Yes _____ No _____
6. Do I eat in between meals? Yes _____ No _____
7. Do I drink liquor OCCASIONALLY? _____ SELDOM? _____
   DAILY? _____
8. Do I eat rich desserts and candy? _____ HOW OFTEN? _____
   HOW MUCH? _____
9. Do I eat at home? Yes _____ No _____
10. Do I eat out? How often? _____
11. Do I do my own cooking? _____ If No, who does? _____

REST

1. Do I go to bed before 12 nightly?   Yes _____   No _____
2. How many hours of sleep do I have?   _____
3. How many do I need?   _____
4. Do I stay up all night?   Yes _____   No _____
   How often?   Regularly _____   Seldom _____
     Occasionally _____
5. Do I have my own room?   Yes _____   No _____
6. If not, how many in my room?   _____
7. Do I have privacy?   Yes _____   No _____
8. Are my sleeping quarters quiet?   Yes _____   No _____

EXERCISE

1. What kind of exercise do I have daily?   _____
2. Do I go in for sports? If so, what kind?   _____
3. Do I work out in a gym?   Yes _____   No _____
4. Do I belong to a recreation center or club? If so, what kind?

   _____
5. What sport do I like to watch?   _____

CARE OF BODY

1. Do I bathe daily?   Yes _____   No _____
2. Do I use deodorants?   Yes _____   No _____
Women: 3. Do I use hand lotion?   _____
Men: 4. Do I use after-shave lotion?   Yes _____   No _____
5. Do I go for an annual physical checkup?   Yes _____   No _____

HAIR

1. Do I shampoo my hair weekly?   Yes _____   No _____
   If not, how often?   _____
2. Do I use chemicals on it?   _____
   Women: Dyes and bleaches? _____   *Men:* Hair dressings? _____
3. Do I massage my scalp daily?   Yes _____   No _____
4. Do I brush my hair daily?   Yes _____   No _____

EYES

    1. Do I have infections frequently?   Yes _____   No _____

    2. Do I see a doctor when necessary?   Yes _____   No _____

    3. Do I need glasses?   Yes _____   No _____

    4. Have I done anything about it if I do need them?
    Yes _____   No _____

    5. Am I ashamed to wear them if I have them?
    Yes _____   No _____

    6. Do I have to sit up front in order to see the blackboard?
    Yes _____   No _____

EARS

    1. Have I ever had an ear infection?   Yes _____   No _____

    2. Do I have trouble hearing in either ear?   Yes _____   No _____

    3. Do I have a habit of poking things into my ears — pencils, etc?
    Yes _____   No _____

TEETH

    1. Do I go to the dentist at least twice a year?
    Yes _____   No _____

    2. Do I brush my teeth daily?   Yes _____   No _____
    How many times daily?   _____

    3. When did I go to the dentist last?   _____

FEET

    1. Do I wear shoes that fit properly?   Yes _____   No _____

    2. Have I ever been to a chiropodist?   When? _____
    Why? _____

    3. Have I ever had athlete's foot?   Yes _____   No _____

    4. Do I bathe my feet weekly?   Yes _____   No _____

Vocabulary Development

This is a sample of the vocabulary that developed from class discussions, daily newspaper reading, and expressions used by guests or, inadvertently, by me. The students learn to conceptualize if these words are explained with illustrations from their own lives. You will be amazed at the rapidity with which they use these new words and at their satisfaction with their ability to understand.

PROCEDURES IN VOCABULARY DEVELOPMENT

1. Use unexpected incidents or discussions for introducing new vocabulary.
2. Try to get the meaning of a word from the group first, before explaining it.
3. Put the word on the blackboard.
4. Pronounce it.
5. Have the group pronounce it.
6. Give illustrations related to their lives. Make the illustrations personal and concrete to help the students learn to conceptualize.
7. Review previous vocabulary.

Vocabulary Building

Can you use the following words correctly when you want to express ideas? Have you ever tried? Many of these words arose in our Personal Development course.

1. genocide	14. irrelevant
2. gourmet	15. inept
3. à la carte	16. deft
4. entree	17. infantile
5. connoisseur	18. initiate
6. à la mode	19. initiative
7. gullible	20. legitimate
8. har<u>ass</u>	21. lucrative
9. hazardous	22. maim
10. hemoglobin	23. metabolism
11. <u>im</u>potent	24. mimeograph
12. impudent	25. manifestation
13. influence	

Can you spell the following words correctly without consulting a dictionary? If you read daily, you will meet these words. Try to use them often.

1. simultaneously	13. soliloquy
2. site	14. statistics
3. cite	15. specific
4. sight	16. specifications
5. stimulant	17. sophisticated
6. subtle	18. stable
7. subtlety	19. emotionally unstable
8. superintendent	20. stability
9. supervise	21. subsidize
10. supervisor	22. subject
11. sustain	23. stencil
12. sustenance	24. stereotype

The following words have come up during the course of this program. If used accurately and frequently enough, they may become part of your everyday vocabulary, allowing you to communicate more effectively in the situations of daily life.

1. sympathy	18. conservative	35. personal
2. sympathetic	19. radical	36. personnel
3. superfluous	20. derogatory	37. coincidence
4. scarcity	21. beseeched	38. coincidental
5. supplement	22. endocrinology	39. controversial
6. supplementary	23. strata	40. controversy
7. sporadic	24. anthropology	41. deficit
8. tangent	25. differ	42. assets
9. tentative	26. defer	43. emergency
10. traits	27. deter	44. emphasis
11. turbulent	28. ambiguous	45. emphasize
12. tolerance	29. din	46. employee
13. tolerate	30. den	47. employer
14. transmit	31. dine	48. evolve
15. unique	32. static	49. revolve
16. revered	33. stationary	50. era
17. prodigy	34. stationery	51. evaluate

What do these words mean to you? Do you have a clear idea of how to use them?

1. monogamous	16. polygamy
2. monogamy	17. principal
3. militant	18. principle
4. militancy	19. pseudonym
5. motivate	20. pseudoscientific
6. motivation	21. phase
7. naive	22. phrase
8. ostracize	23. precise
9. perception	24. procrastinate
10. perceptive	25. euphemism
11. perceive	26. euphoria
12. phenomenon	27. promiscuous
13. phenomena	28. genetic
14. phenomenal	29. coagulate
15. physiology	30. meticulous

Are the following words familiar to you? We'll review these before the end of this program. Try to use them. The more frequently you do, the more quickly they will become part of your speaking and writing vocabulary.

1. perspective	16. resume
2. potent	17. résumé
3. potentialities	18. retaliate
4. poise	19. retaliation
5. polygamous	20. regimented
6. provoke	21. retentive
7. provocative	22. rehabilitate
8. ream	23. serious
9. retrench	24. series
10. receipt	25. unstable
11. receive	26. reverberate
12. reluctant	27. incoherent
13. repetition	28. tycoon
14. reside	29. typhoon
15. residue	30. mythology

Listening Techniques: Sample Telephone Messages

The following telephone messages are only samples to get the students used to listening and becoming aware of a speaker's message, and to help them acquire the ability to get the gist of a message and to record it in acceptable English. This kind of material also provides opportunities to review spelling and punctuation. The initial step prepares the student to increase his span of attention. Soon thereafter he is motivated to create messages which require thinking and formulating thoughts in acceptable English.

Communication Skills Development

TELEPHONE MESSAGES FOR DICTATION

Mr. Smith said the office was *too drab*. He will be more *specific* on his *personal* visit. Right now he can only be *vague*. He will call you again to discuss *personnel* and *evaluations*.

Mr. Davis called. He said he couldn't *answer* questions on *personnel* until he had *consulted* the *supervisors*. He expected *their* replies *momentarily*.

Mr. Smith wants *specific complaints*. He cannot make *adjustments* if you are *vague* in your *criticism*. Please *prepare* this *information* for your next *appointment*.

The *two employees* to whom I *referred* are *presently* being *evaluated*. To date they have *shown neither initiative* nor *responsibility. Their appointment* is still *tentative*.

Mr. Sox said it was *impossible* to see the foreman because there was a *huge explosion* in the *factory*. There was much *chaos* and *confusion*, but no one was *incapacitated*. He will keep you *informed* of future events.

Mrs. Duke, a *customer*, complained that the coffee table she *received* was badly *damaged*. One leg was missing. She requests *immediate* pickup and *replacement*.

Student's Self-Evaluation Sheet on Attitudes and Behavior

This sheet, which I prepared, can be used to stimulate discussion at the beginning of each program, for review later, and for frank self-criticism at the end.

HOW DO I THINK I RATE?	High	Above Average	Average	Below Average
1. In willingness to admit mistakes?				
2. In readiness to cooperate on tasks I don't like?				
3. In willingness to accept criticism if it is offered constructively?				
4. In readiness to help my co-worker with a difficult job?				
5. In willingness to compromise when the solution is to the best interest of the employer or company?				
6. In willingness to subordinate my own interest to the good of the majority?				
7. In being a good sport when the majority outvotes me?				
8. In being happy at the success of others close to me?				
9. In being tolerant of others when their weaknesses show?				
10. In ability to know when I need counsel from others who may know more than I?				
11. In willingness to listen to new ideas with an open mind?				
12. In readiness to accept instructions or directions from a supervisor or foreman without getting upset or angry?				

	High	Above Average	Average	Below Average
13. In willingness to share my ideas with others for the benefit of the job?				
14. In ability to discuss rather than to argue?				
15. In ability to reason rather than to lose my temper?				
16. In ability to curb profanity when angry?				
17. In ability to use proper channels in solving problems arising from the job rather than to take matters in my own hands to the detriment of myself and/or the company?				

Preparation for Employment

The *Criteria for Evaluating Effectiveness of Employees* and *Characteristics of a Mature Person* serve as appropriate material for stimulating discussion on what employers expect from an employee. The students are beginning to look at themselves in relation to others — in this case, to employers. When they go out on tours to industrial plants, they are better equipped to observe in everyday office practice applications of what they are learning.

Preparing for an Interview is self-explanatory. This is an essential. It can be mimeographed and distributed in the class to be used for reading and discussion. Role playing may supplement the class discussion.

The *Pre-employment Tests* are samples of the various test formats the students will face when they take employment tests. Including these in the regular course — at least twice a week later in the program — will prepare the students for reality, reduce their nervousness, and thereby increase their self-confidence. Timing the test will help them learn to work under pressure.

The students liked the *Open-ended Questions* about situations they may actually face on the job because these questions made them think. This sort of question also provides opportunities for the students to learn how to express themselves and gives them practice in spelling and in using new vocabulary.

Criteria for Evaluating Effectiveness of Employees

1. Punctuality
2. Consideration for others
3. Manifestation of interest in the job
4. Initiative
5. Ability to plan and organize ideas and activities
6. Avoidance of gossip
7. Respect for privacy
8. Ability to listen
9. Ability to accept criticism
10. Loyalty to company
11. Tact
12. Ability to assume responsibility
13. Ability to turn out accurate work
14. Use of channels of communication
15. Appropriate attire
16. Ability to control temper
17. Effective speech
18. Cooperation
19. Ability to cope with frustrations
20. Willingness to learn
21. Understanding one's relationship to company, employer, and employees

Characteristics of a Mature Person

1. He is self-critical.
2. He can accept criticism from others without getting upset. He considers constructive criticism helpful to his future growth.
3. He doesn't sulk or become hostile if he doesn't get his own way.
4. He faces disappointments as part of daily living.
5. He doesn't expect special consideration from anyone.
6. He learns to control his temper.
7. He tries to understand the consequences of his planned actions *before* they are committed. Consideration for others is important to him.
8. He is not hypersensitive.
9. He meets emergencies with poise.
10. He doesn't view everything as either "all good" or "all bad." He is aware of many possible shades of opinions in between.

11. He recognizes the rights of others to disagree with him.

12. He refrains from jumping to conclusions before he has the needed information.

13. He is not impatient at reasonable delays. He tries to understand the peculiarities of various situations.

14. He is a good loser. He can endure defeat and disappointment without whining or complaining.

15. He doesn't boast or "show off" to get attention.

16. He is interested enough in another person to listen rather than to interrupt.

17. He plans thoughtfully in order to live effectively.

An Employment Interview

PREPARING FOR AN INTERVIEW

The time you spend with an employment interviewer is very important. How you conduct yourself will affect your chances of being hired. To make the right impression you should do the following important things:

1. Know something about the company in question. Company literature is usually available in waiting rooms. An interviewer is trained to perceive your interest in working for the company. Your desire to obtain information, revealed by your knowledge of the company at the interview, will act in your favor.

2. Complete the company's application blank provided by the employment office. Do this while in the office. The company wants to evaluate your ability to write and to understand instructions. Watch your spelling and handwriting. Bring a pocket dictionary with you to help with your spelling. The application is a very important part of your interview.

3. Arrive on time. If an unavoidable delay occurs, notify the employment office *before* the appointed time of your interview. This practice indicates your sense of responsibility.

4. Dress neatly and appropriately—for men, a coat and tie; for women, a suit or a basic dress, but not a sweater. Check hair, nails, shoes, press of suit, etc. Don't dress in extreme styles.

AT THE INTERVIEW

1. Try to be yourself. You will be nervous. The interviewer will allow for this.

2. Greet the interviewer by his name, if you know it; for example, "Mr. Jones," "Miss Smith."

3. Take your cues from the interviewer. If he moves to shake hands, shake hands. Don't sit down until he suggests it.

4. Do not chew gum, and do not smoke unless you are permitted to do so.

5. Look at your interviewer when you talk or when he talks.

6. Sit up in your seat.

7. Be alert and articulate, and, by all means, listen before you reply.

Pre-Employment Tests

VOCABULARY REVIEW

Directions: In each group *underline* the word that means most nearly the same as the capitalized one.

1. DEVIATE
   demonstrate
   follow
   digress

2. MANDATORY
   required
   query
   direction

3. INCOHERENT
   unstable
   unnecessary
   unclear

4. EUPHORIA
   useless
   sense of well-being
   amiable

5. DISSENT
   go down
   ascend
   disagree

6. IRATE
   evaluate
   enraged
   congenial

7. SIMULTANEOUSLY
   taking place at the same time
   sporadic
   omniverous

8. MISCEGENATION
   misconduct
   misanthrope
   interbreeding of races

9. GHETTO
   city
   slang for "getting to work"
   section of a city restricted to
   a racial or ethnic group

10. AGENDA
    index
    additions
    a list of things to
    be done; a schedule

Directions: Fill in the blanks in the sentences with appropriate words from the list on the left. Remember that what you select has to complete the thought.

1. congenial
2. deterrent
3. congenital
4. stereotypes
5. condescending
6. intangible
7. mammal
8. provocative
9. illicit
10. priority
11. liaison
12. metabolism
13. voracious
14. discernible
15. connoisseur
16. fraudulent
17. promiscuous
18. perceptive
19. principal
20. principle
21. slander
22. rapport
23. gesticulate
24. whet
25. council
26. counsel
27. pugnacious
28. hostile
29. belligerent
30. italics

1. Much medical research today is concerned with investigation into causes of _____ diseases.

2. Some people who think in _____ are also _____ in manner. This can be so _____ at times that it can make you _____.

3. If you are _____, you see beneath the surface. _____ advertising will be _____ to you.

4. To _____ someone is against your _____.

5. You don't have to _____ your appetite. It is _____ enough.

6. Your friends often ask for your _____. It is difficult to do so without losing _____ with them.

7. He was the _____ speaker because he was considered a _____ in his field.

Directions: Fill the blank in each sentence with the word that makes the sentence coherent.

1. The plane suddenly _____ with a jolt.

    dissented, descended, decented

2. He introduced a subject that was _____ to the topic.

    criteria, congenial, irrelevant

3. Her design was _____ according to the critics.

    ad infinitum, original, chaos

4. Her speech was _____ to us because we couldn't hear.

    subtle, embryonic, unintelligible

5. I prefer to _____ rather than to rehearse.

    insubordinate, articulate, improvise

Directions: Fill in the blanks in the sentences with appropriate words from the list on the left. Remember to select words that will complete the thought and make sense.

1. congenital
2. congenial
3. stereotype
4. hostile
5. belligerent
6. eligible
7. contaminate
8. illegible
9. principle
10. promiscuous
11. principal
12. appropriate
13. council
14. counsel
15. rapport
16. slander
17. whet
18. connoisseur
19. liaisons
20. contaminate

1. Much medical research today is concerned with investigation into causes of _____ diseases.

2. He was the _____ speaker because he was a _____ of wines.

3. You will be _____ for the job if you pass the entrance tests.

4. Appetizers will _____ your appetite.

5. The students will be the _____ between new students and teachers.

6. It's against your _____ to _____ people because you do not think in _____.

7. Girls who are _____ are not for you. You like them to be _____, however.

WORD GAME

Directions: Each of the following statements contains an italicized word. Determine the meaning of the word by its structure, by its use in the sentence, or by its context. Place the letter of the correct answer in the blank that precedes each statement.

_____ 1. A *grotesque* figure is (a) dignified (b) proud (c) vain (d) ridiculous (e) humble.

_____ 2. To *defer* payment means to (a) pay it monthly (b) put it off (c) pay it immediately (d) cancel

_____ 3. *Obesity* means (a) fatness (b) promptness (c) coarseness (d) naturalness (e) affectedness

_____ 4. *Sedentary* work is (a) animated (b) sanitary (c) warlike (d) peaceful (e) stationary

_____ 5. To be *indicted* means to be (a) cleared (b) charged (c) jailed (d) arrested (e) released

_____ 6. To *affiliate* with a group is to (a) dismiss it (b) join it (c) defame it (d) betray it (e) imitate it

_____ 7. An *anthropologist* is one who studies (a) stars (b) magic (c) law (d) the human race (e) animals

_____ 8. An *insolent* manner is (a) insulting (b) overbearing (c) triumphant (d) immortal (e) modest

_____ 9. A person who is *facetious* is (a) sad (b) happy (c) stingy (d) proud (e) humorous

_____ 10. A *furtive* glance would be (a) friendly (b) sly (c) hateful (d) sneering (e) disgusting

_____ 11. An *egotist* thinks of (a) others (b) himself (c) money (d) politics (e) sports

_____ 12. *Culinary* habits pertain to the (a) bedroom (b) kitchen (c) garage (d) farm (e) ball park

Total right _____

VOCABULARY TESTS

Directions: Match each word in Column A with its meaning in Column B by placing the letter of the meaning in the blank in front of the word it defines.

Column A	*Column B*
1. _____ probe	a. appraise
2. _____ cosmopolitan	b. study of mankind
3. _____ irrelevant	c. dexterity
4. _____ tentative	d. changeable, unpredictable
5. _____ assent	e. twenty-seven sheets
6. _____ criteria	f. keep out
7. _____ inedible	g. sleeping, quiescent
8. _____ descent	h. not able to be eaten
9. _____ incoherent	i. unrelated
10. _____ ad infinitum	j. worldly
11. _____ initiative	k. investigate
12. _____ bilingual	l. standards
13. _____ specific	m. downward motion
14. _____ dormant	n. temporary
15. _____ ostracize	o. agree
16. _____ quire	p. endlessly
17. _____ agility	q. unintelligible
18. _____ capricious	r. ability to begin on own
19. _____ anthropology	s. able to speak two languages
20. _____ evaluate	t. to the point

Directions: Write in the blank the letter of the word that means the opposite or about the opposite of the first word.

1. *brittle*   (a) profound (b) unsocial (c) homely
                    (d) flexible   _____

2. *transparent* (a) studied (b) inclination (c) shawl
                    (d) opaque   _____

3. *extract*   (a) pollute (b) retract (c) inject
                    (d) interrupt   _____

4. *discard*   (a) dedicate (b) obtain (c) consume (d) obligate   _____

5. *positive*   (a) separate (b) negative (c) external (d) rafter   _____

6. *assessment*   (a) dividend (b) efface (c) reduction (d) loom   _____

7. *coincide*   (a) ignore (b) diverge (c) enter (d) proclaim   _____

8. *cancel*   (a) retreat (b) edge (c) zero (d) record   _____

9. *concave*   (a) caramel (b) flaw (c) convex (d) discretion   _____

10. *simplify*   (a) reduce (b) divide (c) complicate (d) sanction   _____

11. *annex*   (a) casket (b) separate (c) balloon (d) adult   _____

12. *sporadic*   (a) irregular (b) addition (c) regular (d) talkative   _____

13. *tenure*   (a) impermanency (b) holding (c) time study (d) regular   _____

14. *repel*   (a) attract (b) staple (c) poisonous (d) motto   _____

15. *confine*   (a) charge (b) slight (c) free (d) congenial   _____

Total right _____

Directions: Select the word that differs in some way from the other words in each group. Write the letter of the word that differs from the others in the box that follows each group.

1. (a) scorch (b) roast (c) freeze (d) toast (e) bake

2. (a) harmonious (b) hostile (c) fraternal (d) cordial (e) amicable

3. (a) alter (b) change (c) swerve (d) deviate (e) persist

4. (a) distinguished (b) disreputable (c) renowned (d) celebrated

5. (a) haughty (b) dictatorial (c) intolerant (d) insolent (e) servile

6. (a) freedom (b) subjection (c) liberty (d) independence
   (e) emancipation

7. (a) assured (b) positive (c) doubtful (d) certain (e) secure

8. (a) terminal (b) ultimate (c) final (d) incipient
   (e) conclusive

9. (a) exquisite (b) refined (c) graceless (d) comely (e) elegant

10. (a) sever (b) cut (c) sectionalize (d) unite (e) uncouple

11. (a) disregard (b) revere (c) respect (d) esteem (e) venerate

12. (a) overlook (b) pardon (c) avenge (d) forgive (e) condone

Total right _____

Open-Ended Questions

Open-ended questions are of use in testing the following:

1. Ability to think
2. Ability to express thoughts in writing
3. Spelling
4. Vocabulary

BUDGETING YOUR INCOME

You receive $85 per week as a trainee.

Question One: Make up a monthly budget for you and your family, if you have one. If you live alone, of course, make one for yourself only.

Question Two: Why did you give certain items priority over others?

Question Three: Have you tried to budget your MDTA allowance so far? If so, why? If not, why not?

Careers and Employment

Answer thoughtfully. Don't worry about the spelling.

1. What kind of employment would interest you?

2. If you had to work with some people you didn't like, would that affect your ability to produce? Explain why.

3. If someone says, "He has good manners and knows office etiquette," what do you understand him to mean?

PROBLEMS

1. You are now employed as a custom engineer for IBM. You have been on the job for a year. You are still in training and have not yet been released from the supervision of the senior custom engineer. You are, however, permitted to visit each customer needing service on your own, without being accompanied by the man training you.

Today your first customer is a challenge. The company knows it. As you enter the office of your customer, he greets you with, "It's about time you came. You know I already lost ten thousand dollars because the computer broke down. This is the third time in two months. Let it happen again and you can tell IBM to take their computer back. I'll deal with their competitor. Your company isn't king yet!"

How would you answer this man? Write your answer below.

2. While you are taking the machine apart to find out the source of trouble, this man peers over your shoulder, talking all the time. He urges you to hurry because he's losing money. You locate the trouble and begin to work on it. He finds fault with your dexterity and talks to you angrily.

Write your report of this visit as you would if you had to present it to your supervisor.

Audiovisual Materials

The visual aids listed below may be used to supplement the material in this book. The films have been grouped by topics, but a film may be applicable to more than one topic. It is recommended that you view them before use whenever possible in order to determine their suitability for a particular group.

Titles of motion pictures (marked MP) and filmstrips (marked FS) are included in the following list. Each title is followed by the name of the producer and the distributor, unless one firm performs both functions. In many instances, the films can be borrowed or rented from local or state 16-mm-film libraries.

ATTITUDES AND BEHAVIOR

Habit Patterns. (MP) McGraw-Hill, 1954. Psychology for Living Series. sd, 15 min., b&w

The habitually late teen-ager, who lacks a sense of order, is sloppy, etc., is contrasted with a girl who has learned the value of good habit patterns.

Marriage Today. (MP) McGraw-Hill, 1950. Marriage Series. sd, 22 min., b&w

Shows effects of personality on the marriage relation and indicates ways of avoiding the pitfalls that cause conflicts.

Obligations. (MP) Simmel, 1950. sd, 17 min., b&w

Contrasts two families: one in which the members do not observe the obligations of family life, with resulting disorder and bad temper; and a second where there is planning of activities, courtesy, and cooperation, with resulting friendliness and accomplishment.

How Honest Are You? (MP) Coronet, 1950. Personal Guidance Series. sd, 14 min., b&w

Simple honesty does not present much trouble, but in some situations honesty is a much deeper problem; it is this kind of situation that is analyzed here. Three tests of character by which this trait can be measured are advanced.

Having Your Say. (MP) McGraw-Hill, 1955. What Do You Think? Series. sd, 6 min., b&w

A community center committee, without a hearing, accuses a teen-age group of destructive behavior and denies them use of the center. The young people hire a hall to voice their protest publicly. The committee feels it should have a hearing at this meeting. The film audience is left to decide the question.

The Honest Truth. (MP) McGraw-Hill, 1953. What Do You Think? Series. sd, 5 min., b&w

Presents a problem situation in dramatic form; a student is forced into a situation where he must tell the truth or hurt someone's feelings. The film doesn't show which course the student takes. The audience is invited to discuss the issue.

How to Concentrate. (MP) Coronet, 1951. sd, 11 min., b&w

The following concentration techniques are shown: looking for answers to questions, selecting one idea at a time, avoiding distractions, and employing periodic relaxation.

Act Your Age. (MP) Coronet, 1949. Guidance Series. sd, 13 min., b&w

Consideration of the pattern of growth in adolescents, with particular emphasis upon the lags and gaps in the pattern. Childish responses by older adolescents to minor irritations are shown.

Control Your Emotions. (MP) Coronet, 1950. Personal Guidance Series. sd, 15 min., b&w

A clinical analysis of three emotions fundamental to the development of personality — rage, fear, and love. The narrator is portrayed as a practicing psychologist who discusses these emotions in two different situations.

How to Say No. (MP) Coronet, 1951. sd, 10 min., b&w

How to attain moral maturity. Teen-agers discuss this subject, considering how to say "No" to a drink, a cigarette, etc. One can say "No" and keep friends by using various devices, such as avoiding the situation or changing the subject, but in any case stressing the importance of maintaining his own moral integrity.

Neighbors. (MP) Canadian Film Board. sd, 18 min., color

Love Thy Neighbor theme. Shows the cumulative effect of violence through the bitter fight and struggle of two men over a flower which grows on the property between two houses. An experimental-type film.

Boundary Lines. (MP) International Film Foundation, 1947. sd, 10 min., color

A plea to eliminate the arbitrary boundary lines which divide people from each other as individuals and as nations — invisible boundary lines of color, origin, wealth, and religion.

Brotherhood of Man. (MP) Brandon Films, 1946. sd, 10 min., color

A clever animated film which makes the point that dissimilarities between people are not basic but result from superficial environmental influences.

House I Live In. (MP) Young America, 1948. sd, 10 min., b&w

An Academy Award picture starring Frank Sinatra. Community relationships, religious tolerance, and democracy are stressed.

PREPARING FOR EMPLOYMENT

Good Table Manners. (MP) Coronet, 1951. sd, 10 min., b&w

Shows that table manners are matters of courtesy, consideration for others, and common sense.

How to Think. (MP) Coronet, 1950. Guidance Series. sd, 13 min., b&w

Shows the process of scientific thinking by illustrating each step in the process of working out a significant problem of adolescents, that of fixing up an old car to pass traffic inspection.

How to Read a Newspaper. (MP) Coronet, 1951. sd, 10 min., b&w

Some of the basic techniques of newspaper reading. Headlines, leads, editorials, etc., are quickly explained.

How to Keep a Job. (MP) Coronet, 1949. sd, 10 min., b&w

Shows a contrast between good and poor qualities in a worker; getting along with fellow workers, conduct of work, attitude toward the company, and several other factors.

HEALTH

What Do You Know About Food? (FS) Society for Visual Education, 1952. 43 frames

Shows how to incorporate the seven basic groups of food into the daily diet. Based on the book *Homemaking for Teenagers* by McDermott and Nichols.

The Human Body: The Circulatory System. (MP) Coronet. sd, 20 min., color

Overall view of the circulatory system — structure and function. Excellent photographs of a working heart. Fine diagrams.

The Human Body: The Nervous System. (MP) Coronet, 1958. sd, 20 min., color

A study of the brain and nervous system, emphasizing the basic functions of the system, its main organs, and the various neurons of which the organs are composed. Microscopic views of nerve tissue, a specimen of human brain, and anatomical charts explain the nervous system and show its control of life processes.

The Human Brain. (MP) Encyclopaedia Britannica Films, 1954. sd, 11 min., b&w

Using a driver in traffic as an example, the film describes the thinking process performed by the cerebrum.

NARCOTICS

Write to:

Narcotic Educational Foundation of America
5055 Sunset Boulevard
Los Angeles 27, California

At a nominal rental you can obtain many excellent films on the subject.

Assassin of Youth. (MP) Narcotic Educational Foundation of America. sd, 19 min., color or b&w

Documents the tragic story of one teen-age girl, typical of youthful addicts. She begins by smoking marijuana, and ends up with a criminal record and a dismal future.

Subject — Narcotics. (MP) NEFA. sd, 21 min., color

The film covers the following: what narcotics are; methods in which they are administered; how they enter the country and the processing they undergo; the narcotics addict and his effect upon society; and the physical and psychological rehabilitation of an addict.

MENTAL HEALTH

Feeling of Rejection. (MP) McGraw-Hill, 1948. sd, 23 min., b&w

Case history of a neurotic twenty-three year-old girl. She suffers from headaches, dizzy spells, extreme fatigue. As no physical cause is evident, she is referred to a psychiatrist who is able to uncover the emotional basis for these physical reactions.

VENEREAL DISEASE

The following films are available from many local health departments or from the State Department of Public Health. They are suitable
for showing to school groups and adults. The films alone have insufficient teaching content, and they should definitely be previewed before
classroom use so that supplementary materials can be selected. Other
venereal-disease teaching materials are also available through your
local or state department of public health.

A Quarter Million Teen-agers. 16 min.

An important and authoritative film on the physiological aspects of
venereal disease, designed specifically for the teen-age audience
among whom V.D. has been increasing sharply. Both gonorrhea and
syphilis are explained in detail: how the organisms enter the body,
how the diseases affect tissues and organs, how they may be recognized. The need for treatment is stressed. Extensive animation is used
throughout to present the information objectively. The best available
film to use in presenting basic facts to junior and senior high school
groups.

The Innocent Party. 17 min.

A film about venereal disease in teen-agers, for teen-agers. A high
school boy discovers he has contracted syphilis from a casual "pickup".
He consults his family physician, who provides him with information
about the disease and the importance of early treatment. The boy is
faced with the decision of telling his steady girl friend, whom he has
exposed, in order to ensure that she also will be treated in time. The
point is made that persons who may have been exposed should seek
medical counsel, rather than take advice of misinformed friends who
believe syphilis is no longer a serious disease.

Syphilis, the Invader. 25 min.

Excellent historical film tracing efforts since the fifteenth century to
cope with the problem of syphilis. Portrays the development of medical
knowledge and changes in public attitudes towards syphilis. The film
is enriched with historical engravings and paintings. Particularly useful
in junior and senior high schools.

Dance Little Children. 25 min.

Designed for general use, but can be used in schools. Highlights conditions leading to an epidemic of syphilis among youths, portraying varying degrees of parental concern and reaction. Emphasizes measures employed to control syphilis and the close working relationships of the health department and the private physician. Probably best suited for initiating discussions with adult groups.

A Respectable Neighborhood. 25 min.

Designed for general use, the film depicts the harm done to young people when improper behavior is coupled with ignorance of venereal diseases. Points out that syphilis is not restricted to any one group and portrays local health activities for control.

VD/Venereal Disease. (FS and tape recording)

On the tape recording, a physician presents the physiological aspects of syphilis and gonorrhea. A coordinated filmstrip emphasizes the major points by line drawings. In addition to how these diseases affect the body, there is discussion of the legal and public health control measures. Suitable for junior and senior high school groups.

DRIVING

The Human Factor in Driving. Progressive. sd, 11 min., b&w

Shows how habits can become subconscious patterns and influence driving. Bad habits thus learned are detrimental to safe driving and must be broken. The objective is to demonstrate possible results of bad driving habits.

WARDROBE PLANNING AND APPEARANCE

Teen-Age Clothing. (FS) McGraw-Hill, 1953. 4 filmstrips, 40 frames each: *Grooming, Care of Your Clothes, Right Clothes for You, Color in Your Clothes*

This film is correlated with the book *How You Look and Dress* by Byrta Carson.

CONSUMER EDUCATION

Too Good to be True. (MP) Association of Better Business Bureaus, 1962. sd, 20 min., color

Dramatizes several typical "bait-and-switch" sales situations, including refrigerators, used cars, sewing machines, and home improvements. Warns consumers and also points up positive values of legitimate advertising and selling to the economy.

The Better Business Bureau Story. (MP) Association of Better Business Bureaus, 1958. sd, 28 min., color

"Investigate before you invest" is the theme of this dramatized version of three typical activities of this agency in its effort to protect the consumer against frauds. Stresses the importance of reading contracts before signing them, checking on honesty in advertising (especially when purchasing cars), and inquiring into the integrity of people soliciting funds for various organizations.

Credits and Loans. (MP) Progressive Pictures, 1960. sd, 17 min., b&w

Discusses all phases of borrowing and credit for financing a home, purchasing a car, and buying merchandise on the installment plan. Stresses importance of reading every item of a contract, methods of repossession for nonpayment, and the importance of shopping for credit.

Home Management: Buying Food. (MP) McGraw-Hill, 1950. sd, 11 min., b&w

The following are stressed: impulse buying as a waste of funds; importance of package size; buying in quantity, and storage problems; the value of information on cars, and the influence on price of season and transportation.

GENERAL INFORMATION

I See Chicago: Story of the High School Dropout. Illinois Bell Telephone Company. sd, 45 min., b&w

Presents in documentary fashion the problems of high school dropouts in a cosmopolitan city and how existing agencies are trying to combat them.

NOTE: There are catalogs of films available through the school departments of local telephone companies. Contact them.

INTERRACIAL RELATIONS AND THE CULTURALLY DIFFERENT

NOTE: There is a dearth of such films. The Anti-Defamation League of B'Nai B'rith, however, is a nonpartisan organization specializing in the circulation of films and filmstrips with an interracial and multiracial theme. For catalog, write to:

> National Office
> Anti-Defamation League of B'nai B'rith
> 315 Lexington Avenue
> New York, N. Y. 10016

BROADENING PERSPECTIVE

NOTE: Some industries — such as Shell Oil, Aluminum Corporation, Monsanto Chemical, and others — have free films for distribution. The various consulates also have excellent films, as do the airlines.
The following is a sample of films my students found exciting.

Grand Canyon. (MP) Disney, 1959. sd, 29 min., color

An exciting, musical, synchronized interpretation of Ferde Grofe's "Grand Canyon Suite." Spectacular scenery of the Grand Canyon, Colorado River and general region. Unusual.

A Raisin in the Sun. (MP) Columbia. Institutional Cinema Service, 29 East 10 St., N. Y. 10003. sd, 128 min., b&w

A feature film of special interest for a special occasion or holiday. Sidney Poitier, Claudia McNeil, and Ruby Dee. The Broadway play that won the New York Drama Circle Award. The dreams, ambitions, and frustrations of a poor black family in Chicago's South Side are dramatized with great skill and sensitivity.

Sources of Instructional Materials

"Instructional Materials for Antipoverty and Manpower-Training Programs," McGraw-Hill Book Company, New York, 1966-67.

Materials Available from Supt. of Documents, U.S. Government Printing Office, Washington, D. C.

U.S. Department of Health, Education and Welfare: "About Syphilis and Gonorrhea." Price: 5 cents, single copies; $2.50 per 100.
U.S. Department of Health, Education and Welfare: "Strictly for Teenagers," Price: 5 cents, single copies; $3.25 per 100.

Agencies Which Distribute Free or Inexpensive Resource Materials on Blacks

American Council on Education
1785 Massachusetts Ave., N. W., Washington, D. C.

American Council on Race Relations
32 West Randolph Street, Chicago, Illinois.

American Friends Race Relations Committee
20 South 12 Street, Philadelphia, Pennsylvania.

Association for the Study of Negro Life and History
1538 Ninth Street, N. W., Washington, D. C.

Catholic Interracial Council
20 Vesey Street, New York 7, N. Y.

Council on African Affairs
23 West 26 Street, N. Y. 10, N. Y.

Federal Council of Churches of Christian America,
Commission on Church and Minority Peoples
297 Fourth Avenue, New York 10, N. Y.

National Association for the Advancement of Colored People
69 Fifth Avenue, New York, N. Y.

National Council of Negro Women, Inc.
1318 Vermont Avenue, N. W., Washington, D. C.

National Urban League,
1133 Broadway, New York, N. Y.

Southern Conference Educational Fund
808 Perdido Street, New Orleans, Louisiana.

Suggested Supplementary Reading

Bois, Samuel J.: *Explorations in Awareness*, Harper & Row, Publishers, Incorporated, New York, 1957.

Brown, Claude: *Manchild in the Promised Land*, The Macmillan Company, New York, 1965.

Cayton, Horace R.: *Long Old Road*, Trident Press, Affiliated Publishers, New York, 1965.

Clark, Kenneth B.: *Dark Ghetto*, Harper & Row, Publishers, Incorporated, New York, 1965.

Handler, Oscar: *Newcomers: Negroes and Puerto Ricans in a Changing Metropolis*, Harvard University Press, Cambridge, Mass., 1959.

Harrington, Michael: *The Other America: Poverty in the United States*, The Macmillan Company, New York, 1962.

Hayakawa, S. I.: *Language in Thought and Action*, 2d ed., Harcourt, Brace, and Company Inc., New York, 1964.

Kelley, Earl C. *In Defense of Youth*, Prentice-Hall, Inc., Englewood Cliffs, N. J., 1962.

Lewis, Oscar: *La Vida*, Random House, Inc., New York, 1966.

Lincoln, Eric C.: *The Black Muslims in America*, Beacon Press, Boston, 1961.

Lomax, Louis E.: *The Negro Revolt*, Harper & Row, Publishers, Inc., New York, 1962.

Maslow, Abraham Harold: *Toward a Psychology of Being*, Van Nostrand Company, Inc., Princeton, N. J., 1962.

Minteer, Catherine: *Words and What They Do To You*, Institute of General Semantics, Lakeville, Conn., 1966.

Montagu, Ashley: *The Concept of Race*, The Free Press of Glencoe, New York, 1964.

Pearl, Arthur, and Frank Riessman: *New Careers for the Poor*, The Free Press of Glencoe, New York, 1965.

Rogers, Carl Ransom: *On Becoming a Person*, Houghton-Mifflin Company, Boston, 1961.

Silberman, Charles E.: *Crisis in Black and White*, Random House, Inc., New York, 1964.

Tannenbaum, Frank: *The Struggle for Peace and Bread*, Alfred A. Knopf, Inc., New York, 1950.

Williams, John: *The Angry Black*, Lancer Books, Inc., New York, 1962.

Catalog

If you are interested in a list of fine Paperback
books, covering a wide range of subjects
and interests, send your name and address,
requesting your free catalog, to:

McGraw-Hill Paperbacks
330 West 42nd Street
New York, New York 10036